AF522085

LIBRARY AND INFORMATION TECHNOLOGY

By
Dr. Pankaj Kumar Singh
Librarian & H.O.D.
Dept. of Library & Information Science
D.S.N. (P.G.) College
Unnao - 209 801 (U.P.)
(India)

DISCOVERY PUBLISHING HOUSE PVT. LTD.
NEW DELHI-110 002

Published by:

DISCOVERY PUBLISHING HOUSE PVT. LTD.
4383/4B, Ansari Road, Darya Ganj
New Delhi-110 002 (India)
Phone : +91-11-23279245; 23253475; 43596065
E-mail : discoverybooksindia@gmail.com
discoverypublishinghouse@gmail.com
namitwasan9@gmail.com
web : www.discoverypublishinggroup.com

First Edition: **2014**
Reprinted: **2022**

ISBN: 978-93-5056-425-7

Library and Information Technology

Printed at:
Infinity Imaging Systems
Delhi

Preface

The effectiveness of management of library information is accomplished by a combination of basic management function, roles and skill. The fundamental structural change caused by information technologies not only affects the technical services of libraries but also shapes the library services that are being offered to the public libraries as possibly faced with a much more dangerous kind of competition than the one customary among direct competitors: the substitution competition caused by new information technologies. Management skills are needed when dealing with all types of organized activities and all types of organization indeed, managing a library requires. One of the key contributors to future library success, for libraries will be the exploitation of IT, which will facilitate the use and management of information. Through the use of IT, libraries are presently engineering the way in which they carry out their activities.

—*Author*

Contents

1

Introduction to Information Technology

COMPUTER SAVVY BENEFITS FOR PRACTICAL USER

MEANINING AND IT'S PRACTICAL PAYOFFS

There is no doubt now that for most of us information technology is becoming like a second skin-an extension of our intellects and even emotions, creating almost a parallel universe of 'digital selves.' Perhaps you have been using computers a long time and in a multitude of ways, or perhaps not. Either way, this book hopes to deliver important practical rewards by helping you become 'computer streetwise'–that is, computer savvy. Being computer savvy means knowing what computers can do and what they can't, knowing how they can benefit you and how they can harm you, knowing when you can solve computer problems and when you have to call for help.

Better Buying Decisions

No matter how much computer prices come down, you will always have to make Judgements about quality and usefulness when buying equipment and software. In fact, we start you off right in this chapter by identifying the constituent parts of a computer system, what they do, and how much they cost.

Upgrade Equipment and Integrate

Whether it's replacing a printer cartridge, obtaining a software improvement, or pulling photos from your digital camera or camera cellphone, we hope this book will give you the confidence to deal with the continual challenges that arise with computers—and know when and how to call for help.

New gadgetry and software are constantly being developed. A knowledgeable user learns under what conditions to upgrade, how to do so, and when to start over by buying a new machine.

Effectively Use the Internet

The sea of data that exists on the internet and other online sources is so great that finding what's best or what's really needed can be a hugely timeconsuming activity. We hope to show you the most workable ways to approach this problem.

How to Protect Yourself against Online Villains

The online world poses real risks to your time, your privacy, your finances, and your peace of mind—spammers, hackers, virus senders, identity thieves, and companies and agencies constructing giant databases of personal profiles—as suggested, explain. This book aims to make you streetwise about these threats.

Computer Uses can Advance Your Career

Even top executives now use computers, as do people in careers ranging from police work to politics, from medicine to music, from retail to recreation. We hope you will come away from this book with ideas about how the technology can benefit you in whatever work you choose. Along the way—in the experience boxes, practical action boxes, survival tips, and more infos—we offer many kinds of practical advice that we hope will help you become truly computer savvy in a variety of ways, large and small.

INFORMATION TECHNOLOGY AND YOUR LIFE

This stage is about computers, of course. But not just about computers. It is also about the way computers communicate with one another. When computer and communications technologies are combined, the result is information technology, or 'infotech.' Information technology *(IT)* is a general term that describes any technology that helps to produce, manipulate, store, communicate, and/or disseminate information. IT merges computing with high-speed communications links carrying data, sound, and video. Examples of information technology include personal computers but also new forms of telephones, televisions, appliances, and various handheld devices.

THE TWO PARTS OF I.T. COMPUTERS AND COMMUNICATIONS

Distinguish Computer Technology and Communications Technology

Computer Technology

You have certainly seen and, we would guess, used a computer. Nevertheless, let's define what it is. A computer is a programmable, multiuse machine that accepts data—raw facts and figures—and processes, or manipulates, it into information we can use, such as summaries, totals, or reports. Its purpose is to speed up problem solving and increase productivity.

Communications Technology

Unquestionably you've been using communications technology for years. *Communications* technology, also called *telecommunications technology,* consists of electromagnetic devices and systems for communicating over long distances. The principal examples are telephone, radio, broadcast television, and cable TV.

In more recent times, there has been the addition of communication among computers—which is what happens when people 'go online' on the internet. In this context, *online* means using a computer or some other information device, connected through a network, to access information and services from another computer or information device. A network is a communications system connecting two or more computers; the internet is the largest such network. Information technology is already affecting your life in exciting ways and will do so even more in the future.

EDUCATION THE PROMISE OF MORE INTERACTIVE AND INDIVIDUALISED LEARNING

Information Technology and its Uses in Education

In her sociology classes at Indiana University, professor Melissa Wilde uses a small wireless keypad linked to a computer to enable students to answer questions not by raising their hands but by pressing buttons, with the results appearing on a screen in the front of the room. Wilde has her students answer multiple-choice questions to see whether they understand her lecture points and to make necessary adjustments.

"I can instantly see that three-quarters of the class doesn't get it," she says. She also uses the technology to get students to answer questions about themselves—race, income, political affiliation—skewed, for example, Towards wealthier or poorer students, an event that fired up a half hour of excited class discussion. Maybe the classrooms at your school haven't reached this level of interactivity yet, but there's no question that information technology is universal on college campuses, and at lower levels the internet has penetrated 99 per cent of schools. Most college students have been exposed to computers Since, the lower grades; indeed, one-fifth of college students report they were using computers between ages 5 and 8, and all had begun using computers by the time they were 16–18 years old. At the college level, the great majority (85 per cent) of students have their own computers, and two-thirds use at least two e-mail addresses.

As you no doubt know, *e-mail* is 'electronic mail,' messages transmitted over a computer network, most often the internet. Three-quarters of college students use the internet 4 or more hours a week, and about onefifth use it 12 or more hours a week. About half are required to use e-mail in their classes. For academic purposes, most students use e-mail to set up appointments (62 per cent) with professors, discuss grades (58 per cent), or get clarification of an assignment (75 per cent). Besides using the internet to help in teaching, today's college instructors also use *presentation graphics software* such as PowerPoint to show their lecture outlines and other materials on classroom screens.

In addition, they use Blackboard, WebCT, and other *course management software* for administering online assignments, schedules, examinations, and grades. One of the most intriguing developments in education at all levels, however, is the rise of *distance learning*, or *e-learning*, the name given to online education Programmes, which has more than 3.2 million online students enrolled nationwide and grows more than 20 per cent a year. E-learning has had some interesting effects: for example, the home-schooling movement, whereby children are taught at home, usually by parents, has come of age thanks to internet resources. e-Learning has also propelled the rise of for-profit institutions, such as Devry and the University of Phoenix, which 8 per cent of full-time college students now attend.

More than a third of institutions of higher education—and 97 per cent of public universities—offer online courses, and many have attracted on-campus students, who say they like the flexibility of not having to attend their classes at a set time. e-learning has been put to such varied uses as bringing career and technical courses to high school students in remote prairie towns, pairing gifted science students with master teachers in other parts of the country, and helping busy professionals obtain further credentials outside business hours. But the reach of information technology into education has only begun.

In the future, as suggested, see software called 'intelligent tutoring systems' that gives students individualised instruction when personal attention is scarce—such as the software Cognitive Tutor, which not only helps high school students to improve their performance in math but also sparks them to enjoy a subject they might have once hated.

In colleges, more students may use interactive simulation games, such as McGraw-Hill's *Business Strategy Game*, to apply their knowledge to real-world kinds of problems. And employees in company training Programmes may find themselves engaged in mock conversations with *avatars*—computer depictions of humans, as are often found in online video-games—that represent imaginary customers and coworkers, combining the best parts of computer-based learning with face-to-face interaction.

HEALTH: HIGH TECH FOR WELLNESS

Computers Used in Health and Medicine

Viktor Yazykov, competing in the perilous Around Alone solo sailing competition, found himself in the stormy South Atlantic with a seriously infected arm that needed emergency surgery. So, with the help of step-bystep instructions sent by e-mail from Boston-based Dr. Daniel Carlin to his solar-powered laptop computer, Yazykov operated on his own arm. Yazykov's story is a dramatic example of *telemedicine*—medical care delivered via telecommunications. For some time, physicians in rural areas lacking local access to radiologists have used 'teleradiology' to exchange computerised images such as X-rays via telephone-linked networks with expert physicians in metropolitan areas.

Now telemedicine is moving to an exciting new level, as the use of digital cameras and sound, in effect, moves patients to doctors rather than the reverse. Already telemedicine is being embraced by administrators in the American prison system, where by law inmates are guaranteed medical treatment—and where the increase in prisoners every year has led to the need to control health costs.

Computer technology is also radically changing the tools of medicine. All medical information, including that generated by X-ray, lab test, and pulse monitor, can now be transmitted to a doctor in digital format. And image transfer technology allows radiologic images such as CT scans and MRIs to be immediately transmitted to electronic charts and physicians' offices. Patients in intensive care, who are usually monitored by nurses during offtimes, can also be watched over by doctors in remote 'control towers' miles away. Electronic medical records and other computerised tools enable heart attack patients to get follow-up drug treatment and diabetics to have their blood sugar measured. Software can compute a woman's breast cancer risk. Patients can use e-mail to query their doctors about their records.

Various *robots*—automatic devices that perform functions ordinarily performed by human beings, with names such as robo doc, RoboCart, TUG, and HelpMate—help free medical workers for more critical tasks; the four-armed da Vinci surgical robot, for instance, can do cuts and stitches deep inside the body, so that surgery is less traumatic and recovery time faster. Hydraulics and computers are being used to help artificial limbs get 'smarter.' And a patient paralysed by a stroke has received an implant that allows communication between his brain and a computer; as a result, he can move a cursor across a screen by brainpower and convey simple messages—as in *Star Trek.*

Want to calculate how long you will live? Want to go about gathering your family health history to see if you're at risk for particular inherited diseases? These are only two examples of health Web sites available to patients and health consumers. Although online health information can be misleading and even dangerous, many people now tap into health care databases, e-mail health professionals, or communicate with people who have similar conditions. For instance, hours after 10-year-old Robert Lord of San Diego fractured his spine in a fall from a tree, his father found an experimental drug on the internet, saving the boy from lifetime paralysis.

Often patients are already steeped in information about their conditions when they arrive in the offices of health care professionals. This represents a fundamental shift of knowledge, and therefore power, from physicians to patients. In addition, health care consumers are able to share experiences and information with one another. Young parents, for example, can find an online gathering spot at pediatrician Alan Greene's Web site.

MONEY: TOWARDS THE CASHLESS SOCIETY

Computers Affect and Financial Matters

"The future of money is increasingly digital, likely virtual, and possibly universal," says one writer. *Virtual* means that something is created, simulated, or carried on by means of a computer or a computer network, and we certainly have come a long way Towards becoming a cashless society. Indeed, the percentage of all financial transactions done electronically, both phone-initiated and computer-initiated, was projected to rise to 18.4 per cent in 2013, up from 0.9 per cent in 1993.

Besides currency, paper checks, and credit and debit cards, the things that serve as 'money' include cashvalue cards, automatic transfers, and digital money. Many readers of this book will probably already have engaged in online buying and selling, purchasing CDs and DVDs, books, airline tickets, or computers.

But what about groceries? After all, you can't exactly squeeze the cantaloupes through your keyboard. Even so, online groceries are expected to reach $7.5 billion in U.S., sales by 2012. To change decades of shopping habits, e-grocers keep their delivery charges low and delivery times convenient, and they take great pains in filling orders, knowing that a single bad piece of fruit will produce a devastating word-of-mouth backlash. Only about 46 per cent of U.S. workers have their paychecks electronically deposited into their bank accounts, but this is sure to change as Americans discover that direct deposit is actually safer and faster. Online bill paying is also picking up steam. For more than two decades, it has been possible to pay bills online, such as those from phone and utility companies, with special software and online connections to your bank. About 19 million American households do some bill paying online, and the number was expected to reach 61 million households in 2008.

Some banks and other businesses are backing an electronic-payment system that allows internet users to buy goods and services with *micropayments,* electronic payments of as little as 25 cents in transactions for which it is uneconomical to use a credit card. Micropayment, suggests futurist Paul Saffo, 'allows you to buy things by the sip rather than the gulp.' The success of Apple Computer's iTunes online music service, which sells songs for 99 cents each, suggests that micro sales are now feasible.

All kinds of businesses and organisations, from independent songwriters to comic book writers to the Legal Aid Society of Cleveland, now accept micropayments, using intermediaries such as BitPass and Peppercoin. Thus, you could set up your own small business simply by constructing a Web site and accepting micropay-ments.

LEISURE: INFOTECH IN ENTERTAINMENT AND THE ARTS

Leisure Activities be affected by Information Technology

Information technology is being used for all kinds of entertainment, ranging from videogames to telegambling. It is also being used in the arts, from painting to photography. Let's consider just two examples, music and film. Computers, the internet, and the World Wide Web (WWW) are standing the system of music recording and distribution on its head—and in the process are changing the financial underpinnings of the music industry. Because of their high overhead, major record labels typically need a band to sell half a million CDs in order to be profitable, but independent bands, using online marketing, can be reasonably successful selling 20,000 or 30,000 albums. Team Love, a small music label established in 2003, found it could promote its first two bands, Tilly and the Wall and Willy Mason, by offering songs online fRee for *downloading*—transferring data from a remote computer to one's own computer—so that people could listen to them before paying $12 for a CD. It also puts videos online for sharing and uses quirky Web sites to reach fans.

"There's something exponential going on," says one of Team Love's founders. "The more music that's downloaded, the more it sells." Many independent musicians are also using the internet to get their music heard, hoping that giving away songs will help them build audiences. The web also offers sources for instantly downloadable sheet music. One research engineer has devised a computerised scoring system for judging musical competitions that overcomes the traditional human-jury approach, which can be swayed by personalities and politics.

A Spanish company, PolyphonicHMI, has created Hit Song Science software, which they say can analyse the hit potential of new songs by "reference to a finely parsed universe of attributes derived from millions of past songs." As for movies, now that blockbuster movies routinely meld live action and animation, computer artists are in big demand. The 1999 film *Star Wars: Episode I*, for instance, had fully 1,965 digital shots out of about 2,200 shots.

Even when film was used, it was scanned into computers to be tweaked with animated effects, lighting, and the like. Entire beings were created on computers by artists working on designs developed by producer George Lucas and his chief artist. What is driving the demand for computer artists? One factor is that animation, though not cheap, looks more and more like a bargain, because hiring movie actors costs so much—some make $20 million a film. Moreover, special effects are readily understood by audiences in other countries, and major studios increasingly count on revenues from foreign markets to make a film profitable.

Digital manipulation also allows a crowd of extras to be multiplied into an army of thousands. It can also be used to create settings: in the film *Sky Captain and the World of Tomorrow*, the actors—Gwyneth Paltrow, Angelina Jolie, and Jude Law—shot all their scenes in front of a blue screen, and computer-generated imagery was then used to transport them into an imaginary world of 1939. Computer techniques have even been used to develop digitally created actors—called 'synthespians.' Actors ranging from the late James Dean to the late John Wayne, for instance, have been recruited for television commercials. And computerised animation is now so popular that Hollywood studios and movie directors are finding they can make as much money from creating videogames as from making movies.

But animation is not the only area in which computers are revolutionising movies. Digital editing has radically transformed the way films are assembled.

Whereas traditional film editing involved reeling and unreeling spools of film and cutting and gluing pieces of highly scratchable celluloid together, nearly burying the editor in film, today an editor can access 150 miles of film stored on a computer and instantly find any visual or audio moment, allowing hundreds of variations of a scene to be called up for review. Even Non-professionals can get into movie making as new computerrelated products come to market.

Now that digital video capture-and-edit systems are available for under $1,000, amateurs can turn home videos into digital data and edit them. Also, digital camcorders, which offer outstanding picture and sound quality, have steadily dropped in price.

GOVERNMENT AND ELECTRONIC DEMOCRACY

A Rutgers University study suggests that the internet has great potential for civic betterment because it is fast and cheap for users and facilitates communication among citisens better than do mass media such as radio and TV. And a study by the Pew Internet and American Life Project found that internet users are much more likely to contact government than are Non-users because of the ease of finding information online and of contacting officials through e-mail.

Some cities have adopted Neighbourhood Link, a free, easy-to-use system of Neighbourhood Web sites in which residents can communicate with one another and with local governments. In Denver, for instance, the system serves 405 Neighbourhoods. In Austin, Texas, an entrepreneur formed

E-The People, which describes itself as 'America's Interactive Town Hall' and is designed to connect citisens with their government officials, local and national, everywhere in the United States. In Nevada, citisens visit the state legislature's hearings and floor voting sessions by accessing the legislature's Web site, where they can either listen to internet broadcasts or read the text of legislation. In Seattle, citisens can go to their city's Web site to deal with everything from absentee ballots to youth and family services. Besides cutting expenses for stamps, paper, and employees, e-government helps reduce lines and offers people more convenience in paying taxes and parking tickets, renewing vehicle registration and driver's licenses, viewing birth and marriage certificates, and applying for public sector jobs.

The internet and other information technology have also changed much of the political process, both for good and for ill. On the one hand, the net has enabled political candidates and political interest groups to connect with voters in new ways, to raise money from multiple small donors instead of just rich fat cats, and to organise street protests.

On the other hand, computers have allowed incumbent legislators to design voting districts that make it nearly impossible for them to be dislodged; electronic tools have also made it easier than ever for political parties to skirt or break campaign laws, and computerised voting machines still don't always count votes as they are supposed to. Still, Web sites and bloggers have become important watchdogs on government. The Web site E-Democracy, for instance, can help citisens dig up government conflicts of interest, and Web sites such as Project Vote Smart outline candidates' positions.

JOBS AND CAREERS

Career and Use of Computers

Today almost every job and profession requires computer skills of some sort. Some are ordinary jobs in which computers are used as ordinary tools. Others are specialised jobs in which advanced computer training combined with professional training gives people dramatically new kinds of careers.

Consider:

- In the hotel business, even front-desk clerks need to know how to deal with computerised reservation systems. Some hotels, however, also have a so-called computer concierge, someone with knowledge of computer systems who can help computer-carrying guests with online and other problems.
- In law enforcement, police officers need to know how to use computers while on patrol or at their desks to check out stolen cars, criminal records, outstanding arrest warrants, and the like. However, investigators with specialised computer backgrounds are also required to help solve fraud, computer break-ins, accounting illegalities, and other high-tech crimes.
- In entertainment, computers are used for such ordinary purposes as budgets, payroll, and ticketing. However, there are also new careers in virtual set design, combining training in architecture and 3-D computer modeling, and in creating cinematic special effects.

Clearly, information technology is changing old jobs and inventing new ones. To prosper in this environment, you need to combine a traditional education with training in computers and communications. You also need to be savvy about job searching, resume writing, interviewing, and postings of employment opportunities.

Advice about careers, job hunting, occupational trends, and employment laws is available at Yahoo!, Google, and other Web sites. Some starting annual salaries for recent college graduates are shown; note that jobs involving degrees in computers and information systems occupy four of the seven top-paying starting salaries. Computers can be used both for you to find employers and for employers to find you.

Ways for you to Find Employers

As you might expect, the first to use cyberspace as a job

bazaar were companies seeking people with technical backgrounds and technical people seeking employment. However, as the public's interest in commercial services and the internet has exploded, the focus of online job exchanges has broadened. Now, interspersed among ads for programmers on the internet are openings for forest rangers in Idaho, physical therapists in Atlanta, models in Florida, and English teachers in China. Most Web sites are free to job seekers, although many require that you fill out an online registration form.

Ways for Employers to Find You

Posting your résumé online for prospective employers to view is attractive because of its low cost and wide reach. But does it have any disadvantages? Certainly it might if the employer who sees your posting happens to be the one you're already working for. In addition, you have to be aware that you lose control over anything broadcast into cyberspace. You're putting your credentials out there for the whole world to see, and you need to be somewhat concerned about who might gain access to them. If you have a technical background, it's definitely worth posting your résumé with an electronic jobs registry, Since, technology companies in particular find this an efficient way of screening and hiring.

However, posting may also benefit people with less technical backgrounds. Online recruitment is popular with companies because it prescreens applicants for at least basic computer skills. If you've mastered the internet, you're likely to know something about word processing, spreadsheets, and database searching as well, knowledge required in most good jobs these days.

One wrinkle in job seeking is to prepare a résumé with web links and/or clever graphics and multimedia effects and then put it on a Web site to entice employers to chase after you. If you don't know how to do this, there are many companies that—for a fee—can convert your résumé and publish it on their own Web sites. Some of these services can't dress it up with fancy graphics or multimedia, but Since, complex pages take longer for employers to download anyway, the extra pizzazz is probably not worth the effort.

A number of Web sites allow you to post your résumé for free. Another wrinkle is to pay extra to move your résumé higher in the listings so that it will stand out compared with competing résumés. For example, for an extra $20–$150 apiece, Careerbuilder.com will move your listing Towards the top of the search heap, and the company says that employers click on upgraded résumés 200 per cent more often than regular ones.

INFOTECH IS ALL-PERVASIVE

One of the first computers, the outcome of military-related research, was delivered to the U.S., Army in 1946. ENIAC weighed 30 tons and was 80 feet long and two stories high, but it could multiply a pair of numbers in the then-remarkable time of three-thousandths of a second. This was the first general-purpose, programmable electronic computer, the grandparent of today's lightweight handheld machines—including the smart cellphone.

Cellphone mania has swept the world. All across the globe, people have acquired the portable gift of gab, with some users making 45 or more calls a day. Strategy Analytics has estimated that worldwide mobile phone subscriptions will rise to 3.9 billion in 2013; more than half the world's population will be using mobile phones by 2010.

It has taken more than 100 years for the telephone to get to this point—getting smaller, acquiring push buttons, losing its cord connection. In 1964, the * and # keys were added to the keypad. In 1973, the first cellphone call was processed. In its most basic form, the telephone is still so simply designed that even a young child can use it.

However, it is now becoming more versatile and complex—a way of connecting to the internet and the World Wide Web. Indeed, internet smartphones—such as the Apple iPhone, the Samsung Instinct, the palm Centro, and the

Motorola Q9c—represent another giant step for information technology. Now you no longer need a personal computer to get on the internet.

Smartphones in their various forms enable you not only to make voice calls but also to send and receive text messages, browse the World Wide Web, and obtain news, research, music, photos, movies, and TV Programmes. The percentage of people who use Non-voice applications for text messages is 27 per cent; e-mail 11 per cent; internet 9 per cent; and photography 6 per cent—and the numbers of users for these options are growing all the time.

E-mail Distinctive from Earlier Technologies

It took the telephone 40 years to reach 10 million customers, and fax machines 20 years. Personal computers made it into that many American homes 5 years after they were introduced. E-mail, which appeared in 1981, became popular far more quickly, reaching 10 million users in little more than a year. No technology has ever become so universal so fast. Thus, one of the first things new computer and internet users generally learn is how to send and receive e-mail.

Until 1998, hand-delivered mail was still the main means of correspondence. But in that year, the volume of e-mail in the United States surpassed the volume of hand-delivered mail. In 2007, the total number of e-mail messages sent daily has been estimated at 183 billion worldwide. Already, in fact, e-mail is the leading use of PCs. Because of this explosion in usage, suggests a *BusinessWeek* report, 'e-mail ranks with such pivotal advances as the printing press, the telephone, and television in mass impact.'

Using electronic mail clearly is different from calling on a telephone or writing a conventional letter. As one writer puts it, e-mail "occupies a psychological space all its own. It's almost as immediate as a phone call, but if you need to, you can think about what you're going to say for days and reply when it's convenient." E-mail has blossomed, points out another writer, not because it gives us more immediacy but because it gives us *less*.

'The new appeal of e-mail is the old appeal of print,' he says. "It isn't instant; it isn't immediate; it isn't in your face." E-mail has succeeded for the same reason that the videophone—which allows callers to see each other while talking— has been so slow to catch on: because "what we actually want from our exchanges is the minimum human contact commensurate with the need to connect with other people." It will be interesting to see, however, whether this observation holds up during the next few years if marketers roll out more videophones. What is interesting, though, is that in these times when images often seem to overwhelm words, e-mail is actually *reactionary*. 'The internet is the first new medium to move decisively backward,' points out one writer, because it essentially involves writing. Twenty years ago, "even the most literate of us wrote maybe a half a dozen letters a year; the rest of our lives took place on the telephone." E-mail has changed all that—and has put pressure on businesspeople in particular to sharpen their writing skills.

Difference between the Net, the Web, and Cyberspace

As the success of the cellphone shows, communications has extended into every nook and cranny of Civillization, a development called the 'plumbing of cyberspace.' The term *cyberspace* was coined by William Gibson in his novel *Neuromancer* to describe a futuristic computer network into which users plug their brains. In everyday use, this term has a rather different meaning. Today many people equate cyberspace with the internet.

But it is much more than that. Cyberspace includes not only the web, chat rooms, online diaries, and member-based services such as America Online—all features we explain in this book—but also such things as conference calls and automatic teller machines, says David Whittler. We may say, then, that *cyberspace* encompasses not only the online world and the internet in particular but also the whole wired and wireless world of communications in general—the Non-physical terrain created by computer and communications systems. Cyberspace is where you go when you go online with your computer.

The Net and Web

The two most important aspects of cyberspace are the internet and that part of the internet known as the World Wide Web. To give them formal definition:

- *The Internet*—'the mother of all networks': The internet is at the heart of the Information Age. Called 'the mother of all networks,' the *internet* is a worldwide computer network that connects hundreds of thousands of smaller networks. These networks link educational, commercial, Non-profit, and military entities, as well as individuals.
- *The World Wide Web*—the multimedia part of the internet: The internet has been around for more than 40 years. But what made it popular, apart from e-mail, was the development in the early 1990s of the *World Wide Web*, often called simply the 'Web' or the "web—an interconnected system of internet computers that support specially formatted documents in multimedia form. The word *multimedia*, from 'multiple media,' refers to technology that presents information in more than one medium, such as text, still images, moving images, and sound. In other words, the web provides information in more than one way.

The Internet's Influence

There is no doubt that the influence of the net and the web is tremendous. At present, 75 per cent of American adults use the internet, according to the Pew Internet and American Life Project. Seventy-two per cent of American adult internet users use the net on an average day, with 60 per cent using it to send or read e-mail. But just how revolutionary is the internet?

Is it equivalent to the invention of television, as some technologists say? Or is it even more important—equivalent to the invention of the printing press? "Television turned out to be a powerful force that changed a lot about society," says *USA Today* technology reporter Kevin Maney. "But the printing press changed everything—religion, government, science, global distribution of wealth, and much more. If the internet equals the printing press, no amount of hype could possibly overdo it."

COLLEGE STUDENTS AND THE E-WORLD

One thing we know already is that cyberspace is saturating our lives. The worldwide internet population was projected to be 1.21 billion in 2006, with 185 million of that number American. While the average age of users is rising, there's no doubt that people ages 18–27 love information technology, with 85 per cent using computers and 78 per cent using the net.

Among college students, 99 per cent use e-mail, four out of five carry cellphones, and more than 80 per cent of on-campus students access the net through high-speed lines, which make it easier to obtain music and videos. Most students multitask—switching between listening to music, watching TV, trolling the internet, talking on the phone, and e-messaging friends—and still somehow are able to do some studying. They are also big-participants in e-commerce, e-shopping, and e-business. For the Net Generation, the digital media are like air. The electronic world is everywhere. The net and the web are everywhere. Cyberspace permeates everything.

THE VARIETIES OF COMPUTERS

When the alarm clock blasts you awake, you leap out of bed and head for the kitchen, where you check the coffee maker. After using your electronic toothbrush and showering and dressing, you stick a bagel in the microwave, and then pick up the TV remote and click on the TV to catch the weather forecast. Later, after putting dishes in the dishwasher, you go out and start up the car and head Towards campus or work. Pausing en route at a traffic light, you turn on your iPod to listen to some music.

You haven't yet touched a PC, a personal computer, but you've already dealt with at least 10 computers. All these familiar appliances rely on tiny 'computers on chips' called *microprocessors*. Maybe, then, the name 'computer' is inadequate. As computer pioneer John von Neumann has said, the device should not be called the computer but rather the 'all-purpose machine.' It is not, after all, just a machine for doing calculations. The most striking thing about it is that it can be put to *any number of uses*. What are the various types of computers? Let's take a look.

The Five Sizes of Computers

At one time, the idea of having your own computer was almost like having your own personal nuclear reactor. In those days, in the 1950s and 1960s, computers were enormous machines affordable only by large institutions. Now they come in a variety of shapes and sizes, which can be classified according to their processing power:

- Supercomputers,
- Mainframe computers,
- Workstations,
- Microcomputers, and
- Microcontrollers.

Supercomputers

Typically priced from $1 million to more than $350 million, *supercomputers* are high-capacity machines with thousands of processors that can perform more than several trillion calculations per second. These are the most expensive and fastest computers available.

'Supers,' as they are called, have been used for tasks requiring the processing of enormous volumes of data, such as doing the U.S., census count, forecasting weather, designing aircraft, modeling molecules, and breaking encryption codes. More recently they have been employed for business purposes—for instance, sifting demographic marketing information—and for creating film animation.

The fastest computer in the world, costing $100 million and with roughly the computing power of 100,000 of today's most powerful laptops, is the Roadrunner, developed by engineers from the Los Alamos National Laboratory and IBM Corp., primarily for nuclear weapons research, including simulating nuclear explosions.

Roadrunner's speed is 1 petaflop, or 1,000 trillion operations per second. Supercompu-ters are still the most powerful computers, but a new generation may be coming that relies on *nanotechnology,* in which molecule-size nanostructures are used to create tiny machines for holding data or performing tasks. Computers the size of a pencil eraser could become available that work 10 times faster than today's fastest supercomputer. Eventually nanotech could show up in every device and appliance in your life.

Mainframe Computers

The only type of computer available until the late 1960s, *mainframes* are water- or air-cooled computers that cost $5,000–$5 million and vary in size from small, to medium, to large, depending on their use. Small mainframes are often called *midsize computers;* they used to be called *minicomputers,* although today the term is seldom used.

Mainframes are used by large organisations—such as banks, airlines, insurance companies, and colleges—for processing millions of transactions. Often users access a mainframe by means of a *terminal,* which has a display screen and a keyboard and can input and output data but cannot by itself process data. Mainframes process billions of instructions per second.

Workstations

Introduced in the early 1980s, *workstations* are expensive, powerful personal computers usually used for complex scientific, mathematical, and engineering calculations and for computer-aided design and computer-aided manufacturing. Providing many capabilities comparable to those of midsize mainframes, workstations are used for such tasks as designing airplane fuselages, developing prescription drugs, and creating movie special effects.

Workstations have caught the eye of the public mainly for their graphics capabilities, which are used to breathe three-dimensional life into movies such as *WALL.E* and *Harry Potter*. The capabilities of low-end workstations overlap those of high-end desktop microcomputers.

Microcomputers

Microcomputers, also called *personal computers* (*PCs*), which cost $500 to over $5,000, can fit next to a desk or on a desktop or can be carried around. They either are stand-alone machines or are connected to a computer network, such as a local area network.

A *local area network (LAN)* connects, usually by special cable, a group of desktop PCs and other devices, such as printers, in an office or a building. Microcomputers are of several types: desktop PCs, tower PCs, notebooks (laptops), mobile internet devices (MIDs), and personal digital assistants— handheld computers or palmtops.

Desktop Pcs

Desktop PCs are older microcomputers whose case or main housing sits on a desk, with keyboard in front and monitor often on top.

Tower Pcs

Tower PCs are microcomputers whose case sits as a 'tower,' often on the floor beside a desk, thus freeing up desk surface space. Some desktop computers, such as Apple's iMac, no longer have a boxy housing; most of the computer components are built into the back of the flat-panel display screen.

Notebooks

Notebook computers, also called *laptop computers,* are lightweight portable computers with built-in monitor, keyboard, hard-disk drive, CD/DVD drive, battery, and AC adapter that can be plugged into an electrical outlet; they weigh anywhere from 1.8 to 9 pounds.

Mobile Internet Devices (Mids)

A new category of mobile devices, smaller than notebook computers but larger and more powerful than PDAs, *mobile internet devices (MIDs)* are for consumers and business professionals. Fully internet integrated, they are highly compatible with desktop microcomputers and laptops. The initial models focus on data communication, not voice communication.

Personal Digital Assistants

Personal digital assistants (PDAs), also called *handheld computers* or *palmtops,* combine personal organisation tools—schedule planners, address books, to-do lists—with the ability in some cases to send e-mail and faxes. Some PDAs have touch-sensitive screens. Some also connect to desktop computers for sending or receiving information.

Microcontrollers

Microcontrollers, also called *embedded computers,* are the tiny, specialised microprocessors installed in 'smart' appliances and automobiles. These microcontrollers enable microwave ovens, for example, to store data about how long to cook your potatoes and at what power setting. Microcontrollers have been used to develop a new universe of experimental electronic appliances—e-pliances.

For example, they are behind single-function products such as digital cameras, MP3 players, and organisers, which have been developed into hybrid forms such as gadgets that store photos and videos as well as music. They also help run tiny web servers embedded in clothing, jewelry, and household appliances such as refrigerators. In addition, microcontrollers are used in bloodpressure monitors, air bag sensors, gas and chemical sensors for water and air, and vibration sensors.

SERVERS

The word *server* describes not a size of computer but rather a particular way in which a computer is used. Nevertheless, because servers have become so important to telecommunications, especially with the rise of the internet and the web. A *server,* or *network server,* is a central computer that holds collections of data and Programmes for connecting or supplying services to PCs, workstations, and other devices, which are called *clients.*

These clients are linked by a wired or wireless network. The entire network is called a *client/server network.* In small organisations, servers can store files, provide printing stations, and transmit e-mail.

In large organisations, servers may also house enormous libraries of financial, sales, and product information. You may never lay eyes on a supercomputer or mainframe or even a tiny microcontroller. But most readers of this book will already have laid eyes and hands on a personal computer. We consider this machine next.

UNDERSTANDING YOUR COMPUTER

Perhaps you know how to drive a car. But do you know what to do when it runs badly? Similarly, you've probably been using a personal computer. But do you know what to do when it doesn't act right—when, for example, it suddenly 'crashes'? Cars are now so complicated that professional mechanics are often required for even the smallest problems. With personal computers, however, there are still many things you can do yourself—and should learn to do, so that, as we've suggested, you can be effective, efficient, and employable. To do so, you first need to know how computers work.

COMPUTERS WORK: THREE KEY CONCEPTS

Could you build your own personal computer? Some people do, putting together bare-bones systems for just a few hundred dollars. "If you have a logical mind, are fairly good with your hands, and possess the patience of Job, there's no reason you can't... build a PC," says science writer David Einstein. And, if you do it right, 'it will probably take only a couple of hours," because industry-standard connections allow components to go together fairly easily.

Actually, probably only techies would consider building their own PCs. But many ordinary users *order* their own custom-built PCs. Let's consider how you might do this. We're not going to ask you to build or order a PC—just to pretend to do so. The purpose of this exercise is to give you a basic overview of how a computer works. That information will help you when you go shopping for a new system or, especially, if you order a custom-built system. It will also help you understand how your existing system works, if you have one. Before you begin, you will need to understand three key concepts.

First: Purpose of a Computer: Turning Data into Information

Very simply, the purpose of a computer is to process data into information.

- *Data* : *Data* consists of the raw facts and figures that are processed into information—for example, the votes for different candidates being elected to student-government office.
- *Information*: *Information* is data that has been summarised or otherwise manipulated for use in decision making—for example, the total votes for each candidate, which are used to decide who won.

Second: Difference between Hardware and Software

You should know the difference between hardware and software.You should know the difference between hardware and software.

- *Hardware*: *Hardware* consists of all the machinery and equipment in a computer system. The hardware includes, among other devices, the keyboard, the screen, the printer, and the 'box'—the computer or processing device itself. Hardware is useless without software.
- *Software*: *Software,* or *Programmes,* consists of all the electronic instructions that tell the computer how to perform a task. These instructions come from a software developer in a form that will be accepted by the computer. Examples are Microsoft Windows and Office XP/Vista.

Third: The Basic Operations of a Computer

Regardless of type and size, all computers use the same four basic operations:

- *Input Operation*: *Input* is whatever is put in ('input') to a computer system. Input can be nearly any kind of data—letters, numbers, symbols, shapes, Colourss, temperatures, sounds, pressure, light beams, or whatever raw material needs processing. When you type some words or numbers on a keyboard, those words are considered input data.
- *Processing Operation*: *Processing* is the manipulation a computer does to transform data into information. When the computer adds 2 + 2 to get 4, that is the act of processing. The processing is done by the *central processing unit*—frequently called just the *CPU*—a device consisting of electronic circuitry that executes instructions to process data.
- *Storage Operation*: Storage is of two types—temporary storage and permanent storage, or primary storage and secondary storage. *Primary storage,* or *memory,* is the internal computer circuitry that temporarily holds data waiting to be processed. *Secondary storage,* simply called *storage,* refers to the devices and media that store data or information permanently. A hard disk or CD/DVD is an example of this kind of storage.
- *Output Operation*: *Output* is whatever is output from the computer system—the results of processing, usually information. Examples of output are numbers or pictures displayed on a screen, words printed out on paper by a printer, or music piped over some loudspeakers.
- *Communications Operation*: These days, most computers have communications ability, which offers an extension capability—in other words, it extends the power of the computer. With wired or wireless communications connections, data may be input from afar, processed in a remote area, stored in several different locations, and output in yet other places. However, you don't need communications ability to write letters, do calculations, or perform many other computer tasks.

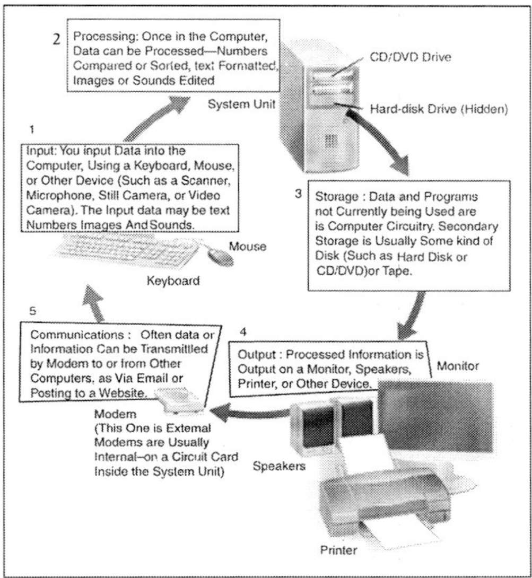

Fig 1.1. Five Operations of a Computer

PRETENDING TO ORDER A CUSTOM-BUILT DESKTOP COMPUTER

Now let's see how you would order a custom-built desktop PC, or even build one yourself. Remember, the purpose of this is to help you understand the internal workings of a computer so that you'll be knowledgeable about using one and buying one. Although prices of components are always subject to change, we have indicated general ranges of prices for basic equipment current as of 2008 so that you can get a sense of the relative importance of the various parts. *Note:* All the system components you or anyone else chooses *must be compatible*—in other words, each brand must work with other brands. If you work with one company—such as Dell, or Hewlett-Packard—to customise your system, you won't have to worry about compatibility. If you choose all the components yourself—you will have to check on compatibility as you choose each component. And you'll have to make sure each component comes with any necessary cables, instructions, and component-specific software that makes the component run. This section of the chapter gives you a brief overview of the components.

We describe them in the following order:

- *Input hardware*: keyboard and mouse;
- Processing and Memory Hardware;
- *Storage Hardware*: disk Drives;
- *Output Hardware*: video and sound cards, monitor, speakers, and printer;
- *Communication hardware*: the modem; and
- *Software*: system and application.

INPUT HARDWARE: KEYBOARD AND MOUSE

Input hardware consists of devices that allow people to put data into the computer in a form that the computer can use. At minimum, you will need two things: a *keyboard* and a *mouse*.

Keyboard

On a microcomputer, a keyboard is the primary input device. A *keyboard* is an input device that converts letters, numbers, and other characters into electrical signals readable by the processor. A microcomputer keyboard looks like a typewriter keyboard, but besides having keys for letters and numbers it has several keys intended for computer-specific tasks. After other components are assembled, the keyboard will be plugged into the back of the computer in a socket intended for that purpose.

Mouse

A *mouse* is a Non-keyboard input device that is used to manipulate objects viewed on the computer display screen. The mouse cord is plugged into the back of the computer or into the back of the keyboard after the other components are assembled.

PROCESSING AND MEMORY HARDWARE: INSIDE THE SYSTEM CABINET

The brains of the computer are the *processing* and *memory* devices, which are installed in the case or system cabinet.

Case and Power Supply

Also known as the *system unit*, the *case* or *system cabinet* is the box that houses the processor chip (CPU), the memory chips, and the motherboard with power supply, as well as some secondary-storage devices—floppy-disk drive, hard-disk drive, and CD or DVD drive, as suggested, explain. The case generally comes in desktop or tower models. It includes a power supply unit and a fan to keep the circuitry from overheating.

Processor Chip

It may be small and not look like much, but it could be the most expensive hardware component of a build-it-yourself PC—and doubtless the most important. A *processor chip* is a tiny piece of silicon that contains millions of miniature electronic circuits. The speed at which a chip processes information is expressed in *megahertz (MHz)*, millions of processing cycles per second, or *gigahertz (GHz)*, billions of processing cycles per second.

The faster the processor, the more expensive it is. For $50, you might get a 2-GHz chip, which is adequate for most student purposes. For $100, you might get a 3-GHz chip, which you would want if you're running software with spectacular graphics and sound, such as those with some new videogames. Only older processors' speed is measured in megahertz now, but if you want a cheap processor—for instance, because you plan to work only with text documents—you could get a 233-MHz processor for about $40.

Memory Chips

These chips are also small. *Memory chips*, also known as *RAM (random access memory) chips*, represent *primary* storage, or temporary storage; they hold data before processing and information after processing, before it is sent along to an output or storage device. You'll want enough memory chips to hold at least 512 megabytes, or roughly 512 million characters, of data, which is adequate for most student purposes. If you work with large graphics files, you'll need more memory capacity, perhaps 1 gigabyte or more.

Motherboard

Also called the *system board,* the *motherboard* is the main circuit board in the computer. This is the big green circuit board to which everything else—such as the keyboard, mouse, and printer—attaches through connections in the back of the computer. The processor chip and memory chips are also installed on the motherboard. The motherboard has *expansion slots*—for expanding the PC's capabilities—which give you places to plug in additional circuit boards, such as those for video, sound, and communications.

Putting the Components to Gether

Now the components can be put together.

As the illustration below shows,

- The memory chips are plugged into the motherboard.
- Then the processor chip is plugged into the motherboard.
- Now the motherboard is attached to the system cabinet.
- Then the power supply unit is connected to the system cabinet.
- Finally, the wire for the power switch, which turns the computer on and off, is connected to the motherboard.

STORAGE HARDWARE

With the motherboard in the system cabinet, the next step is installation of the storage hardware. Whereas memory chips deal only with temporary storage, *secondary storage,* or *permanent storage,* stores your data for as long as you want. For today's student purposes, you'll need a hard drive and a CD/DVD drive, and in older systems, you might have a floppy disk drive.

These storage devices slide into the system cabinet from the front and are secured with screws. Each drive is attached to the motherboard by a flat cable. Also, each drive must be hooked up to a plug extending from the power supply. A computer system's data/information storage capacity is represented by bytes, kilobytes, megabytes, gigabytes, terabytes, and petabytes, as follows:

Table. 1.1 A Computer System's Date/ Information Storage Capacity

1 Byte	=	1 Character of data (A character can be alphabetic-A,B or C–or numeric–1,2, or 3–or a special character–1,?, •, $ %.)
1 Kilobyte	=	1,024 characters
1 Megabyte	=	1,048,576 characters
1 Gigabyte	=	More than 1 Billion Characters
1 Terabyte	=	More than 1 Trillion Characters
1 Petabye	=	About 1 quadrillion Characters

Floppy-Disk Drive

A floppy-disk drive is a storage device that stores data on removable 3.5-inchdiameter diskettes. These diskettes, which are now used mostly on fairly old microcomputer sysytems, don't seem to be 'floppy,' because they are encased in hard plastic, but the mylar disk inside is indeed flexible or floppy. Each can store 1.44 million bytes or more of data. With a floppy-disk drive installed, you'll later be able to insert a diskette through a slot in the front and remove it by pushing the eject button.

Hard-Disk Drive

A *hard-disk drive* is a storage device that stores billions of characters of data on a Non-removable disk platter. With 120–200 gigabytes of storage, you should be able to handle most student needs.

CD/DVD Drive

A *CD (compact-disk) drive,* or its more recent variant, a *DVD (digital videodisk) drive,* is a storage device that uses laser technology to read data from optical disks. Today new software is generally supplied on CDs or via the net. The system cabinet has lights on the front that indicate when these drives are in use. The wires for these lights need to be attached to the motherboard.

OUTPUT HARDWARE

Output hardware consists of devices that translate information processed by the computer into a form that humans can understand—print, sound, graphics, or video, for example. Now a video card and a sound card need to be installed in the system cabinet. Next the monitor, speakers, and a printer are plugged in. This is a good place to introduce the term *peripheral device.* A *peripheral device* is any component or piece of equipment that expands a computer's input, storage, and output capabilities. In other words, a peripheral device is not part of the essential computer. Peripheral devices can be inside the computer or connected to it from the outside. Examples include printers and disk drives.

Video Card

You doubtless want your monitor to display Colour images. Your system cabinet will therefore need to have a device to make this possible. A *video card* converts the processor's output information into a video signal that can be sent through a cable to the monitor. Remember the expansion slots we mentioned? Your video card is plugged into one of these on the motherboard.

Sound Card

You may wish to listen to music on your PC. If so, you'll need a *sound card,* which enhances the computer's sound-generating capabilities by allowing sound to be output through speakers. This, too, would be plugged into an expansion slot on the motherboard. With the CD drive connected to the card, you can listen to music CDs.

Monitor

As with television sets, the inch dimension on monitors is measured diagonally corner to corner. The *monitor* is the display device that takes the electrical signals from the video card and forms an image using points of ed light on the screen. Later, after the system cabinet has been closed up, the monitor will be connected by means of a cable to the back of the computer, using the clearly marked connector. The power cord for the monitor will be plugged into a wall plug.

Pair of Speakers

Speakers are the devices that play sounds transmitted as electrical signals from the sound card. They may not be very sophisticated, but unless you're into high-fidelity recordings they're probably good enough. The two speakers are connected to a single wire that is plugged into the back of the computer once installation is completed.

Printer

Especially for student work, you certainly need a *printer*, an output device that produces text and graphics on paper. There are various types of printers, as we discuss later. The printer has two connections. One, which relays signals from the computer, goes to the back of the PC, where it connects with the motherboard. The other is a power cord that goes to a wall plug. Colour printers are more expensive than black-and-white printers, and fast printers cost more than slow ones.

COMMUNICATIONS HARDWARE: MODEM

Computers can be stand-alone machines, unconnected to anything else. If all you're doing is word processing to write term papers, you can do it with a stand-alone system. However, the communications component of the computer system vastly extends the range of a PC. Thus, while the system cabinet is still open, there is one more piece of hardware to install.

Modem

A standard *modem* is a device that sends and receives data over telephone lines to and from computers. The modem is mounted on an expansion card, which is fitted into an expansion slot on the motherboard.

Later you can run a telephone line from the telephone wall plug to the back of the PC, where it will connect to the modem. Other types of communications connections exist. However, standard modems are still often used. Now the system cabinet is closed up. The person building the system will plug in all the input and output devices and turn on the power 'on' button. Your microcomputer system will look similar to the one opposite.

SOFTWARE

With all the pieces put together, the person assembling the computer needs to check the motherboard manual for instructions on starting the system. One of the most important tasks is to install software, the electronically encoded instructions that tell the computer hardware what to do. Software is what makes the computer worthwhile. There are two types—*system software* and *application software.*

System Software

First, system software must be installed. *System software* helps the computer perform essential operating tasks and enables the application software to run. System software consists of several electronically coded Programmes. The most important is the *operating system,* the master control Programme that runs the computer.

Examples of operating system software for the PC are various Microsoft Programmes, Unix, and Linux. The Apple Macintosh microcomputer is another matter altogether. It has its own hardware components and software, which often aren't directly transferable to the PC. System software comes most often on CDs.

The person building your computer system will insert these into your CD drive and follow the on-screen directions for installation. After the system software is installed, setup software for the hard drive, the video and sound cards, and the modem must be installed. These setup Programmes will probably come on CDs. Once again, the installer inserts these into the appropriate drive and then follows the instructions that appear on the screen.

Application Software

Now we're finally getting somewhere! After the application software has been installed, you can start using the PC. *Application software* enables you to perform specific tasks—solve problems, perform work, or entertain yourself. For example, when you prepare a term paper on your computer, you will use a word processing Programme. Application software is specific to the system software you use.

If you want to run Microsoft Word, for instance, you'll need to first have Microsoft Windows system software on your system, not Unix or Linux. Application software comes on CDs packaged in boxes that include instructions. You insert the CDs into your computer and then follow the instructions on the screen for installation.

Later on you may obtain entire application Programmes by getting them off the internet, using your modem or another type of communications connection.

CUSTOM-BUILT PC WORTH THE EFFORT

Does the foregoing description make you want to try putting together a PC yourself? If you add up the costs of all the components, and then start checking ads for PCs, you might wonder why anyone would bother going to the trouble of building one. And nowadays you would probably be right. "If you think you'd save money by putting together a computer from scratch," says David Einstein, "think again. You'd be lucky to match the price PC-makers are charging these days in their zeal to undercut the competition."

But had you done this for real, it would not have been a wasted exercise: by knowing how to build a system yourself, not only would you be able to impress your friends but you'd also know how to upgrade any store-bought system to include components that are better than standard. For instance, as Einstein points out, if you're into videogames, knowing how to construct your own PC would enable you to make a system that's right for games. You could include the latest three-dimensional graphics video card and a state-of the-art sound card, for example. More important, you'd also know how to order a custom-built system that's right for you. As suggested, expand on this discussion so that you can really know what you're doing when you go shopping for a microcomputer system.

Impact of information technology and role of libraries in the age of information and knowledge societies information technology has transformed the whole world into a global village with a global economy, which is increasingly dependant on the creative management and distribution of information. Over the past decades the world has been experiencing significant changes in which the need to acquire, utilise and share knowledge has become increasingly essential. Now, in the 21st century, the age of knowledge and information is in its higher gear.

This is an age when invisible knowledge and information take the role of prime movers leading all sector. The World Bank has used metaphor 'knowledge is development'. Lack of knowledge is largely responsible for underdevelopment. In a knowledge and information-oriented society, creative brains become leaders of economy and knowledge workers are in great demand. If knowledge can be equated with development, then the wider the knowledge gap, the broader the development gap.

EMERGENCE OF INFORMATION AND KNOWLEDGE SOCIETIES

Some 10,000 year ago the early ancestor of mankind, subsisted by hunting and gathering, started to building agrarian societies. The old agrarian societies began their transitions to industrial societies in mid-18th centuries. Expansion of intellectual activities in industrial societies, such as industrial production, international trade and transactions, and technological advancement, stimulated mass distribution of education and creation of libraries. Industrial societies continued their enormous material development throughout the 20th century.

The information society has passed through four transformational stages of development, the most radical stage starting at the tail end of the 20th century. This stage has brought a never-ending revolution, particularly with the introduction of information and communication technologies. During this period, there have been unprecedented developments, profoundly affecting the social structure–the decline of manufacturing sector as compared to the prospering information-rich service sector is one example of such developments. The concept of knowledge societies is often used to denote a development in or second generation of information society.

Whereas the information society aims to make information available and provide the necessary technology, the knowledge society aims to generate knowledge, create culture of sharing and develop applications that operate mainly via the Internet. The goal of knowledge society is to fill social needs, create wealth and enhance the quality of life in a sustainable manner. India is moving fast towards becoming an information society as the Government of India is paying due attention to the use of information technology (IT).

The Prime Minister of India constituted a National Task Force on IT and Software Development in May 1998 with the purpose of formulating a long-term National IT Policy to convert India into an IT software superpower. These steps are helping India to shift from an 'economy of goods' to a 'knowledge economy' or 'knowledge driven economy'. The beginning of the knowledge society has been made through creation of parks and corridors, and the Prime Minister has given a mission of converting India into a 'knowledge society' by the year 2008. Today, India is one of the largest exporters of knowledge workers.

ROLE OF LIBRARIES

In the modern knowledge society libraries have a new role and there are various types of library models. In the modern society, where the use of electronic services and Web-based information sources constantly increases, libraries are managed in a more democratic way, have more flexible communication system and work organisation, and their service development is based on the quality and user-orientation of services. In the modern knowledge society libraries have a new role and there are various types of library models.

These are as follows:

- Traditional library as a memory institution
- Library as a learning and research centre
- Library as a cultural and communication centre
- Electronic library
- Digital library
- Virtual library as library without walls.

Libraries had been performed many important roles in the past agrarian and industrial societies. But those roles were limited in scope. In the 21st century, libraries have to perform pivotal roles in disseminating and sharing the culture of knowledge. In this age of knowledge libraries should be repositories of all of the knowledge and information accumulated by human kind.

They will have to store all kinds and forms of material and information and disseminate beyond the geographical boundaries. Today's advanced information technology is enabling libraries to accomplish this immense task. Exchange of knowledge has always been the most important objectives of libraries. Various systems have been developed to share and exchange the records of human knowledge. Universal Bibliographic Control and Universal Availability of Publications are two major Programmes of IFLA (International Federation of Library Associations and Institutions) to exchange knowledge world over. OCLC is the world leading library network in USA for sharing intellectual knowledge among academic community in all over the world. But libraries in the 21st century should fulfill more dynamic role. They should exchange knowledge and information with users inside and outside their country, thus going beyond their traditional reference and lending services. This would possible when libraries agreed to expand their roles beyond the geographical boundaries by using sate of art technologies.

The modern libraries certainly can not be passive repository for books and other printed materials. The opposite requirements of storing increasing collection in various forms and of maintaining easy access to most part of it can only be balanced by deploying information and communication technologies. Libraries should upgrade their services by digitising their resources for online use.

These services should be accessible to anyone, regardless of time or location, through digital communication devices. Libraries can play significant role in providing a good education and knowledge of high quality. Individuals around the world, no matter how poor they may be, can access whatever knowledge and information they need by visiting libraries via the internet, such as the library of congress.

PROBLEMS AND OPPORTUNITIES FACING LIBRARIES IN INDIA

Library and information services are fundamental to the goals of creating, disseminating, optimally utilising and preserving knowledge. They are instrumental in transforming an unequal society into an egalitarian, progressive knowledge-based society. It is well known that in India most of the libraries function in the government sector.

These are in academic and research institutions and under the public library system, which is again under the state and central governments. At present, education being a state subject and coming under the purview of different apex agencies, there is no common direction or coordination among them. It is imperative that all libraries (public, academic, research and special) change gear and develop at an accelerated pace. Developments in information communication technology (ICT) have enabled libraries to provide access to all, and also bridge the gap between the local, the national and the global. Yet the Library and Information Services (LIS) sector in India has not kept pace with the paradigmatic changes taking place in society.

There are a few libraries which are using state of art technologies to disseminate knowledge to their respective user community. There is lack of cooperation among the libraries of different organisations and which cause the lack of union catalogues at national level.

The national library failed even to do this immense task. One of the major problems faced by LIS sector in India is lack of bibliographic control at national level which causes duplication in research. A considerable number of libraries had not been developed bibliographic databases of their documents for putting them on network. To summarise, the major constraints faced by the libraries which militate against effective dissemination and use of information are:

- A considerable percentage of the population is illiterate or functionally literate making libraries of minimal use to them.
- Poor resource allocation for infrastructure improvement and collection development for public libraries.
- Lack of sufficient sanctioned posts, forcing most services to be operated by voluntary Non-professional staff, which damages information organisation and services.
- Lack of national policies promoting ICT as a tool for development of library systems and services.
- Lack of adequate trained manpower in the use of IT.
- Lack of funds for acquiring necessary hardware and software facilities.
- Resistance on the part of library staff to change from their traditional practices to the use of IT.

Despite the problems, Library and Information Services (LIS) sector in India has got remarkable achievements. Efforts had been made to set up networks at local, regional and national level to deploy information and communication technologies and to build electronic information sources. Besides INFLIBNET at the national level to support university and college libraries, a number of other national networks and various library networks have also been developed including

NICNET (National Informatics Centers Network), ERNET (Education and Research Network), CALIBNET (Calcutta Library Network), DELNET (Developing Library Network), etc.

A number of educational institutions are members of such networks. These networks, especially INFLIBNET and DELNET, are engaged in compiling union catalogs, creating various databases of experts, providing training to library staff, ILL, online facilities, reference service, assistance in retrospective conversion, etc. To overcome the problem of financial crunch and the rising costs of journals, librarians have formed consortia to subscribe all the required journals and databases. Some special libraries and research organisations have established consortia known as FORSA (Forum for Resource Sharing in Astronomy) to share electronic access to journal literature.

NISCAIR (National Institutes of Science Communication and Information Resources), one of CSIR labs, has formed a consortium for CSIR labs for accessing e-journals and databases. In order to solve the problem of universities and college libraries, UGC launched a major initiative called UGC-INFONET that provides high speed Internet connections so as to have electronic access to professional literature including research journals, abstracts, review publications, and databases from all areas in science and technology, as well as in social sciences and humanities.

The Ministry of Human Resource Development (MHRD) has set up the "Indian National Digital Library in Science and Technology (INDEST) Consortium" for the subscription to electronic resources for 38 academic institutions, including the Indian Institute of Sciences, Indian Institute of Technology, Regional Engineering Colleges, Indian Institute of Managements, and about 60 centrally-funded/aided government institutions through the consortium. For the improvement of quality of library and information services through the systematic acquisition, organisation and dissemination of knowledge, various library associations have been set up at national and state level.

They annually organised conferences, seminars and training Programmes to trained and update library professionals with latest development in LIS. Recently libraries and research organisations realise the importance of digital libraries and they started the work of digitisation of important documents. NISCAIR and the Department of Indian Systems of Medicine and Homoeopathy (ISMandH) have entered into an agreement for establishing a Traditional Knowledge Digital Library (TKDL) on Ayurveda. TKDL will be available in English, German, French, Spanish and Japanese Since, these languages account for more than 98 per cent of the international patent applications.

TKDL in the first phase targets Ayurveda. But as a whole it would encompass, in addition to Ayurveda, Siddha, Unani, Yoga, Naturopathy and Folklore medicine. The Indian Institute of Science (IISc), Carnegie Mellon University (CMU), the International Institute of Information Technology, Hyderabad (IIITH) and many other academic, religious and government organisations, totaling about 21 'Content Creation Centers', have become partners in the Digital Library of India (DLI) initiative for the digitisation and preservation of Indian heritage present in the form of books, manuscripts, art and music.

Each centre brings its own unique collection of literature into the digital library. DLI has a vision to build a universal digital library of world knowledge. One million books have already been available through this project. India perhaps has one of the oldest and largest collections of Manuscripts in the world. These manuscripts are in different languages and scripts; written on different materials such as birch bark, palm leaf, cloth, paper, etc. They are in the custody of libraries, museums, monasteries, mutts and individuals.

A significant proportion is not preserved scientifically. Experts estimate that almost all palm leaf manuscripts may perish due to wear and tear over next 50 to 100 years. In this regard the National Mission for Manuscripts has taken a step to save the most valuable, intellectual property of our cultural inheritance. The missions has started a pilot project for digitising the manuscripts in five states across India covering five caches of manuscripts and for the same four digitising agencies have been selected.

Importance of open access archives, institutional repositories and open access journals has been realised by the library and information professionals in India. This movement has been accelerated by the availability of open source software namely DSpace, EPrints, Greenstone, etc., Indian Institute of Science, Bangalore, INFLIBNET Centre, Ahmedabad and Documentation Research and Training Centre (DRTC), Bangalore are the leading institutions who made this movement a great success. Among the top 25 publishing countries, India ranks 12th for the overall number of journals, but drops to 18th for journals with online content. At present there are more than 150 open access journals in India.

The open access journals in India are mainly initiated by six journal publishers, namely, Indian Academy of Sciences, Indian National Science Academy, Indian Medlars Centre of National Informatics Centre, Medknow Publications, indianjournals. com and Kamla-Raj Enterprises. The Indian Institute of Science was the first in the country to set up and interoperable institutional archive ePrints@IIScr. The archive now has more than 7000 records, with over 90 per cent having full text. Presently there are 25 institutional archives in India which are registered in the Registry of Open Access Repositories (ROAR). An open access statement is likely to be ready by this year. The CSIR also has a plan to setup a national digital repository of research literature. NISCAIR has already started to work on the project known as National Science Digital Library. National knowledge Commission is also formulating similar open access policies and guidelines for the higher education and R and D sectors to improve access to research literature and disseminate research literature to the global communities. The National Knowledge Commission has submitted its report to the government on how to redefine the information services sector. The report of Knowledge Commission on library sector suggests that "Every state should establish a registry and archives of knowledge based digital resources which should be made accessible to all".

CONCLUSION

The acquisition of knowledge has therefore been the thrust area throughout the world. The economy of present times depends no longer on visible resources and capital goods but on invisible knowledge and information. Therefore, poor nations as well as poor individuals can create wealth through active contacts and use of knowledge and information. Libraries of the 21st century can help fight poverty and narrow the gap between rich and poor. For the first time in history poor are getting opportunity to enhance their wealth through the creation and use of knowledge. And libraries are taking a central role in this notable movement.

2

Library Survival in the Face of Change

There is an impending crisis in library services. Ongoing research, funded by the Institute for Museum and Library Science (IMLS) in the US, has revealed that while there is an increasing number of remote users of library services, actual visits to libraries have diminished in recent years. That does not mean, however, that librarians are no longer needed. In fact, estimates show that by 2016 there will be a need for 14,120 special librarians and 26,000 public librarians.

With just 4000 graduates entering the sector each year – a consistent number. Since, 1982 – there are likely to be staff shortages before long. The situation may also be exacerbated by a lack of PhD candidates who can provide the younger generation with the educational and professional development requirements they need to prosper in the library/ informationservices sector. And the only reason problems haven't already arisen is because the baby-boomer generation has perhaps taken longer to retire than expected.

For all the talk of how the library profession will need to work harder to recruit and retain talent to forestall the problems, there is surely an underlying concern: that the whole traditional concept of the physical library, whether in business, or in the public domain, is actually becoming obsolete. In a recent issue of *Inside Knowledge* magazine Oliver Schwabe, a specialist in value networks and knowledge innovation, talks about the rise of Wikipedia. Although it has been derided as pandering to the 'masses', there is no doubt that it has, nevertheless, become a huge resource. The great libraries of antiquity, lovingly put together over decades, a project that has harnessed the knowledge of the global community, not just a handful of 'wise men', and which is available to everyone, everywhere, for no charge. He then goes on to argue that the new business model in this online, collaborative age is 'distributed intelligence', a concept of acquiring knowledge that lies within the online control of the many, rather than the physical direction or leadership of the few.

Managing director of Trend Monitor, has also written on this changing environment. The boxout 'Changing times' is an extract from an article also for *Inside Knowledge* magazine, in which he talks about how everyone, assuming they have a broadband connection, can now broadcast their own thoughts by blogs, wikis, podcasts or video-chats. Finding information for ourselves is the resounding trait in this new landscape; anyone over the age of 10 is probably now familiar with searching the internet, for free, via Google or any other number of search engines.

We no longer need to go to anyone else for help and we are no longer passive recipients, waiting on the mass media to fulfil our information needs. The new world is interactive and collaborative, and for the large part, selfsufficient. In this landscape, is there really any room for the traditional librarian?

THE ONLINE BUSINESS WORLD

Nor is technology merely impacting the way we interact with information on a personal level. No doubt, many of us will have been surprised by how popular social-networking sites such as Facebook or MySpace have become. But the new collaborative capabilities of Web 2.0 have not just rung in lifestyle changes on a personal level, they are now being used to change the very way business is conducted.

Even in the most seemingly traditional of professions such as law, some firms are now positively embracing the opportunities of this collaborative online experience. Allen and

Overy LLP, for instance, one of the largest UK law firms, has spent the past few years experimenting with social software. From an initial trial of just three social software sites in 2006, the firm now has around 50 sites, supporting internal and external client communities around the Allen and Overy globe. Different legal, support and project teams develop and use the tools on the site – a group blog and wiki, categorisation and social tagging, and shared newsfeeds and bookmarks – in different ways to meet their own particular needs.

The firm is now working on improving the user interface and functionality of the sites, integrating the tools within the firm's broader intranet and extranet portals based on Microsoft Sharepoint 2007. As Ruth Ward, the firm's head of knowledge systems and development, recently explained, this will enable the firm to make more use of individual social tools for different business purposes and to use really-simple syndication (RSS) to help manage and consolidate information flows. And, of course, feedback and ideas on the project development have been shared between the project team and the site community, via a wiki.

THE IMPACT OF TECHNOLOGY ON EXISTING GENERATIONAL DIFFERENCES

This online collaborative environment has enabled people to access information, as well as interact with each other to share knowledge, like never before. It is no coincidence that in the face of this online landscape, the physical library is getting smaller. There is much debate in the library profession right now as to how the future will shape up, but there is little doubt that many libraries, public and special, are currently facing budgetary cuts and a reduction in the physical space available to them.

Teams of librarians are being replaced by the rise of solo operations, with little career development or ability to recruit more staff. In addition, services may be increasingly outsourced or long-established information centres closed. Quite simply, where people can go online to fulfil many of their information needs, there is little perceived need to visit a library or use the services of a librarian. There is also a generational shift, reinforced by technology advances, which may also be threatening the survival of the library. Quite simply, many still perceive the library to be a physical space, filled with books and policed by a bespectacled librarian, probably from an older generation, and trained in advanced forms of library cataloguing and indexing.

While they are valuable skills, the younger generation may little relish the thought of following in their footsteps – after all, they have grown up into a world that appears completely different, and that is dominated by instantly accessible online information. In the business world, for example, the proliferation of technology has had a completely transformative effect, enabling vast global expansion because the tools allow for different offices in all locations to streamline operations and communicate. Most people now use technology applications on a day-to-day basis, if only to function effectively in the workplace.

For younger generations, though, this technology drive has been even more revolutionary. From childhood, younger people have been using technology to help with everything, from doing their homework to socialising. And as those younger people have grown up and entered the workplace, so have the days of reading books or even just sitting in a classroom seemed increasingly numbered. E-learning, for instance, is becoming more popular, with many businesses employing sophisticated techniques for delivering employees with 'just-in-time' training at their desks.

Younger employees will also be far more adaptable to these technology tools, having most likely graduated from colleges that also employ tools, such as webinars, to deliver vital training. For this younger generation, the whole concept of the 'library', including the people who staff them, may appear somewhat old-fashioned and irrelevant. Meanwhile, the older generation may not be well-equipped to adapt to this new environment or to educate younger people on the continuing and, indeed, evolving value of library services. While certainly not ignorant of technology advances, the older generation is less likely to view technology as such an integral part of daily life.

Al Podboy has worked as director of library services at law firm Baker Hostetler for 30 years; he knows the firm's culture and its lawyers inside out, and he's also familiar with these changing times. "My generation and a lot of my peers have been working in their firms for a long time. I've seen a couple of generations come through the firm and I've seen the differences between them," he comments. He has also been a witness to intergenerational conflict – he refers to one example where a familiar criticism targeted at the younger generation is that they just don't read.

"I get a bit annoyed by this to be honest. We live in a much faster environment than when I started. Younger people do read, just not necessarily books," he says. Such differences highlight a real problem: a potentially growing generation gap that could be particularly harmful for the survival of library services, where the older generation is less likely to keep up with new applications and younger people are less likely to be open to, or understand the worth of library services. And if that means fewer people even enter the library profession, the impending crisis could soon be worse than feared.

For Podboy, such generational differences need to be addressed proactively: "We have to introduce older people to technology and convince them that the younger people are not necessarily doing things wrong," he explains. "We need to ensure that people of my age understand what those technologies are and try to encourage them to adapt to them.

At the same time, though, we need to be able to teach younger people the older forms – the value of a book or of an older mentor, for example, where they can benefit from somebody's direct experience of a particular work or task." But bringing together different generations, so that they can appreciate the merits of different methods of working, may be particularly difficult in this modern landscape. Where Podboy, like many of his peers, stayed with the one firm for his whole career, the younger generations are far more likely to change jobs and even careers several times. According to a 2006 survey by *The American Lawyer*, for example, many associates in US law firms see jumping ship as a 'fundamental career milestone'.

Nearly two-thirds of third and fourth-year associates responding to the survey said they didn't expect to be, or didn't know if they'd be, at the same firm in five years as a partner or senior associate. Quite simply, attitudes to the workplace and lifestyle expectations between generations are often vastly different. Generations X and Y want flexibility, challenges, career-advancement opportunities, learning and development opportunities, and fast appreciation and recognition.

And much of their experience of this will be in a fast-paced, technologicallyenabled, online environment. In contrast, older generations are far more used to working in one company, and having one career for a lifetime, learning via traditional routes, and probably using, but not relying, on technology to function effectively. Not only do their attitudes differ widely, but it is less likely today that they'll even be in the same company for long enough to really benefit from the teachings of each other.

THE DANGER FOR LIBRARIANS

For the library profession, these changes may well prove to be fundamental stumbling blocks in the years ahead. According to America's Career Resource Network (ACRN), the number of people aged 55 and over will increase sharply by 2050, but their labour force participation will increase only slightly.

This means that the labour force overall will shrink. In addition, ACRN expects that by 2014, the workforce will have openings for nine million more degree-holders than will be available. There will be three million surplus openings for two-year degreeholders, four million for four-year degreeholders, and two million for advanced degree-holders. And such a shortage of skilled/professional workers is not just a US phenomenon – the retiring baby-boomer generation is also likely to cause problems for employers in the UK, and beyond. And for librarians, the difficulties may be even more pronounced.

US government statistics show that there were 5490 librarians working in business industries (manufacturing, finance, insurance, trade, publishing and transportation) in 2002. It predicts that there will be 6632 librarian jobs by 2012 – a significant rise of 1142 or 21 per cent. In keeping with overall workforce statistics, not only does the library profession face the aforementioned shortage of graduates entering the informationservices field, but a larger number of those currently working as librarians will be older and close to retirement age.

They need to find a way now of attracting younger people by demonstrating how the library profession can meet the needs of a younger generation with very different personal and career perspectives. If the profession fails to do this now, there may be significant problems in delivering any kind of library services in the future, once the baby-boomers have retired. In June 2006, Mary Ellen Bates, principal of Bates Information Service Research Association, spoke at the Special Libraries Association (SLA) annual conference on the future of library services.

As part of her presentation, she remarked on how library services were experiencing a period of older librarians, with the question arising of how they would be replaced – or how the library profession could go about attracting younger people. In addition, she touched upon the increasingly technology-savvy graduates who have a Masters in Library Science (MLS) – but might be put off the idea of entering a library environment perhaps because of perceptions of it being outdated or old-fashioned, the remit of an older generation more used to books and classrooms, rather than social software and online collaboration. Indeed, SLA surveys of members suggest that an increasing number of information graduates that might traditionally have entered the library environment, are actually choosing jobs outside the library or information resources centre.

In 2003, the SLA 'Annual Salary Survey' revealed that as many as 18 per cent of Canadian and US SLA members were not working in the library or information resource centre. This compares to 13 per cent in 1999. Other areas of work attracting information professionals today include publishing, the database, directory and software industry, as well as the computer systems design industry.

The trend also shows a growing number of information professionals not only working outside the library, but also taking on different responsibilities compared to the traditionally accepted library remit:

- Analysis is the primary responsibility of 8.1 per cent of SLA members who do not claim to work in libraries. This compares to just 0.7 per cent of those who work in libraries;
- Of those not working in libraries, 3.4 per cent said that information product/ database development was their primary responsibility, compared to 1.0 per cent of those who work in libraries;
- While 2.5 per cent of those claiming to work in libraries have primary responsibility for knowledge management (KM), a higher percentage (3.8 per cent) of those not working in libraries primarily manage KM; and
- Records management is the primary responsibility of 4.1 per cent of those not working in libraries, compared to just 0.7 per cent of those working in libraries.

This means that traditional libraries may not just find themselves struggling to recruit fresh graduates to the field, but they may also find themselves competing for talent against other functions, including records management and KM.

THE GOOD NEWS

There is little doubt that the library profession is presently facing something of a perception problem. As Mary Ellen Bates said at the 2006 SLA annual conference, there is much work to be done to market librarians and library services as something 'sexy', attractive and new. The rather stale and outdated image of a glasses-wearing, book-laden librarian will just not hold up against the fast-paced expectations of the younger business generation. To some, indeed, there now appears to be a very real prospect that libraries as we understand them will soon cease to have a purpose at all; that they will before long be consigned to the history books – which in themselves will disappear down some dark, disused library corridor. But there are also signs that the librarian may be emerging from these difficult times to become something altogether new. Ramon Barquin, president of consulting firm Barquin International, recently argued that librarians are perhaps key to making sense of a world that has certainly moved on technologically, but actually struggles more than ever to manage the sheer amount of information circulating in this online dimension. Librarianship has, and will continue to evolve, beyond books to helping to connect people with what they need to know, in whatever format they need to receive the information.

3

Technology Across the Curriculum

If information technology skills are increasingly important in the world outside of higher education, then certainly educators need to examine the Programmes of study at their institution to see how they are preparing students to survive and thrive in the technology rich environment that has now permeated all areas of life. Information literacy, fluency in *information technology* (IT), technology across the curriculum, general education requirements, ubiquitous computing—there are many models for introducing technology into academic Programmes, but no silver bullet that meets the needs of every institution.

We are not attempting here to define one approach that every institution should take. Instead, we focus on factors that every institution needs to consider in successful curriculum development for fluency in information technology and information literacy, and we offer examples of strategies that can address these factors. Although we present these factors linearly, they are really recursive—consideration of any one factor may lead back to reconsideration of others.

In addition, although we focus here on curriculum development for undergraduate education, we recognise that the strategies we identify also have broader application to the design of continuing training Programmes for workforce development at the college or university level or in the work setting. The growing industry of IT-related training needs to be cognizant of the same range of factors as academic institutions in order to create successful Programmes. Supplying information technology workers and IT-enabled workers is a task that higher education shares with employers, and both sectors need carefully planned strategies to be effective in meeting that responsibility.

In our discussion, we have used examples from George Mason University's Technology Across the Curriculum (TAC) initiative because we are most familiar with it, but we would be the first to acknowledge that George Mason's Programme was designed to fit this institution's particular circumstances and is not necessarily appropriate at another institution.

PRELIMINARY DEFINITIONS

Information literacy and information technology fluency are overlapping but distinct competencies. They are complementary to each other—in today's world an information technology fluent person must also be information literate, and vice versa. In this context, the aim of *fluency* in information technology tends to focus on the technology itself; the goal of *literacy* is primarily concerned with the intellectual framework of dealing with information.

Mastery of the three types of knowledge characterises fluency in information technology, or FITness. These are the essential building blocks for acquiring knowledge of and sustaining the process of lifelong learning for FITness, bolstering a person's ability to succeed in the dynamic environment of information technology. Although the concept of FITness clearly goes well beyond the mechanical type of learning typically associated with computer literacy, its focus nevertheless remains information technology itself—hardware, software, networks, and so forth. In contrast, the central concern of information literacy "is an intellectual framework for understanding, finding, evaluating, and using information—activities which may be accomplished in part by fluency with information technology, in part by sound investigative methods, but most important, through critical discernment and reasoning". Development of information literacy focuses on information itself:

- Determining the nature and extent of information needed
- Finding and accessing needed information effectively and efficiently, whether it is available in the library, on the Web, from a government agency, in a book or journal, or in a map
- Critically evaluating information and its sources and using it effectively
- Understanding the ethical, legal, economic, and social uses of information

Like FITness, information literacy aims to develop, foster, and sustain lifelong learning. But unlike FITness, information literacy abilities are not exclusively or ultimately intertwined with or dependent on information technology.

KEYS TO A SUCCESSFUL PROGRAMME

In thinking about how to integrate either or both of the related concepts of IT fluency and information literacy into the curricula of an institution, we have identified ten factors as crucial elements in a successful Programme.

DETERMINE YOUR INSTITUTIONAL STAKEHOLDERS

An environmental scan is an important early step in addressing technology in the curriculum. Who cares, or might potentially care, about this issue? The list is certain to vary from institution to institution, but here are a few suggestions:

- Does your governing board take a strong interest in curriculum?
- Has your regional accrediting agency or state higher education board set guidelines for technology or information literacy competencies?
- Has the business community in your area expressed a need for employees with technology skills?
- Do some academic departments already offer technology-related courses?

- Are there faculty committees involved in curriculum development?
- How important is it to your students to develop their technology and information literacy skills?
- How do your alumni feel about an effort to include more technology skills in your institution's degree Programmes?

Don't overlook in your environmental scan academic support units such as the library, student services, and information technology—and even the public relations department, the development office, and institutional research staff.

The staff in these units are very likely to have not only an interest in the issue but the expertise to contribute to developing a successful initiative. Any or all of these groups can be a tremendous ally in developing a unified and coherent institutional approach to improving student technology and information literacy skills.

Conversely, they can also be a tremendous roadblock if they feel that their perspectives or interests in the issue are not being addressed by the proposed Programme. At the very least, your Programme will be deprived of their potential contributions of time, funding, or expertise if the Programme coordinators are unaware of their interest in the issue.

For George Mason's Programme, the governor and the state legislature turned out to be key players in initiating TAC. But the actual design and implementation required many participants within the institution. Not every group of stakeholders has the same strategic importance, of course, but institutional change being as difficult as it is, one supporter more or one resister less can make a difference in the success of the overall Programme.

ENGAGE YOUR STAKEHOLDERS

Having identified stakeholders or potential stakeholders in the issue of student technology and information literacy skills and their respective levels of strategic importance, you need to engage them appropriately. At a minimum, you can engage stakeholders by sharing information through a Web site, brochure, e-mail announcement, and the like.

At a higher level of engagement, you can actively solicit input on the project through a survey or focus group. For example, in designing TAC, faculty were surveyed quite early in the process to find out the degree to which they were already asking students to use technology in their courses and what kinds of technology they were using. By being able to give a big-picture view of what was already happening, we could show that our proposal aligned with a direction in which faculty were already moving.

We used focus groups both with faculty and members of our local business community to get ideas about exactly what technology skills students needed to succeed in an academic discipline and in a business environment. The high degree of overlap between the two groups helped faculty recognise that TAC had academic value and was not a vocational sellout to Non-academic concerns. Other levels of active engagement include membership on a working group or project team, a proposal review board, and an advisory group.

Whatever you can do to translate interest to participation and ultimately into ownership benefits the Programme. If it is seen as the work of only one or two people, it is much more difficult for the Programme to have long-term staying power, impact, and acceptance. The TAC Programme also uses showcases to continue engaging stakeholders. At our annual celebration of student learning, for example, TAC sponsors a prise for the learning project that demonstrates the best incorporation of technology in learning. We also have a prise sponsored by the university libraries for the best original student research to encourage development of information literacy skills. Hundreds of students and faculty visit the event and are impressed with what their colleagues are learning and doing with technology.

DEFINE YOUR TERMS

Now, with all these interested parties engaged in your Programme, there are a lot of ideas floating around about what the Programme should be. Multiple perspectives and a multitude of ideas can be healthy and helpful at some stages of development, but eventually the participants have to come to consensus on what the Programme really is and what they are actually buying into.

What would technology integrated into the curriculum look like at your institution? Does it mean every student takes a technology course? That every faculty member uses technology in delivering instruction? That every course requires students to use technology to complete the learning? That some courses or some students or some faculty use technology—and if so, which ones?

Perhaps more basically, what does 'technology' encompass? Are you focusing on office applications such as word processing and spreadsheets? Do you also include on-line search and research skills, information literacy skills broadly defined, multimedia skills? What about legal and ethical issues related to technology, such as privacy, security, and copyright?

Do you include use of such technology equipment as digital cameras and data projectors, computer operating systems, and programming languages? None of these possible definitions is necessarily the best for every type of institution. There can be excellent reasons for including or excluding certain features from your institutional approach. But to make the Programme work, everyone needs to know what is included and what is excluded so that the participants' energy is focused on the former. The strategies of engagement already mentioned also facilitate definition of terms and buy-in on the Programme definition. One cornerstone of TAC is a list of ten technology goals. It took almost a year of collaboration to come up with this list, but once it was established, we could work more easily with many groups to build a Programme around that set of skills.

Table 3.1. Technology Goals for George Mason University Students

Students will be Able to:	Essential (Examples)	Advanced (Examples)
1. Engage in electronic collaboration	Send and receive e-mail; understand 'netiquette'	Participate in collaborative writing; participate in an electronic conference
2. Use and create structured electronic documents	Create, format, and edit a document using a word processing	Use templates, macros, and mail merge to automate Programme repetitious tasks
3. Do technology-enhanced presentations	Use a presentation software package to create, format, and edit an electronic presentation	Modify standard tools and templates for presentations and develop their own
4. Use electronic tools for research and evaluation	Understand and apply search strategies appropriate to the Web and on-line databases	Select databases and other resources according to discipline, timeliness, and coverage
5. Use databases to manage information	Enter data into a Pre-existing database; conduct simple queries of a database	Set up a relational data-base of two or three tables: construct aquery for a simple rela-tional database
6. Use spreadsheets to manage information	Enter data into a new or existing spreadsheet; format the layout of a spreadsheet	Use templates and macros to repetitious tasks: use statistical, logical, and financial formulas
7. Use electronic tools for analysing qualitative and quantitative data	Use a statistical pack lage to enter data, name variables, and define variable values	Perform reliabi-lity and validity analyses

(*Contd...*)

8.	Use graphical and multimedia representational technologies resize, crop change format)	Perform simple manipulations on existing images (download, lighting reverse, etc.)	Add special effects to an image (Colour,
9.	Demonstrate familiarity with major issues legal, ethical, privacy, and security issues in information technology	Understand the basics of copyright and property law as they apply to electronic materials	Understand the ethical raised by artificial intelligence, virtual reality, etc.
10.	Have a working knowledge of hardware and software	Perform basic computer operations on at least one computer platform	Install basic peripheral devices (printer, scanner, etc.

IDENTIFY DESIRED OUTCOMES

Another important clarification for a successful Programme is identifying desired outcomes. This enables development of guidelines for participants about activities appropriate to the Programme, and it helps everyone know how you intend to measure the success of the Programme. Desired outcomes may include improvement of student technology skills, improved academic performance for students, more student satisfaction with academic Programmes, greater faculty use of technology, better job placement for graduates, or an enhanced reputation for the institution in an area of strategic importance to it.

Outcomes can also focus on building a specific partnership with the business community or with another college or university in the region or beyond. With TAC, George Mason's primary desired outcome is that every student graduates from the university with a range of technology skills based on the program's goals. As we revised those technology goals, we added specific performance descriptions so that faculty who were redesigning a course would know what kind of assignment—encompassing both technology fluency and information literacy as appropriate—they would need to build in.

Taking the domain of technology fluency as an example, the first definition of the technology goals indicated that graduates would be able to use a spreadsheet; in our revised version, we have specified more exactly what they need to be able to do with a spreadsheet in a beginning or general education course and what they need to be able to do with one in an advanced course in the major.

This focus on student achievement and student learning means that TAC does not fund proposals that focus on faculty delivery of instruction. At another institution, delivery of instruction may be an important step in achieving the goals of the Programme and thus well worth funding.

After three years, we reviewed and revised the list to reflect our changing understanding of the technology goals we wanted our students to achieve.

In the newest version, we have put more emphasis on being able to use representational technologies; consistent with the university's general education requirements, we have also explicitly identified information literacy skills as part of the desired goals.

IDENTIFY RESOURCES

Armed with understanding of exactly what you want to achieve, you must find existing resources or develop new ones that can help you meet your institution's goals. Take another look at that list of stakeholders and see what financial, personnel, or organisational resources they might have that can help build your proposed Programme. The more your program's goals align with the goals and interests of potential stakeholders, the more likely they are to share or contribute resources.

The availability of resources may determine priorities for implementing the Programme. In higher education, leveraging existing resources is an effective, time-honored strategy. If the provost, dean, department chair, chief librarian, head of student services, or development office supports your initiative, then you may be able to take advantage of funding already available for such purposes as curriculum development, faculty and staff development, workforce development, or even classroom renovation.

Or you may be able to use these funds to interest a business partner, state or local government, or a foundation in helping implement your project. If funds aren't available to accomplish everything you want, then target one part of the project whose success is assured and that is highly likely to engender additional funding.

In some institutions, technology enhancement may be considered to add value to the educational experience, so students and their parents pay an extra technology fee or buy a computer for student use. Likewise, the more the Programme can build on existing staff and existing organisational structures, the easier it is to implement. Is there an organisational or administrative structure in place at your institution that can manage this Programme? The goals of the Programme determine to a certain extent how elaborate a structure you need. If the Programme involves distributing money, then part of the administration has to be an institutional agent with fiscal authority. If the Programme is built as part of the regular faculty teaching load and no extra money is involved, then perhaps an existing academic committee structure at the departmental, school or college, or institutional level, as appropriate, can review and approve curricular changes that meet the Programme goals.

In implementing TAC, George Mason University did create a few new structures but as much as possible we used the existing resources and organisational structure of the College of Arts and Sciences and the Information Technology unit, the two principle partners in the initiative. When the university libraries began to restructure their instruction Programme with an information literacy focus, discussion began immediately to see how we could collaborate and help each other achieve mutual goals.

When the university added an IT proficiency component

to its general education requirements, we worked closely with the universitywide general education committee to make sure that the TAC Programme was in harmony with general education goals and that the committee was aware of the TAC and library goals in planning its implementation.

CHECK YOUR TECHNOLOGY INFRASTRUCTURE

A Programme to enhance student technology learning needs technology resources and may flounder if they are not readily available. It can be extremely frustrating to plan new ways to get students and faculty to use technology, only to discover that there are few facilities on campus where they can learn or use these skills, or that the network or server capacity is insufficient to support your plans, or that the technology cannot be accessed when and where it is needed, or that insufficient networked digital scholarly resources are available. It is wise to start with an understanding of your institution's existing technology infrastructure and any plans already in place to enhance that infrastructure. Working with your IT staff and librarians, you may be able to target improvements in the areas most important to your Programme.

Besides looking at the existing structure, you should also take into account whatever increased demand for technology resources your Programme may generate. Once people start using certain kinds of technology in instruction, more faculty and students want to use them, and expectations grow. Not only do they want to do electronic presentations in every classroom; now they want electronic presentations with audio and video clips accessible over the network.

If there's no possibility that the institution can make that level of technology available, then you must manage expectations or else risk seeing your Programme labeled as a failure even as it succeeds. In the case of TAC, we had two major concerns about technology. Faculty wanted to be sure that students would be supported in learning technology skills outside of the classroom and that there would be enough technology-enhanced classrooms to allow faculty and students to demonstrate the targeted technology skills. We dedicated part of the IT staff to the task of mentoring students in technology skills; we focused our equipment funds on making more classroom technology available.

BUILD YOUR SUPPORT TEAM

New curricula using technology require planning on how you will support the students and the faculty who are to use that technology. Faculty support may include financial incentives or release time as well as student assistants, professional staff trained in instructional design and instructional technology, training classes in instructional technology, librarians to consult regarding research assignments and resources, printed and on-line resource materials, models of the kind of assignment or evaluation you want them to use, and peer mentors. Students likewise need a range of support if they are expected to use technology in new ways as part of their learning process. Except for those in some technical disciplines, faculty generally do not want to dedicate class time for teaching technology skills or information literacy. So although they may expect students to be able to create an electronic presentation for class, they are not going to spend class time teaching this application.

Likewise, they may not devote instructional time to the process of conducting topical literature research and reporting of findings. Students who need it must be able to get the basics of these skills somewhere else. How will your institution facilitate this? Perhaps you can offer short training sessions through one of the technology-related academic departments. Perhaps you can include this kind of training in instructional sessions held by the library or IT staff.

In the TAC Programme, we made use of existing instructional support staff to work with faculty in developing and implementing course revision proposals. We also developed a new Programme to make available graduate and undergraduate student assistants for technology projects. In addition, we expanded an existing student technology facility to include a broader range of support and licensed on-line instructional modules for several hundred software applications.

DEVELOP AN ASSESSMENT PLAN

Assessment constitutes a key feature of educational endeavors. In practical terms, it helps you to keep on improving your Programme and assures your participants and funders that the Programme is doing what was intended. Therefore, think early on about how you will show that the Programme is achieving its outcomes.

Can you repurpose data that are already being collected at the institution, as through graduating senior or alumni surveys that ask about student use of technology during or after their educational experience? Or do you need to collect new sets of data? Perhaps you can work with admissions or student services to collect benchmark information about the technology and associated skills students bring with them to the institution. It is also important to work with the faculty who are teaching technology-enhanced courses so that they find ways to assess how students' skills change or how their learning changes as a result of introducing technology or information literacy skills development.

You may also want to look at specific tests of competency for all students or a random sample of students to demonstrate the impact of your Programme. The organisational structure of the Programme should include provision for how assessment data are collected and disseminated. Whoever is managing the Programme has to develop regular reports about how many students and faculty in which areas of the institution participate in the Programme, and collect data from faculty and other sources about its impact. In addition, thought should be given to how data are applied to improve the Programme.

Who is empowered to make adjustments to it? What are the processes for changing the Programme? In our TAC Programme, we began with a focus on the faculty who were redesigning the curriculum. Proposal guidelines called for inclusion of an assessment component. We didn't always get one, and we spent a lot of time helping faculty to develop that component, including recruiting the head of institutional assessment to give workshops in assessment strategies.

But we kept right on asking for those assessment plans and assessment reports until we got results. We also developed some programmatic strategies for tracking data, such as a grid of which courses included which technology skills; we published regular reports about the number of students, faculty, and departments participating in the Programme. The leadership of the Programme also had operational authority to implement change as a result of assessment information.

THINK PROGRAMMATICALLY

Curricular change is most effective when it is programmatic rather than episodic. If curricular change is left to each individual faculty member to implement, the institution is unlikely to be in a position to know if the end result matches the original intention. With technology fluency and information literacy skills in particular, it is critical to plan for building a range of skills across a number of courses; this can't happen unless there is programwide thinking about the connections between one set of skills and other more advanced ones.

Instead of asking individual faculty to think about technology in their individual courses, consider asking all faculty who teach a particular course to set technology or information literacy goals for the course. That way, every student who takes the course, no matter who teaches it, is working Towards the same outcomes as the other students are. If the faculty know, for example, that every first-year biology student uses spreadsheets to accomplish certain tasks, then faculty teaching more advanced courses can build on that to help students use spreadsheets for sophisticated data collection and analysis.

If use of spreadsheets in the first year is only hit-or-miss, depending on who is teaching the class, then it is difficult for faculty in other courses to build in advanced uses. Similarly, developing information literacy skills is a gradual and cumulative process. Abilities and skills acquired early on, beginning with introductory or general courses, serve students well in the courses of their chosen major.

George Mason's TAC Programme offered extra incentives for group and departmental proposals to encourage the broadest possible collaboration and development across an entire Programme of study. If your Programme is built around a single technology course for all students, then it is important that all faculty be aware of the skills introduced in that course so they can give students additional practice in using the skills in other courses later in their Programme of study. If there is no Programme for ensuring that students use a range of technology and information literacy skills, then they will probably be reintroduced to the same basic skills over and over—never having the opportunity to develop or use more advanced skills at all. In the TAC initiative, for example, we got many proposals for introducing students to Internet research and Web page design, but far fewer that focused on using spreadsheets or electronic presentations, making critical assessment of information and its sources and incorporating selected information in students' written projects, or understanding legal and ethical issues in technology use. We were able to use our tracking grid and our request for proposals to encourage course development across the whole range of skills that we wanted our students to learn.

THINK COLLABORATIVELY

Thinking collaboratively may be the most important strategy in working on your project. Terry O'Banion sets forth a model that is particularly relevant when applied to curriculum development: "Everyone employed in the learning college will be a learning facilitator, including categories formerly designated administration and support or clerical staff.... The goal is to have every employee... thinking about how his or her work facilitates the learning process". If the job of helping students develop interrelated technology fluency and information literacy is left to any one group—faculty, librarians, IT staff, career services—then many opportunities are lost. Understanding and using information and information technology is a multifaceted process that can be facilitated from many perspectives. The more the goal of helping students in that process pervades the institution, the more opportunities students have to learn and hone their skills in these areas.

Building as large a community of interest as possible brings more resources to bear and allows them to be used most productively. If an academic department can share instructional materials, directly or indirectly, then it can avoid duplicating work that is being done in other departments. For example, if many departments are introducing spreadsheets or electronic presentations into their courses, there is really no need for every one of them to develop independent tutorials, assignments, evaluation instruments, and so forth. The same holds true for courses incorporating assignments related to information literacy. At the least, if faculty members see what other colleagues have prepared, they can build on each other's work. At best, faculty from several departments might collaborate, assisted by librarians and instructional technologists, in building a library of assignments or tutorials or other instructional resources from which they all can draw. The TAC Programme builds on a collaborative relationship between the

College of Arts and Sciences and the *Information Technology Unit* (ITU)—including increasingly the libraries, which are an administrative component of ITU—that involves shared goal setting, shared decisions about priorities and resource allocation, and shared commitment to student learning and success. Collaborative partnerships can also extend outside the institution— for example, with the business community—in developing internships that help students practice information and technology skills.

4

Computer Architecture

In computer science and engineering, computer architecture is the practical art of defining the structure and relationship of the subcomponents of a computer. As in designing the architecture of buildings, *architecture* can comprise many levels of information. The highest level of the definition conveys the concepts implement, whereas in building architecture this over-view is normally visual, computer architecture is primarily logical, positing a conceptual system that serves a particular purpose. In both instances, many levels of detail are required to completely specify a given implementation.

As in building architecture, some of these details are often implied as common practice. An early example of an architectural definition of a computer was John Von Neumann's 1945 paper, *First Draft of a Report on the EDVAC,* which described an organisation of logical elements. IBM used this to develop the IBM 701, the company's first commercial stored Programme computer, delivered in early 1952. For example, at a high level, computer architecture is concerned with how the central processing unit (CPU) acts and how it accesses computer memory. Some currently fashionable computer architectures include cluster computing and Non-Uniform Memory Access.

The art of computer architecture has three main subcategories:

- *Instruction set architecture,* or ISA. The ISA is the code that a central processor reads and acts upon. It is the machine language, including the instruction set, word size, memory address modes, processor registers, and address and data formats.

- *Microarchitecture,* also known as *Computer organisation* describes the data paths, data processing elements and data storage elements, and describes how they should implement the ISA. The size of a computer's CPU cache for instance, is an organisational issue that generally has nothing to do with the ISA.
- *System Design* includes all of the other hardware components within a computing system. These include:
  - Data paths, such as computer buses and switches
  - Memory controllers and hierarchies
  - Data processing other than the CPU, such as direct memory access (DMA)
  - Miscellaneous issues such as virtualisation or multiprocessing.

From early days, computers have been used to design the next generation. Programmes written in the proposed instruction language can be run on a current computer via emulation. At this stage, it is now commonplace for compiler designers to collaborate, suggesting improvements in the ISA. Modern simulators normally measure time in clock cycles, and give power consumption estimates in watts, or, especially for mobile systems, energy consumption in joules. Once instruction set and microarchitecture are described, a practical machine must be designed. This design process is called the *implementation*. Implementation is usually not considered architectural definition, but rather hardware design engineering.

Implementation can be further broken down into several steps:

- *Logic Implementation*—design of blocks defined in the microarchitecture at the register-transfer level and logic gate level.
- *Circuit Implementation*—transistor-level design of

basic elements as well as of some larger blocks that may be implemented at this level, or even at the physical level, for performance reasons.

- *Physical Implementation*—physical circuits are drawn out, the different circuit components are placed in a chip floorplan or on a board and the wires connecting them are routed.
- *Design Validation*—The computer as a whole is tested to see if it works in all situations and all timings. Once implementation starts, the first design validations are simulations using logic emulators. However, this is usually too slow to run realistic Programmes. So, after making corrections, next, prototypes are constructed using field-programmable gate-arrays FPGAs. Many hobby projects stop at this stage. The final step is to test prototype integrated circuits. Integrated circuits may require several redesigns to fix problems.

For CPUs, the entire implementation process is often called CPU design.

HISTORY

The term 'architecture' in computer literature can be traced to the work of Lyle R. Johnson, Muhammad Usman Khan and Frederick P. Brooks, Jr., members in 1959 of the Machine Organisation department in IBM's main research center. Johnson had the opportunity to write a proprietary research communication about Stretch, an IBM-developed supercomputer for Los Alamos Scientific Laboratory. In attempting to characterise his chosen level of detail for discussing the luxuriously embellished computer, he noted that his description of formats, instruction types, hardware parameters, and speed enhancements was at the level of 'system architecture' – a term that seemed more useful than 'machine organisation.' Subsequently, Brooks, one of the Stretch designers, "Computer architecture, like other architecture, is the art of determining the needs of the user of a structure and then designing to meet those needs as effectively as possible within economic and technological constraints."

Brooks went on to play a major role in the development of the IBM System/360 line of computers, where 'architecture' gained currency as a noun with the definition as 'what the user needs to know'. Later the computer world would employ the term in many less-explicit ways.

COMPUTER ARCHITECTURE TOPICS

SUB-DEFINITIONS

Some practitioners of computer architecture at companies such as Intel and AMD use more fine distinctions:

- *Macroarchitecture*—Architectural layers that are more Instruction Set Architecture (ISA)
- *Assembly ISA*—A smart assembler may convert an abstract assembly language common to a group of machines into slightly different machine language for different implementations
- *Programmer Visible Macroarchitecture*—Higher level language tools such as compilers may define a consistent interface or contract to programmers using them, abstracting differences between underlying ISA, UISA, and microarchitectures. , *e.g.*, the C, C++, or Java standards define different Programmer Visible Macroarchitecture — although in practice the C microarchitecture for a particular computer includes
- *UISA (Microcode Instruction Set Architecture)*—A family of machines with different hardware level microarchitectures may share a common microcode architecture, and Hence, a UISA.
- *Pin Architecture*—The set of functions that a microprocessor is expected to provide, from the point of view of a hardware platform, *e.g.,*, the × 86 A20M, FERR/IGNNE or FLUSH pins, and the messages that

the processor is expected to emit after completing a cache invalidation so that external caches can be invalidated. Pin architecture functions are more flexible than ISA functions—external hardware can adapt to changing encodings, or changing from a pin to a message—but the functions must be provided in successive implementations even if the manner of encoding them changes.

THE ROLE OF COMPUTER ARCHITECTURE

Computer Architecture: the Definition

The coordination of abstract levels of a processor under changing forces, involving design, measurement and evaluation. It also includes the overall fundamental working principle of the internal logical structure of a computer system. It can also be defined as the design of the task-performing part of computers, *i.e.*, how various gates and transistors are interconnected and are caused to function per the instructions given by an assembly language programmer.

Instruction Set Architecture

Instruction set architecture (ISA) is the interface between the software and hardware. Computers do not understand high level languages. A processor only understand instructions encoded as binary numbers. Besides instructions, the ISA defines items in the computer that are available to a Programme—including data types, registers, addressing modes, and memory organisation. Register indexes and memory addressing modes are the ways that instructions locate their operands. Software tools, special computer Programmes such as compilers, translate high level languages into instructions for a particular instruction set architecture. The ISA of a computer is usually described in a small book or pamphlet. This guide describes the binary numbers that encode the instructions. Most often, short three-letter human names for the instructions can be recognised by a software development tool called an assembler. An assembler is a computer Programme that translates a human-readable form of the ISA into a computer-readable form. Disassemblers are also widely available, usually in debuggers, software Programmes to isolate and correct malfunctions in binary computer Programmes. ISAs vary in quality and completeness. A good ISA compromises between programmer convenience, cost of the computer to interpret the instructions, speed of the computer, and size of the code. For example, a single-instruction ISA is possible, inexpensive, and fast, but not convenient or helpful to make Programmes small. Memory organisation defines how instructions interact with the memory.

Computer Organisation

Computer organisation helps optimise performance-based products. For example, software engineers need to know the processing ability of processors. They may need to optimise software in order to gain the most performance at the least expense. This can require quite detailed analysis of the computer organisation. For example, in a multimedia decoder, the designers might need to arrange for most data to be processed in the fastest data path and the various components are assumed to be in place and task is to investigate the organisational structure to verify the computer parts operates. Computer organisation also helps plan the selection of a processor for a particular project. Multimedia projects may need very rapid data access, while supervisory software may need fast interrupts. Sometimes certain tasks need additional components as well. For example, a computer capable of virtualisation needs virtual memory hardware so that the memory of different simulated computers can be kept separated. Computer organisation and features also affect power consumption and processor cost.

Design Goals

The exact form of a computer system depends on the constraints and goals it is optimised for. Computer architectures usually trade off standards, cost, memory capacity, latency and throughput. Sometimes other considerations, such as features, size, weight, reliability, expandability and power consumption are factors. The most common scheme carefully chooses the bottleneck that most reduces the computer's speed. Ideally, the cost is allocated proportionally to assure that the data rate is nearly the same for all parts of the computer, with the most costly part being the slowest. This is how skillful commercial integrators optimise personal computers.

Performance

Modern computer architectural performance is often described in MIPS per MHz. This metric explicitly measures the efficiency of the architecture at any clock speed. Since, a faster clock can make a faster computer, this is a useful, widely applicable measurement. Historic complex instruction set computers had MIPs/MHz as low as 0.1. Simple modern processors easily reach near 1. Superscalar processors may reach three to five by executing several instructions per clock cycle. Multicore and vector processing CPUs can multiply this further by acting on a lot of data per instruction, and have several CPUs executing in parallel. Counting machine language instructions would be misleading because they can do varying amounts of work in different ISAs. The 'instruction' in the standard measurements is not a count of the ISA's actual machine language instructions, but a historical unit of measurement, usually based on the speed of the VAX computer architecture. Historically, many people measured the speed by the clock rate. This refers to the cycles per second of the main clock of the CPU.

However, this metric is somewhat misleading, as a machine with a higher clock rate may not necessarily have higher performance. As a result manufacturers have moved away from clock speed as a measure of performance. Other factors influence speed, such as the mix of functional units, bus speeds, available memory, and the type and order of instructions in the Programmes being run. In a typical home computer, the simplest, most reliable way to speed performance is usually to add random access memory (RAM). More RAM increases the likelihood that needed data or a Programme is in RAM—so the system is less likely to need to move memory data from the disk. The disk is often ten thousand times slower than RAM because it has mechanical parts that must move to access its data.

There are two main types of speed, latency and throughput. Latency is the time between the start of a process and its completion. Throughput is the amount of work done per unit time. Interrupt latency is the guaranteed maximum response time of the system to an electronic event. Performance is affected by a very wide range of design choices — for example, pipelining a processor usually makes latency worse but makes throughput better.

Computers that control machinery usually need low interrupt latencies. These computers operate in a real-time environment and fail if an operation is not completed in a specified amount of time. For example, computer-controlled anti-lock brakes must begin braking within a predictable, short time after the brake pedal is sensed. The performance of a computer can be measured using other metrics, depending upon its application domain.

A system may be CPU bound, I/O bound or memory bound. Power consumption has become important in servers and portable devices like laptops. Benchmarking tries to take all these factors into account by measuring the time a computer takes to run through a series of test Programmes. Although benchmarking shows strengths, it may not help one to choose a computer. Often the measured machines split on different measures. For example, one system might handle scientific applications quickly, while another might play popular video games more smoothly. Furthermore, designers may add special features to their products, in hardware or software, that permit a specific benchmark to execute quickly but don't offer similar advantages to general tasks.

Power Consumption

Power consumption is another design criterion that factors

in the design of modern computers. Power efficiency can often be traded for performance or cost benefits. The typical measurement in this case is MIPS/W (millions of instructions per watt).

With the increasing power density of modern circuits as the number of transistors per chip scales (Moore's law), power efficiency has increased in importance. Recent processor designs such as the Intel Core 2 put more emphasis on increasing power efficiency. Also, in the world of embedded computing, power efficiency has long been and remains an important goal next to throughput and latency.

COMPUTER HARDWARE

Computer hardware is the collection of physical elements that comprise a computer system. Computer hardware refers to the physical parts or components of computer such as monitor, keyboard, hard disk, mouse, etc. Refers to objects that you can actually touch, like disks, disk drives, display screens, keyboards, printers, boards, and chips. In contrast, software is untouchable. Software exists as ideas, concepts, and symbols, but it has no substance. A combination of hardware and software forms a usable computing system.

HISTORY OF COMPUTING HARDWARE

Computing hardware evolved from machines that needed separate manual action to perform each arithmetic operation, to punched card machines, and then to stored-Programme computers. The history of stored-Programme computers relates first to computer architecture, that is, the organisation of the units to perform input and output, to store data and to operate as an integrated mechanism.

Before the development of the general-purpose computer, most calculations were done by humans. Mechanical tools to help humans with digital calculations were then called 'calculating machines', by proprietary names, or even as they are now, calculators. It was those humans who used the machines who were then called computers. Aside from written numerals, the first aids to computation were purely mechanical devices which required the operator to set up the initial values of an elementary arithmetic operation, then manipulate the device to obtain the result. A sophisticated (and comparatively recent) example is the slide rule in which numbers are represented as lengths on a logarithmic scale and computation is performed by setting a cursor and aligning sliding scales, thus adding those lengths.

Numbers could be represented in a continuous 'analog' form, for instance a voltage or some other physical property was set to be proportional to the number. Analog computers, like those designed and built by Vannevar Bush before World War II were of this type. Numbers could be represented in the form of digits, automatically manipulated by a mechanical mechanism. Although this last approach required more complex mechanisms in many cases, it made for greater precision of results.

The invention of electronic amplifiers made calculating machines much faster than their mechanical or electro-mechanical predecessors. Vacuum tube (thermionic valve) amplifiers gave way to solid state transistors, and then rapidly to integrated circuits which continue to improve, placing millions of electrical switches (typically transistors) on a single elaborately manufactured piece of semi-conductor the size of a fingernail.

By defeating the tyranny of numbers, integrated circuits made high-speed and low-cost digital computers a widespread commodity. There is an ongoing effort to make computer hardware faster, cheaper, and capable of storing more data. Computing hardware has become a platform for uses other than mere computation, such as process automation, electronic communications, equipment control, entertainment, education, etc.

Each field in turn has imposed its own requirements on the hardware, which has evolved in response to those requirements, such as the role of the touch screen to create a more intuitive and natural user interface. As all computers rely on digital storage, and tend to be limited by the size and speed of memory, the history of computer data storage is tied to the development of computers.

CPU DESIGN

CPU design is the design engineering task of creating a central processing unit (CPU), a component of computer hardware. It is a subfield of electronics engineering and computer engineering. CPU design focuses on these areas:

- Datapaths (such as ALUs and pipelines)
- control unit: logic which controls the datapaths
- Memory components such as register files, caches
- Clock circuitry such as clock drivers, PLLs, clock distribution networks
- Pad transceiver circuitry
- Logic gate cell library which is used to implement the logic

CPUs designed for high-performance markets might require custom designs for each of these items to achieve frequency, power-dissipation, and chip-area goals.

CPUs designed for lower performance markets might lessen the implementation burden by:

- Acquiring some of these items by purchasing them as intellectual property
- Use control logic implementation techniques (logic synthesis using CAD tools) to implement the other components - datapaths, register files, clocks

Common logic styles used in CPU design include:

- Unstructured random logic
- Finite-state machines
- Microprogramming (common from 1965 to 1985)
- Programmable logic array (common in the 1980s, no longer common)

Device types used to implement the logic include:

- Transistor-transistor logic Small Scale Integration logic chips - no longer used for CPUs
- Programmable Array Logic and Programmable logic devices - no longer used for CPUs

- Emitter-coupled logic (ECL) gate arrays - no longer common
- CMOS gate arrays - no longer used for CPUs
- CMOS ASICs - what's commonly used today, they're so common that the term ASIC is not used for CPUs
- Field-programmable gate arrays (FPGA) - common for soft microprocessors, and more or less required for reconfigurable computing

A CPU design project generally has these major tasks:

- Programmer-visible instruction set architecture, which can be implemented by a variety of microarchitectures
- Architectural study and performance modeling in ANSI C/C++ or SystemC
- High-level synthesis (HLS) or RTL (, *e.g.*, logic) implementation
- RTL Verification
- Circuit design of speed critical components (caches, registers, ALUs)
- Logic synthesis or logic-gate-level design
- Timing analysis to confirm that all logic and circuits will run at the specified operating frequency
- Physical design including floorplanning, place and route of logic gates
- Checking that RTL, gate-level, transistor-level and physical-level representations are equivalent
- Checks for signal integrity, chip manufacturability

Re-designing a CPU core to a smaller die-area helps achieve several of these goals.

- Shrinking everything (a 'photomask shrink'), resulting in the same number of transistors on a smaller die, improves performance (smaller transistors switch faster), reduces power (smaller wires have less parasitic capacitance) and reduces cost (more CPUs fit on the same wafer of silicon).
- Releasing a CPU on the same size die, but with a smaller CPU core, keeps the cost about the same but

allows higher levels of integration within one VLSI chip (additional cache, multiple CPUs, or other components), improving performance and reducing overall system cost.

As with most complex electronic designs, the logic verification effort (proving that the design does not have bugs) now dominates the project schedule of a CPU. Key CPU architectural innovations include index register, cache, virtual memory, instruction pipelining, superscalar, CISC, RISC, virtual machine, emulators, microprogram, and stack.

Micro-architectural Concepts

In computer engineering, microarchitecture (sometimes abbreviated to μarch or uarch), also called computer organisation, is the way a given instruction set architecture (ISA) is implemented on a processor. A given ISA may be implemented with different microarchitectures. Implementations might vary due to different goals of a given design or due to shifts in technology. Computer architecture is the combination of microarchitecture and instruction set design.

Relation to Instruction set Architecture

The ISA is roughly the same as the programming model of a processor as seen by an assembly language programmer or compiler writer. The ISA includes the execution model, processor registers, address and data formats among other things. The microarchitecture includes the constituent parts of the processor and how these interconnect and interoperate to implement the ISA. The microarchitecture of a machine is usually represented as (more or less detailed) diagrams that describe the interconnections of the various microarchitectural elements of the machine, which may be everything from single gates and registers, to complete arithmetic logic units (ALU)s and even larger elements. These diagrams generally separate the datapath (where data is placed) and the control path (which can be said to steer the data). Each microarchitectural element is in turn represented by a schematic describing the interconnections of logic gates used to implement it. Each logic gate is in turn represented by a circuit diagram describing the connections of the transistors used to implement it in some particular logic family.

Machines with different microarchitec-tures may have the same instruction set architecture, and thus be capable of executing the same Programmes. New microarchitectures and/ or circuitry solutions, along with advances in semiconductor manufacturing, are what allows newer generations of processors to achieve higher performance while using the same ISA. In principle, a single microarchitec-ture could execute several different ISAs with only minor changes to the microcode.

Aspects of Microarchitecture

The pipelined datapath is the most commonly used datapath design in microarchitecture today. This technique is used in most modern microprocessors, microcontrollers, and DSPs. The pipelined architecture allows multiple instructions to overlap in execution, much like an assembly line.

The pipeline includes several different stages which are fundamental in microarchitecture designs. Some of these stages include instruction fetch, instruction decode, execute, and write back. Some architectures include other stages such as memory access. The design of pipelines is one of the central microarchitectural tasks.

Execution units are also essential to microarchitecture. Execution units include arithmetic logic units (ALU), floating point units (FPU), load/store units, branch prediction, and SIMD. These units perform the operations or calculations of the processor. The choice of the number of execution units, their latency and throughput is a central microarchitectural design task.

The size, latency, throughput and connectivity of memories within the system are also microarchitectural decisions. System-level design decisions such as whether or not to include peripherals, such as memory controllers, can be considered part of the microarchitectural design process. This includes decisions on the performance-level and connectivity of these peripherals. Unlike architectural design, where achieving a specific performance level is the main goal, microarchitectural design pays closer attention to other constraints. Since, microarchitecture design decisions directly affect what goes into a system, attention must be paid to such issues as:

- Chip area/cost
- Power consumption
- Logic complexity
- Ease of connectivity
- Manufacturability
- Ease of debugging
- Testability

Microarchitectural Concepts

Instruction Cycle

In general, all CPUs, single-chip microprocessors or multi-chip implementations run Programmes by performing the following steps:

- Read an instruction and decode it
- Find any associated data that is needed to process the instruction
- Process the instruction
- Write the results out

The instruction cycle is repeated continuously until the power is turned off.

Increasing Execution Speed

Complicating this simple-looking series of steps is the fact that the memory hierarchy, which includes caching, main memory and Non-volatile storage like hard disks (where the Programme instructions and data reside), has always been slower than the processor itself. Step often introduces a lengthy (in CPU terms) delay while the data arrives over the computer bus.

A considerable amount of research has been put into designs that avoid these delays as much as possible. Over the years, a central goal was to execute more instructions in parallel, thus increasing the effective execution speed of a Programme. These efforts introduced complicated logic and circuit structures. Initially, these techniques could only be implemented on expensive mainframes or supercomputers due to the amount of circuitry needed for these techniques. As semiconductor manufacturing progressed, more and more of these techniques could be implemented on a single semiconductor chip.

Instruction Set Choice

Instruction sets have shifted over the years, from originally very simple to sometimes very complex (in various respects). In recent years, load-store architectures, VLIW and EPIC types have been in fashion. Architectures that are dealing with data parallelism include SIMD and Vectors.

Some labels used to denote classes of CPU architectures are not particularly descriptive, especially so the CISC label; many early designs retroactively denoted 'CISC' are in fact significantly simpler than modern RISC processors (in several respects). However, the choice of instruction set architecture may greatly affect the complexity of implementing high performance devices. The prominent strategy, used to develop the first RISC processors, was to simplify instructions to a minimum of individual semantic complexity combined with high encoding regularity and simplicity.

Such uniform instructions were easily fetched, decoded and executed in a pipelined fashion and a simple strategy to reduce the number of logic levels in order to reach high operating frequencies; instruction cache-memories compensated for the higher operating frequency and inherently low code density while large register sets were used to factor out as much of the (slow) memory accesses as possible.

Instruction Pipelining

One of the first, and most powerful, techniques to improve performance is the use of the instruction pipeline. Early processor designs would carry out all of the steps for one instruction before moving onto the next. Large portions of the circuitry were left idle at any one step; for instance, the instruction decoding circuitry would be idle during execution and so on. Pipelines improve performance by allowing a number of instructions to work their way through the processor at the same time.

In the same basic example, the processor would start to decode a new instruction while the last one was waiting for results. This would allow up to four instructions to be 'in flight' at one time, making the processor look four times as fast. Although any one instruction takes just as long to complete (there are still four steps) the CPU as a whole 'retires' instructions much faster. RISC make pipelines smaller and much easier to construct by cleanly separating each stage of the instruction process and making them take the same amount of time — one cycle.

The processor as a whole operates in an assembly line fashion, with instructions coming in one side and results out the other. Due to the reduced complexity of the Classic RISC pipeline, the pipelined core and an instruction cache could be placed on the same size die that would otherwise fit the core alone on a CISC design. This was the real reason that RISC was faster. Early designs like the SPARC and MIPS often ran over 10 times as fast as Intel and Motorola CISC solutions at the same clock speed and price.

Pipelines are by no means limited to RISC designs. By 1986 the top-of-the-line VAX implementation was a heavily pipelined design, slightly predating the first commercial MIPS and SPARC designs. Most modern CPUs (even embedded CPUs) are now pipelined, and microcoded CPUs with no pipelining are seen only in the most area-constrained embedded processors. Large CISC machines, from the VAX 8800 to the modern Pentium 4 and Athlon, are implemented with both microcode and pipelines. Improvements in pipelining and caching are the two major microarchitectural advances that have enabled processor performance to keep pace with the circuit technology on which they are based.

Cache

It was not long before improvements in chip manufacturing allowed for even more circuitry to be placed on the die, and designers started looking for ways to use it. One of the most common was to add an ever-increasing amount of cache memory on-die. Cache is simply very fast memory, memory that can be accessed in a few cycles as opposed to many needed to 'talk' to main memory. The CPU includes a cache controller which automates reading and writing from the cache, if the data is already in the cache it simply 'appears', whereas if it is not the processor is 'stalled' while the cache controller reads it in.

RISC designs started adding cache in the mid-to-late 1980s, often only 4 KB in total. This number grew over time, and typical CPUs now have at least 512 KB, while more powerful CPUs come with 1 or 2 or even 4, 6, 8 or 12 MB, organised in multiple levels of a memory hierarchy. Generally speaking, more cache means more performance, due to reduced stalling.

Caches and pipelines were a perfect match for each other. Previously, it didn't make much sense to build a pipeline that could run faster than the access latency of off-chip memory. Using on-chip cache memory instead, meant that a pipeline could run at the speed of the cache access latency, a much smaller length of time. This allowed the operating frequencies of processors to increase at a much faster rate than that of off-chip memory.

Branch Prediction

One barrier to achieving higher performance through instruction-level parallelism stems from pipeline stalls and flushes due to branches. Normally, whether a conditional branch will be taken isn't known until late in the pipeline as conditional branches depend on results coming from a register. From the time that the processor's instruction decoder has figured out that it has encountered a conditional branch instruction to the time that the deciding register value can be read out, the pipeline needs to be stalled for several cycles, or if it's not and the branch is taken, the pipeline needs to be flushed. As clock speeds increase the depth of the pipeline increases with it, and some modern processors may have 20 stages or more.

On average, every fifth instruction executed is a branch, so without any intervention, that's a high amount of stalling. Techniques such as branch prediction and speculative execution are used to lessen these branch penalties. Branch prediction is where the hardware makes educated guesses on whether a particular branch will be taken. In reality one side or the other of the branch will be called much more often than the other.

Modern designs have rather complex statistical prediction systems, which watch the results of past branches to predict the future with greater accuracy. The guess allows the hardware to prefetch instructions without waiting for the register read. Speculative execution is a further enhancement in which the code along the predicted path is not just prefetched but also executed before it is known whether the branch should be taken or not. This can yield better performance when the guess is good, with the risk of a huge penalty when the guess is bad because instructions need to be undone.

Superscalar

Even with all of the added complexity and gates needed to support the concepts, improvements in semiconductor manufacturing soon allowed even more logic gates to be used. In the processor processes parts of a single instruction at a time. Computer Programmes could be executed faster if multiple instructions were processed simultaneously.

This is what superscalar processors achieve, by replicating functional units such as ALUs. The replication of functional units was only made possible when the die area of a single-issue processor no longer stretched the limits of what could be reliably manufactured. By the late 1980s, superscalar designs started to enter the market place. In modern designs it is common to find two load units, one store (many instructions have no results to store), two or more integer math units, two or more floating point units, and often a SIMD unit of some sort. The instruction issue logic grows in complexity by reading in a huge list of instructions from memory and handing them off to the different execution units that are idle at that point. The results are then collected and re-ordered at the end.

Out-of-order Execution

The addition of caches reduces the frequency or duration of stalls due to waiting for data to be fetched from the memory hierarchy, but does not get rid of these stalls entirely. In early designs a *cache miss* would force the cache controller to stall the processor and wait. Of course there may be some other instruction in the Programme whose data *is* available in the cache at that point.

Out-of-order execution allows that ready instruction to be processed while an older instruction waits on the cache, then re-orders the results to make it appear that everything happened in the programmed order. This technique is also used to avoid other operand dependency stalls, such as an instruction awaiting a result from a long latency floating-point operation or other multi-cycle operations.

Register Renaming

Register renaming refers to a technique used to avoid unnecessary serialised execution of Programme instructions because of the reuse of the same registers by those instructions. Suppose we have two groups of instruction that will use the same register. One set of instructions is executed first to leave the register to the other set, but if the other set is assigned to a different similar register, both sets of instructions can be executed in parallel.

Multiprocessing and Multithreading

Computer architects have become stymied by the growing mismatch in CPU operating frequencies and DRAM access times. None of the techniques that exploited instruction-level parallelism within one Programme could make up for the long stalls that occurred when data had to be fetched from main memory. Additionally, the large transistor counts and high operating frequencies needed for the more advanced ILP techniques required power dissipation levels that could no longer be cheaply cooled. For these reasons, newer generations of computers have started to exploit higher levels of parallelism that exist outside of a single Programme or Programme thread.

This trend is sometimes known as *throughput computing*. This idea originated in the mainframe market where online transaction processing emphasised not just the execution speed of one transaction, but the capacity to deal with massive numbers of transactions. With transaction-based applications such as network routing and web-site serving greatly increasing in the last decade, the computer industry has Re-emphasised capacity and throughput issues. One technique of how this parallelism is achieved is through multiprocessing systems, computer systems with multiple CPUs.

Once reserved for high-end mainframes and super-computers, small scale (2-8) multiprocessors servers have become commonplace for the small business market. For large corporations, large scale (16-256) multiprocessors are common. Even personal computers with multiple CPUs have appeared Since, the 1990s. With further transistor size reductions made available with semiconductor technology advances, multicore CPUs have appeared where multiple CPUs are implemented on the same silicon chip.

Initially used in chips targeting embedded markets, where simpler and smaller CPUs would allow multiple instantiations to fit on one piece of silicon. By 2005, semiconductor technology allowed dual high-end desktop CPUs *CMP* chips to be manufactured in volume. Some designs, such as Sun Microsystems' UltraSPARC T1 have reverted back to simpler (scalar, in-order) designs in order to fit more processors on one piece of silicon. Another technique that has become more popular recently is multithreading. In multithreading, when the processor has to fetch data from slow system memory, instead of stalling for the data to arrive, the processor switches to another Programme or Programme thread which is ready to execute. Though this does not speed up a particular Programme/thread, it increases the overall system throughput by reducing the time the CPU is idle.

Conceptually, multi-threading is equivalent to a context switch at the operating system level. The difference is that a multithreaded CPU can do a thread switch in one CPU cycle instead of the hundreds or thousands of CPU cycles a context switch normally requires.

This is achieved by replicating the state hardware (such as the register file and Programme counter) for each active thread. A further enhancement is simultaneous multithreading. This technique allows superscalar CPUs to execute instructions from different Programmes/threads simultaneously in the same cycle.

PERFORMANCE ANALYSIS AND BENCH-MARKING

Because there are too many programmes to test a CPU's speed on all of them, benchmarks were developed. The most famous benchmarks are the SPECint and SPECfp benchmarks developed by Standard Performance Evaluation Corporation and the ConsumerMark benchmark developed by the Embedded Microprocessor Benchmark Consortium EEMBC. Some important measurements include:

- *Instructions per second*: Most consumers pick a computer architecture (normally Intel IA32 architecture) to be able to run a large base of Pre-existing pre-compiled software. Being relatively uninformed on computer benchmarks, some of them pick a particular CPU based on operating frequency.
- *Flops*: The number of floating point operations per second is often important in selecting computers for scientific computations.
- *Performance per Watt*: System designers building parallel computers, such as Google, pick CPUs based on their speed per watt of power, because the cost

of powering the CPU outweighs the cost of the CPU itself.

- *Some system designers*: Building parallel computers pick CPUs based on the speed per dollar.
- *System designers building real:* Time computing systems want to guarantee worst-case response. That is easier to do when the CPU has low interrupt latency and when it has deterministic response.
- Computer programmers who Programme directly in assembly language want a CPU to support a full featured instruction set.
- *Low power*: For systems with limited power sources.
- *Small size or low weight*: For portable embedded systems, systems for spacecraft.
- *Environmental impact*: Minimising environmental impact of computers during manufacturing and recycling as well during use. Reducing waste, reducing hazardous materials.

Some of these measures conflict. In particular, many design techniques that make a CPU run faster make the 'performance per watt', 'performance per dollar', and 'deterministic response' much worse, and vice versa.

MARKETS

Developing new, high-end CPUs is a very costly proposition. Both the logical complexity (needing very large logic design and logic verification teams and simulation farms with perhaps thousands of computers) and the high operating frequencies (needing large circuit design teams and access to the state-of-the-art fabrication process) account for the high cost of design for this type of chip.

The design cost of a high-end CPU will be on the order of US $100 million. Since, the design of such high-end chips nominally takes about five years to complete, to stay competitive a company has to fund at least two of these large design teams to release products at the rate of 2.5 years per product generation.

As an example, the typical loaded cost for one computer engineer is often quoted to be $250,000 US dollars/year. This includes salary, benefits, CAD tools, computers, office space rent, etc. Assuming that 100 engineers are needed to design a CPU and the project takes 4 years.

Total cost = $250,000/ Engineer-Man/Year × 100 engineers × 4 years = US $100,000,000.

The amount is just an example. The design teams for modern day general purpose CPUs have several hundred team members.

There are several different markets in which CPUs are used. Since, each of these markets differ in their requirements for CPUs, the devices designed for one market are in most cases inappropriate for the other markets.

General Purpose Computing

The vast majority of revenues generated from CPU sales is for general purpose computing, that is, desktop, laptop, and server computers commonly used in businesses and homes. In this market, the Intel IA-32 architecture dominates, with its rivals PowerPC and SPARC maintaining much smaller customer bases.

Yearly, hundreds of millions of IA-32 architecture CPUs are used by this market. A growing percentage of these processors are for mobile implementations such as netbooks and laptops. Since, these devices are used to run countless different types of Programmes, these CPU designs are not specifically targeted at one type of application or one function. The demands of being able to run a wide range of Programmes efficiently has made these CPU designs among the more advanced technically, along with some disadvantages of being relatively costly, and having high power consumption.

Scientific Computing

Scientific computing is a much smaller niche market (in revenue and units shipped). It is used in government research labs and universities. Before 1990, CPU design was often done for this market, but mass market CPUs organised into large clusters have proven to be more affordable. The main remaining area of active hardware design and research for scientific computing is for high-speed data transmission systems to connect mass market CPUs.

Embedded Design

As measured by units shipped, most CPUs are embedded in other machinery, such as telephones, clocks, appliances, vehicles, and infrastructure. Embedded processors sell in the volume of many billions of units per year, however, mostly at much lower price points than that of the general purpose processors. These single-function devices differ from the more familiar general-purpose CPUs in several ways:

- Low cost is of utmost importance.
- It is important to maintain a low power dissipation as embedded devices often have a limited battery life and it is often impractical to include cooling fans.
- To give lower system cost, peripherals are integrated with the processor on the same silicon chip.
- Keeping peripherals on-chip also reduces power consumption as external GPIO ports typically require buffering so that they can source or sink the relatively high current loads that are required to maintain a strong signal outside of the chip.
  - Many embedded applications have a limited amount of physical space for circuitry; keeping peripherals on-chip will reduce the space required for the circuit board.
  - The Programme and data memories are often integrated on the same chip. When the only allowed Programme memory is ROM, the device is known as a microcontroller.
- For many embedded applications, interrupt latency will be more critical than in some general-purpose processors.

Embedded Processor Economics

The embedded CPU family with the largest number of total units shipped is the 8051, averaging nearly a billion units per year. The 8051 is widely used because it is very inexpensive. The design time is now roughly zero, because it is widely available as commercial intellectual property. It is now often embedded as a small part of a larger system on a chip. The silicon cost of an 8051 is now as low as US$0.001, because some implementations use as few as 2200 logic gates and take 0.0127 square millimeters of silicon As of 2009, more CPUs are produced using the ARM architecture instruction set than any other 32-bit instruction set.

The ARM architecture and the first ARM chip were designed in about one and a half years and 5 human years of work time. The 32-bit Parallax Propeller micro-controller architecture and the first chip were designed by two people in about 10 human years of work time. It is believed that the 8-bit AVR architecture and first AVR micro-controller was conceived and designed by two students at the Norwegian Institute of Technology. The 8-bit 6502 architecture and the first MOS Technology 6502 chip were designed in 13 months by a group of about 9 people.

Research and Educational CPU Design

The 32 bit Berkeley RISC I and RISC II architecture and the first chips were mostly designed by a series of students as part of a four quarter sequence of graduate courses. This design became the basis of the commercial SPARC processor design. For about a decade, every student taking the 6.004 class at MIT was part of a team—each team had one semester to design and build a simple 8 bit CPU out of 7400 series integrated circuits.

One team of 4 students designed and built a simple 32 bit CPU during that semester. Some undergraduate courses require a team of 2 to 5 students to design, implement, and test a simple CPU in a FPGA in a single 15 week semester.

Soft Microprocessor Cores

For embedded systems, the highest performance levels are often not needed or desired due to the power consumption requirements. This allows for the use of processors which can be totally implemented by logic synthesis techniques. These synthesised processors can be implemented in a much shorter amount of time, giving quicker time-to-market.

ORTHOGONAL INSTRUCTION SET

In computer engineering, an orthogonal instruction set is an instruction set architecture where all instruction types can use all addressing modes. It is 'orthogonal' in the sense that the instruction type and the addressing mode vary independently. An orthogonal instruction set does not impose a limitation that requires a certain instruction to use a specific register.

ORTHOGONALITY IN PRACTICE

In many CISC computers, an instruction could access either registers or memory, usually in several different ways. This made the CISC machines easier to Programme, because rather than being required to remember thousands of individual instruction opcodes, an orthogonal instruction set allowed a programmer to instead remember just thirty to a hundred operation codes ('ADD', 'SUBTRACT', 'MULTIPLY', 'DIVIDE', etc.,) and a set of three to ten addressing modes ('FROM REGISTER 0', 'FROM REGISTER 1', 'FROM MEMORY', etc.,). The DEC PDP-11 and Motorola 68000 computer architectures are examples of nearly orthogonal instruction sets, while the ARM11 and VAX are examples of CPUs with fully orthogonal instruction sets.

The PDP-11

With the exception of its floating point instructions, the PDP-11 was very strongly orthogonal. Every integer instruction could operate on either 1-byte or 2-byte integers and could access data stored in registers, stored as part of the instruction, stored in memory, or stored in memory and pointed to by addresses in registers. Even the PC and the stack pointer could be affected by the ordinary instructions using all of the ordinary data modes. In fact, 'immediate' mode (hardcoded numbers within an instruction, such as ADD #4,

R1 (R1 = R1 + 4) was implemented as the mode 'register indirect, autoincrement' and specifying the Programme counter (R7) as the register to use reference for indirection and to autoincrement.

Since, the PDP-11 was an octal-oriented (3-bit sub-byte) machine (addressing modes 0 - 7, registers R0 - R7), there were (electronically) 8 addressing modes. Through the use of the Stack Pointer (R6) and Programme Counter (R7) as referenceable registers, there were 10 conceptual addressing modes available.

The VAX-11

The VAX-11 extended the PDP-11's orthogonality to all data types, including floating point numbers (although instructions such as 'ADD' was divided into data-size dependent variants such as ADDB, ADDW, ADDL, ADDP, ADDF for add byte, word, longword, packed BCD and single-precision floating point, respectively). Like the PDP-11, the Stack Pointer and Programme Counter were in the general register file (R14 and R15).

The general form of a VAX 11 instruction would be:

- opcode [operand] [operand]...

Each component being one byte, the opcode a value in the range 0 - 255, and each operand consisting of two nibbles, the upper 4 bits specifying an addressing mode, and the lower 4 bits (usually) specifying a register number (R0 - R15). Unlike the octal-oriented PDP-11, the VAX-11 was a hexadecimal-oriented machine (4-bit sub-byte).

This resulted in 16 logical addressing modes (0-15), however, addressing modes 0-3 were 'short immediate' for immediate data of 6 bits or less (the 2 low-order bits of the addressing mode being the 2 high-order bits of the immediate data, when prepended to the remaining 4 bits in that data-addressing byte). Since, addressing modes 0-3 were identical, this made 13 (electronic) addressing modes, but as in the PDP-11, the use of the Stack Pointer (R14) and Programme Counter (R15) created a total of over 15 conceptual addressing modes (with the assembler Programme translating the source code into the actual stack-pointer or Programme-counter based addressing mode needed).

The MC68000

Motorola's designers attempted to make the assembly language orthogonal while the underlying machine language was somewhat less so. Unlike PDP-11, the MC68000 used separate registers to store data and the addresses of data in memory.

At the bit level, the person writing the assembler (or debugging machine code) would clearly see that symbolic instructions could become any of several different op-codes. This compromise gave almost the same convenience as a truly orthogonal machine, and yet also gave the CPU designers freedom to use the bits in the instructions more efficiently than a purely orthogonal approach might have.

The 8080 and Follow on Designs

The 8-bit Intel 8080 (as well as the 8085 and 8051) microprocessor was basically a slightly extended accumulator-based design and therefore not orthogonal. An assembly-language programmer or compiler writer had to be mindful of which operations were possible on each register: Most 8-bit operations could be performed only on the 8-bit accumulator (the A-register), while 16-bit operations could be performed only on the 16-bit pointer/accumulator (the HL-register pair), whereas simple operations, such as increment, were possible on all seven 8-bit registers.

This was largely due to a desire to keep all opcodes one byte long and to maintain source code compatibility with the original Intel 8008 (an LSI-implementation of the Datapoint 2200's CPU). The binary-compatible Z80 later added prefix-codes to escape from this 1-byte limit and allow for a more powerful instruction set. The same basic idea was employed for the Intel 8086, although, to allow for more radical extensions, *binary*-compatibility with the 8080 was not attempted here; instead the 8086 was designed as a more regular and fully 16-bit processor that was *source*-compatible with the 8008, 8080, and 8085. It maintained some degree of Non-orthogonality for the sake of high code density (even though this was derided as being 'baroque' by some computer scientists at the time).

The 32-bit extension of this architecture that was introduced with the 80386, was somewhat more orthogonal despite keeping all the 8086 instructions and their extended counterparts. However, the *encoding-strategy* used still shows many traces from the 8008 and 8080 (and Z80); for instance, single-byte encodings remain for certain frequent operations such as push and pop of registers and constants, and the primary accumulator, eax, employ shorter encodings than the other registers on certain types of operations; observations like this are sometimes exploited for code optimisation in both compilers and hand written code.

Into the RISC Age

A fully orthogonal architecture may not be the most 'bit efficient' architecture. In the late 1970s research at IBM (and similar projects elsewhere) demonstrated that the majority of these 'orthogonal' addressing modes were ignored by most Programmes. Perhaps some of the bits that were used to express the fully orthogonal instruction set could instead be used to express more virtual address bits or select from among more registers.

In the RISC age, computer designers strove to achieve a balance that they thought better. In particular, most RISC computers, while still being highly orthogonal with regard to which instructions can process which data types, now have reverted to 'load/store' architectures.

In these architectures, only a very few *memory reference instructions* can access main memory and only for the purpose of loading data into registers or storing register data back into main memory; only a few addressing modes may be available, and these modes may vary depending on whether the instruction refers to data or involves a transfer of control (jump). Conversely, data must be in registers before it can be operated upon by the other instructions in the computer's instruction set. This trade off is made explicitly to enable the use of much larger register sets, extended virtual addresses, and longer *immediate data* (data stored directly within the computer instruction).

SOFTWARE ARCHITECTURE

The software architecture of a system is the set of structures needed to reason about the system, which comprise software elements, relations among them, and properties of both. The term also refers to documentation of a system's 'software architecture.' Documenting software architecture facilitates communication between stakeholders, documents early decisions about high-level design, and allows reuse of design components and patterns between projects.The field of computer science has encountered problems associated with complexity Since, its formation.

Earlier problems of complexity were solved by developers by choosing the right data structures, developing algorithms, and by applying the concept of separation of concerns. Although the term 'software architecture' is relatively new to the industry, the fundamental principles of the field have been applied sporadically by software engineering pioneers Since, the mid 1980s.

Early attempts to capture and explain software architecture of a system were imprecise and disorganised, often characterised by a set of box-and-line diagrams. During the 1990s there was a concentrated effort to define and codify fundamental aspects of the discipline.

Initial sets of design patterns, styles, best practices, description languages, and formal logic were developed during that time. The software architecture discipline is centered on the idea of reducing complexity through abstraction and separation of concerns. To date there is still no agreement on the precise definition of the term 'software architecture'. However, this does not mean that individuals do not have their own definition of what software architecture is. This leads to problems because many people are using the same terms to describe differing ideas. As a maturing discipline with no clear rules on the right way to build a system, designing software architecture is still a mix of art and science. The 'art' aspect of software architecture arises because a commercial software system supports some aspect of a business or a mission.

How a system supports key business drivers, described via scenarios as Non-functional requirements of a system, also known as quality attributes, determine how a system will behave. This could be thought of as a parallel to a mission statement and value system in business strategy. Every system is unique to the business drivers it supports, therefore the quality attributes of each system such as fault-tolerance, backward compatibility, extensibility, reliability, maintainability, availability, security, usability, and such other -ilities will vary with each implementation.

To bring a software architecture user's perspective into the software architecture, it can be said that software architecture gives the direction to take steps and do the tasks involved in each such user's specialty area and interest, *e.g.*, the stakeholders of software systems, the software developer, the software system operational support group, the software maintenance specialists, the deployer, the tester and also the business end user.

In this sense software architecture is really the amalgamation of the multiple perspectives a system always embodies. The fact that those several different perspectives can be put together into a software architecture stands as the vindication of the need and justification of creation of software architecture before the software development in a project attains maturity.

HISTORY

Software architecture as a concept has its origins in the research of Edsger Dijkstra in 1968 and David Parnas in the early 1970s. These scientists emphasised that the structure of a software system matters and getting the structure right is critical. The study of the field increased in popularity Since, the early 1990s with research work concentrating on architectural styles (patterns), architecture description languages, architecture documentation, and formal methods. Research institutions have played a prominent role in furthering software architecture as a discipline.

Mary Shaw and David Garlan of Carnegie Mellon wrote a book titled *Software Architecture: Perspectives on an Emerging Discipline* in 1996, which brought forward the concepts in Software Architecture, such as components, connectors, styles and so on.

The University of California, Irvine's Institute for Software Research's efforts in software architecture research is directed primarily in architectural styles, architecture description languages, and dynamic architectures.

IEEE 1471-2000, *Recommended Practice for Architecture Description of Software-Intensive Systems,* was the first formal standard in the area of software architecture. It was adopted in 2007 by ISO as ISO/IEC 42010:2007. In November 2011, IEEE 1471-2000 was superseded by ISO/IEC/IEEE 42010:2011, *Systems and software engineering — Architecture description* (jointly published by IEEE and ISO).

SOFTWARE ARCHITECTURE TOPICS

Architecture Description Languages

Architecture description languages (ADLs) are used to describe a software architecture. Several different ADLs have been developed by different organisations, including AADL (SAE standard), Wright (developed by Carnegie Mellon), Acme (developed by Carnegie Mellon), xADL (developed by UCI), Darwin (developed by Imperial College London), DAOP-ADL (developed by University of Málaga), and ByADL (University of L'Aquila, Italy). Common elements of an ADL are component, connector and configuration.

Views

Software architecture descriptions are commonly

organised into views, which are analogous to the different types of blueprints made in building architecture.

A view is a representation of a set of system components and relationships among them. Within the ontology established by IEEE 1471-2000, *views* follow the conventions established by their *viewpoints,* where a viewpoint is a specification that describes the notations, modeling techniques to be used in a view to express the architecture in question from the perspective of a given set of stakeholders and their concerns.

The viewpoint specifies not only the concerns addressed but the presentation, model kinds used, conventions used and any consistency (correspondence) rules to keep a view consistent with other views. Some examples of kinds of views (viewpoints in the 1471/42010 ontology) are:

- Functional/logical viewpoint
- Code/module viewpoint
- Development/structural viewpoint
- Concurrency/process/runtime/thread viewpoint
- Physical/deployment/install viewpoint
- User action/feedback viewpoint
- Data view/data model

Several languages for describing software architectures (*architecture description language* in ISO/IEC/IEEE 42010 (IEEE 1471) terminology) have been devised, but no consensus exists on which symbol-set or language should be used to for each architecture viewpoint. The UML is a standard that can be used *'for analysis, design, and implementation of software-based systems as well as for modeling business and similar processes.'* Thus, the UML is a visual language that can be used to create software architecture.

Architecture Frameworks

Frameworks related to the domain of software architecture are:

- 4+1
- RM-ODP (Reference Model of Open Distributed Processing)
- Service-Oriented Modeling Framework (SOMF)

Other architecture frameworks such as the Zachman

Framework, DODAF, and TOGAF relate to the field of Enterprise architecture.

The Distinction from Functional Design

The IEEE Std 610.12-1990 Standard Glossary of Software Engineering Terminology defines the following distinctions:

- *Architectural Design*: The process of defining a collection of hardware and software components and their interfaces to establish the framework for the development of a computer system.
- *Preliminary Design*: The process of analysing design alternatives and defining the architecture, components, interfaces, and timing/sising estimates for a system or components.
- *Detailed Design*: The process of refining and expanding the preliminary design of a system or component to the extent that the design is sufficiently complete to begin implementation.
- *Functional Design*: The process of defining the working relationships among the components of a system.

Software architecture, also described as strategic design, is an activity concerned with global requirements governing *how* a solution is implemented such as programming paradigms, architectural styles, component-based software engineering standards, architectural patterns, security, scale, integration, and law-governed regularities.

Functional design, also described as tactical design, is an activity concerned with local requirements governing *what* a solution does such as algorithms, design patterns, programming idioms, refactorings, and low-level implementation.

According to the Intension/Locality Hypothesis, the distinction between architectural and detailed design is defined by the Locality Criterion, according to which a statement about software design is Non-local (architectural) if and only if a Programme that satisfies it can be expanded into a Programme which does not. For example, the client-server style is architectural (strategic) because a Programme that is built on this principle can be expanded into a Programme which is not client–server; for example, by adding peer-to-peer nodes.

Architecture is design but not all design is architectural. In practice, the architect is the one who draws the line between software architecture (architectural design) and detailed design (non-architectural design). There aren't rules or guidelines that fit all cases.

Examples of rules or heuristics that architects (or organisations) can establish when they want to distinguish between architecture and detailed design include:

- Architecture is driven by Non-functional requirements, while functional design is driven by functional requirements.
- Pseudo-code belongs in the detailed design document.
- UML component, deployment, and package diagrams generally appear in software architecture documents; UML class, object, and Behaviour diagrams appear in detailed functional design documents.

EXAMPLES OF ARCHITECTURAL STYLES AND PATTERNS

There are many common ways of designing computer software modules and their communications, among them:

- Blackboard
- Client–server model (2-tier, n-tier, Peer-to-peer, cloud computing all use this model)
- Database-centric architecture (broad division can be made for Programmes which have database at its center and applications which don't have to rely on databases, *e.g.*, desktop application Programmes, utility Programmes, etc.)
- Distributed computing
- Event-driven architecture (Implicit invocation)
- Front end and back end

- Monolithic application
- Peer-to-peer
- Pipes and filters
- Plug-in (computing)
- Representational State Transfer
- Rule evaluation
- Search-oriented architecture
- Service-oriented architecture (A pure SOA implements a service for every data access point.)
- Shared nothing architecture
- Software componentry
- Space based architecture
- Structured (Module-based but usually monolithic within modules)
- Three-tier model (An architecture with Presentation, Business Logic and Database tiers)

VON NEUMANN ARCHITECTURE

The term Von Neumann architecture, also known as the Von Neumann model or the Princeton architecture, derives from a 1945 computer architecture proposal by the mathematician and early computer scientist John von Neumann and others, *First Draft of a Report on the EDVAC*. This describes a design architecture for an electronic digital computer with subdivisions of a processing unit consisting of an arithmetic logic unit and processor registers, a control unit containing an instruction register and Programme counter, a memory to store both data and instructions, external mass storage, and input and output mechanisms.

The meaning of the term has evolved to mean a stored-Programme computer in which an instruction fetch and a data operation cannot occur at the same time because they share a common bus. This is referred to as the Von Neumann bottleneck and often limits the performance of the system. The design of a Von Neumann architecture is simpler than the more modern Harvard architecture which is also a stored-Programme system but has one dedicated set of address and data buses for memory, and another set of address and data buses for fetching instructions. A stored-Programme digital computer is one that keeps its programmed instructions, as well as its data, in read-write, random-access memory (RAM). Stored-Programme computers were an advancement over the Programme-controlled computers of the 1940s, such as the Colossus and the ENIAC, which were programmed by setting switches and inserting patch leads to route data and to control signals between various functional units.

In the vast majority of modern computers, the same memory is used for both data and Programme instructions. The earliest computing machines had fixed Programmes. Some very simple computers still use this design, either for simplicity or training purposes. For example, a desk calculator (in principle) is a fixed Programme computer. It can do basic mathematics, but it cannot be used as a word processor or a gaming console.

Changing the Programme of a fixed-Programme machine requires re-wiring, re-structuring, or re-designing the machine. The earliest computers were not so much 'programmed' as they were 'designed'. 'Reprogramming', when it was possible at all, was a laborious process, starting with flowcharts and paper notes, followed by detailed engineering designs, and then the often-arduous process of physically re-wiring and re-building the machine.

It could take three weeks to set up a Programme on ENIAC and get it working. With the proposal of the stored-Programme computer this changed. A stored-Programme computer includes by design an instruction set and can store in memory a set of instructions (a Programme) that details the computation. A stored-Programme design also allows for self-modifying code. One early motivation for such a facility was the need for a Programme to increment or otherwise modify the address portion of instructions, which had to be done manually in early designs. This became less important when index registers and indirect addressing became usual features of machine architecture. Another use was to embed frequently used data in the instruction stream using immediate addressing.

Self-modifying code has largely fallen out of Favour, Since, it is usually hard to understand and debug, as well as being inefficient under modern processor pipelining and caching schemes. On a large scale, the ability to treat instructions as data is what makes assemblers, compilers and other automated programming tools possible. One can 'write Programmes which write Programmes'.

On a smaller scale, repetitive I/O-intensive operations such as the BITBLT image manipulation primitive or pixel and vertex shaders in modern 3D graphics, were considered inefficient to run without custom hardware. These operations could be accelerated on general purpose processors with 'on the fly compilation' ('just-in-time compilation') technology, *e.g.*, code-generating Programmes—one form of self-modifying code that has remained popular.

There are drawbacks to the Von Neumann design. Aside from the Von Neumann bottleneck Programme modifications can be quite harmful, either by accident or design. In some simple stored-Programme computer designs, a malfunctioning Programme can damage itself, other Programmes, or the operating system, possibly leading to a computer crash. Memory protection and other forms of access control can usually protect against both accidental and malicious Programme modification.

DEVELOPMENT OF THE STORED-PROGRAMME CONCEPT

The mathematician Alan Turing, who had been alerted to a problem of mathematical logic by the lectures of Max Newman at the University of Cambridge, wrote a paper in 1936 entitled *On Computable Numbers, with an Application to the Entscheidungsproblem*, which was published in the *Proceedings of the London Mathematical Society*. In it he described a hypothetical machine which he called a 'universal computing machine', and which is now known as the 'Universal Turing machine'. The hypothetical machine had an infinite store (memory in today's terminology) that contained both instructions and data. John von Neumann became acquainted with Turing while he was a visiting professor at Cambridge in 1935, and also during Turing's Ph.D. year at the Institute for Advanced Study in Princeton, New Jersey during 1936 - 37. Whether he knew of Turing's paper of 1936 at that time is not clear. In 1936 Konrad Zuse also anticipated in two patent applications that machine instructions could be stored in the same storage used for data. Independently, J. Presper Eckert and John Mauchly, who were developing the ENIAC at the Moore School of Electrical Engineering, at the University of Pennsylvania, wrote about the stored-Programme concept in December 1943. In planning a new machine, EDVAC, Eckert wrote in January 1944 that they would store data and Programmes in a new addressable memory device, a mercury metal delay line memory. This was the first time the construction of a practical stored-Programme machine was proposed. At that time, he and Mauchly were not aware of Turing's work.

Von Neumann was involved in the Manhattan Project at the Los Alamos National Laboratory, which required huge amounts of calculation. This drew him to the ENIAC project, during the summer of 1944. There he joined into the ongoing discussions on the design of this stored-Programme computer, the EDVAC.

As part of that group, he volunteered to write up a description of it and produced the *First Draft of a Report on the EDVAC* which included ideas from Eckert and Mauchly. It was unfinished when his colleague Herman Goldstine circulated it with only von Neumann's name on it, to the consternation of Eckert and Mauchly. The paper was read by dozens of von Neumann's colleagues in America and Europe, and influenced the next round of computer designs. Hence,, Von Neumann was not alone in developing the idea of the stored-Programme architecture, and Jack Copeland considers that it is 'historically inappropriate, to refer to electronic stored-Programme digital computers as 'von Neumann machines''.

At the time that the 'First Draft' report was circulated, Turing was producing a report entitled *Proposed Electronic Calculator* which described in engineering and programming detail, his idea of a machine that was called the Automatic Computing Engine (ACE).

He presented this to the Executive Committee of the British National Physical Laboratory on February 19, 1946. Although Turing knew from his wartime experience at Bletchley Park that what he proposed was feasible, the secrecy surrounding Colossus, that was subsequently maintained for several decades, prevented him from saying so. Various successful implementations of the ACE design were produced. Both von Neumann's and Turing's papers described stored-Programme computers, but von Neumann's earlier paper achieved greater circulation and the computer architecture it outlined became known as the 'von Neumann architecture'.

EARLY VON NEUMANN-ARCHITECTURE COMPUTERS

The *First Draft* described a design that was used by many universities and corporations to construct their computers. Among these various computers, only ILLIAC and ORDVAC had compatible instruction sets.

- Manchester Small-Scale Experimental Machine (SSEM), nicknamed 'Baby' (University of Manchester, England) made its first successful run of a stored-Programme on June 21st 1948.
- EDSAC (University of Cambridge, England) was the first practical stored-Programme electronic computer
- Manchester Mark 1 (University of Manchester, England) Developed from the SSEM
- CSIRAC (Council for Scientific and Industrial Research) Australia
- ORDVAC (U-Illinois) at Aberdeen Proving Ground, Maryland (completed November 1951)

- IAS machine at Princeton University
- MANIAC I at Los Alamos Scientific Laboratory
- ILLIAC at the University of Illinois,
- AVIDAC at Argonne National Laboratory
- ORACLE at Oak Ridge National Laboratory
- JOHNNIAC at RAND Corporation
- BESK in Stockholm
- BESM-1 in Moscow
- DASK in Denmark
- PERM in Munich
- SILLIAC in Sydney
- WEIZAC in Rehovoth

EARLY STORED-PROGRAMME COMPUTERS

The date information in the following chronology is difficult to put into proper order. Some dates are for first running a test Programme, some dates are the first time the computer was demonstrated or completed, and some dates are for the first delivery or installation.

- The IBM SSEC had the ability to treat instructions as data, and was publicly demonstrated on January 27, 1948. This ability was claimed in a US patent. However it was partially electromechanical, not fully electronic. In practice, instructions were read from paper tape due to its limited memory.
- The Manchester SSEM (the *Baby*) was the first fully electronic computer to run a stored Programme. It ran a factoring Programme for 52 minutes on June 21, 1948, after running a simple division Programme and a Programme to show that two numbers were relatively prime.
- The ENIAC was modified to run as a primitive read-only stored-Programme computer (using the Function Tables for Programme ROM) and was demonstrated as such on September 16, 1948, running a Programme by Adele Goldstine for von Neumann.

- The BINAC ran some test Programmes in February, March, and April 1949, although was not completed until September 1949.
- The Manchester Mark 1 developed from the SSEM project. An intermediate version of the Mark 1 was available to run Programmes in April 1949, but was not completed until October 1949.
- The EDSAC ran its first Programme on May 6, 1949.
- The EDVAC was delivered in August 1949, but it had problems that kept it from being put into regular operation until 1951.
- The CSIR Mk I ran its first Programme in November 1949.
- The SEAC was demonstrated in April 1950.
- The Pilot ACE ran its first Programme on May 10, 1950 and was demonstrated in December 1950.
- The SWAC was completed in July 1950.
- The Whirlwind was completed in December 1950 and was in actual use in April 1951.
- The first ERA Atlas was installed in December 1950.

EVOLUTION

Through the decades of the 1960s and 1970s computers generally became both smaller and faster, which led to some evolutions in their architecture. For example, memory-mapped I/O allows input and output devices to be treated the same as memory. A single system bus could be used to provide a modular system with lower cost. This is sometimes called a 'streamlining' of the architecture. In subsequent decades, simple microcontrollers would sometimes omit features of the model to lower cost and size. Larger computers added features for higher performance.

VON NEUMANN BOTTLENECK

The shared bus between the Programme memory and data memory leads to the *Von Neumann bottleneck,* the limited throughput (data transfer rate) between the CPU and memory compared to the amount of memory. Because Programme memory and data memory cannot be accessed at the same time, throughput is much smaller than the rate at which the CPU can work.

This seriously limits the effective processing speed when the CPU is required to perform minimal processing on large amounts of data. The CPU is continuously forced to wait for needed data to be transferred to or from memory. Since, CPU speed and memory size have increased much faster than the throughput between them, the bottleneck has become more of a problem, a problem whose severity increases with every newer generation of CPU. The term 'von Neumann bottleneck' was coined by John Backus in his 1977 ACM Turing Award lecture. According to Backus:

> Surely there must be a less primitive way of making big changes in the store than by pushing vast numbers of words back and forth through the von Neumann bottleneck. Not only is this tube a literal bottleneck for the data traffic of a problem, but, more importantly, it is an intellectual bottleneck that has kept us tied to word-at-a-time thinking instead of encouraging us to think in terms of the larger conceptual units of the task at hand. Thus programming is basically planning and detailing the enormous traffic of words through the von Neumann bottleneck, and much of that traffic concerns not significant data itself, but where to find it.

The performance problem can be alleviated (to some extent) by several mechanisms. Providing a cache between the CPU and the main memory, providing separate caches or separate access paths for data and instructions (the so-called Modified Harvard architecture), using branch predictor algorithms and logic, and providing a limited CPU stack to reduce memory access are four of the ways performance is increased. The problem can also be sidestepped somewhat by using parallel computing, using for example the Non-Uniform Memory Access (NUMA) architecture—this approach is commonly employed by supercomputers.

It is less clear whether the *intellectual bottleneck* that Backus criticised has changed much Since, 1977. Backus's proposed solution has not had a major influence. Modern functional programming and object-oriented programming are much less geared towards 'pushing vast numbers of words back and forth' than earlier languages like Fortran were, but internally, that is still what computers spend much of their time doing, even highly parallel supercomputers. In some cases, emerging memristor technology may be able to circumvent the von Neumann bottleneck.

NON-VON NEUMANN PROCESSORS

The National Semiconductor COP8 was introduced in 1986; it has a Modified Harvard architecture. Perhaps the most common kind of Non-von Neumann structure used in modern computers is content-addressable memory (CAM).

INFLUENCE OF THE IBM PC ON THE PERSONALCOMPUTER MARKET

Following the introduction of the IBM Personal Computer, or IBM PC, many other personal computer architectures became extinct within just a few years.

BEFORE THE IBM PC'S INTRODUCTION

Before the IBM PC was introduced, the personal computer market was dominated by systems using the 6502 and Z80 8-bit microprocessors, such as the TRS 80 and Apple II series, which used proprietary operating systems, and by computers running CP/M. Around 1978, several 16-bit CPUs became available.

Examples included the Data General Mn601, Fairchild's 9440, the Ferranti F100-1, the General Instrument CP1600 and CP1610, the National Semiconductor INS8900, Panafacom's MN1610, Texas Instruments' TMS9900, and, most notably, the Intel 8086. These new processors were expensive to incorporate in personal computers, as they used a 16-bit data bus and needed rare (and thus expensive) 16-bit peripheral and support chips.

Business-oriented Personal Computers before the IBM PC

More than 50 new business-oriented personal computer systems came on the market in the year before IBM released the IBM PC. Very few of them used a 16- or 32-bit microprocessor, as 8-bit systems were generally believed by the vendors to be perfectly adequate, and the Intel 8086 was too expensive to use. Some of the more important manufacturers selling 8-bit business systems during this period were:

- Apple Computer Inc.
- Commodore International
- Cromemco
- Digital Equipment Corporation
- Hewlett-Packard
- Intersystems
- Morrow Designs
- North Star Computers
- Ohio Scientific
- Olivetti
- Processor Technology
- Sharp
- South West Technical Products Corporation
- Tandy Corporation
- Zenith/Heathkit.

THE IBM PC

On August 12, 1981, IBM released the IBM Personal Computer. The IBM PC used the then-new Intel 8088 processor. Like other 16-bit CPUs, it could access up to 1 megabyte of RAM, but it used an 8-bit-wide data bus to memory and peripherals. This design allowed use of the large, readily available, and relatively inexpensive family of 8-bit-compatible support chips.

IBM decided to use the Intel 8088 after first considering the Motorola 68000 and the Intel i8086, because the other two were considered to be too powerful for their needs. IBM's reputation in business computing, combined with a rapid marketplace of third-party peripherals and the later introduction of IBM PC compatibles from other vendors, allowed the IBM PC architecture to take a substantial market share of business applications. Many other companies at the time were also making 'business personal computers' using their own proprietary designs, some still using 8-bit microprocessors. The ones that used Intel x86 processors often used MS-DOS or CP/M-86, just as 8-bit systems with an Intel 8080 compatible CPU normally used CP/M.

THE USE OF MS-DOS ON NON- IBM PC COMPATIBLE X86 BASED SYSTEMS

In the beginning, when the IBM PC did not yet dominate the market, these x86-based systems were not clones of the IBM PC design, but had different internal designs, like the CP/M-based 8-bit systems that preceded them. Even a few years after the IBM PC's introduction, manufacturers such as Digital, HP, Sanyo, Tandy, Texas Instruments, Tulip Computers, NEC, Wang Laboratories, and Xerox continued to introduce personal computers that were barely, if at all, hardware-compatible with the IBM PC, even though they used x86 processors and ran MS-DOS.

They used MS-DOS the way Microsoft had originally envisioned: in the same way as 8-bits systems used CP/M. They implemented standard ROM BIOS routines to achieve hardware independence as had 8080 (Z80) compatibles. So each machine had a different BIOS that, as long as software made only standard MS-DOS calls, would ensure compatibility. But to get the best results out of the 8088's modest performance, many popular software applications were written specifically for the IBM PC.

The developers of these Programmes opted to write directly to the computer's (video) memory and peripheral chips, bypassing MS-DOS and the BIOS. For example, a Programme might directly update the video refresh memory, instead of using MS-DOS calls and device drivers to alter the appearance of the screen.

Many notable software packages, such as the spreadsheet Programme Lotus 1-2-3, and Microsoft's Microsoft Flight Simulator 1.0, directly accessed the IBM PC's hardware, bypassing the BIOS, and therefore did not work on computers that were even trivially different from the IBM PC. This was especially common among games. As a result, the systems that were not fully IBM PC-compatible couldn't run this software, and quickly became obsolete, and with them the concept of OEM versions of MS-DOS meant to run (through BIOS calls) on Non- IBM-PC hardware.

Cloning the PC BIOS

One of the first computers to use a near-clone of the IBM PC BIOS and achieve 100per cent compatibility was the Compaq portable, released in November 1982. Soon after Phoenix Technologies launched their clone of the IBM PC's BIOS and licensed it, which along with IBM's use of standard off-the-shelf ICs made it possible for anyone to develop a PC compatible computer.

Decline of the Intel 80186

Although based on the i8086 and enabling the creation of relatively low cost x86 based systems, the Intel 80186 quickly lost appeal for x86 based PC builders because the supporting circuitry inside the Intel 80186 chip was incompatible with those used in the standard PC chipset as implemented by IBM. It was very rarely used in personal computers after 1982.

DOMINATION OF THE CLONES

Within a few years of the introduction of fully compatible IBM PC clones, virtually all the rival business personal computer systems, and alternate x86 using architectures, were gone from the market. Despite the inherent dangers of an industry based on a de-facto 'standard', a thriving PC clone industry emerged. The only Non-IBM PC-compatible systems that remained were those systems that were classified as home computers, such as the Apple II series made by Apple Inc., or business systems that offered features not available on the IBM

PC, such as a high level of integration (*e.g.*, bundled accounting and inventory) or fault-tolerance and multitasking and multi-user features. IBM tried to capture the remaining home-computer market with the IBM PCjr, which they announced in November 1983, but did not ship until March 1984.

The PCjr flopped. The remaining home computers, such as the Commodore Amiga, Atari ST, and various MSX2 computers remained on the market until IBM PC compatibles gained sufficient multimedia capabilities to compete with home computers. With the advent of inexpensive versions of the VGA video card and the Sound Blaster sound card (and its clones), most of the remaining home computers were driven from the market. By 1995, almost no new consumer-oriented systems were released that were not IBM PC clones.

Escom's Amiga and Apple's Macintosh remained the competitive holdouts. The Amiga and Macintosh originally used Motorola's 68000 family of processors, later migrating to the PowerPC architecture. Throughout the 1990s Apple would steadily transition the Macintosh platform from proprietary expansion interfaces to use emerging industry standards such as IDE, PCI and USB. In 2002 Amiga Inc and Eyetech made the AmigaOne motherboards, dropping support for Zorro III, Amiga native floppy disks and native Amiga custom chipsets such as AGA which was included in every Amiga Since, 1985.

In 2006, Apple converted the Macintosh to the Intel x86 architecture. Modern Macintosh computers are essentially IBM PC compatibles, capable of booting Microsoft Windows and running most IBM PC-compatible software, but still retain unique design elements that support Apple's Mac OS X operating system. As of 2012 AmigaOS 4 runs still only on the PowerPC architecture.

SYSTEMS LAUNCHED SHORTLY AFTER THE IBM PC

Shortly after the IBM PC was released, an obvious split appeared between systems that opted to use an x86-compatible processor, and those that chose another architecture. Almost all of the x86 systems provided a version of MS-DOS. The others used many different operating systems, although the Z80-based systems typically offered a version of CP/M.

The common usage of MS-DOS unified the x86-based systems, promoting growth of the x86/MS-DOS 'ecosystem.' As the Non-x86 architectures died off, and x86 systems standardised into fully IBM PC compatible clones, a market filled with dozens of different competing systems was reduced to a near-monoculture of IBM PC compatible, MS-DOS compatible systems.

x86-based Systems (Using OEM-specific versions of MS-DOS)

Early after the launch of the IBM PC in 1981, there were still dozens of systems that were not IBM PC-compatible, but did use Intel x86 chips. They used Intel 8088, 8086, or 80186 processors, and almost without exception offered an OEM version of MS-DOS (as opposed to the OEM version customised for IBM's use).

However, they generally made no attempt to copy the IBM PC's architecture, so these machines had different I/O addresses, a different system bus, different video controllers, and other differences from the original IBM PC. These differences, which were sometimes rather minor, were used to improve upon the IBM PC's design, but as a result of the differences, software that directly manipulated the hardware would not run correctly.

In most cases, the x86-based systems that didn't use a fully IBM PC compatible design didn't sell well enough to attract support from software manufacturers, though a few computer manufacturers arranged for compatible versions of popular applications to be developed and sold specifically for their machines. Fully IBM PC-compatible clones appeared on the market shortly thereafter, as the advantages of cloning became impossible to ignore. But before that some of the more notable systems that were x86-compatible, but not real clones, were:

- The ACT Apricot by ACT
- The Dulmont Magnum

- The Epson QX-16
- The Seequa Chameleon
- The HP-150 by Hewlett-Packard and the later HP 95LX, HP 100LX, HP 200LX, HP 1000CX, HP OmniGo 700LX, HP OmniGo 100, and HP OmniGo 120.
- The Hyperion by Infotech Cie used its own H-DOS OEM version of MS-DOS
- The MBC-550 by Sanyo
- The 80186 based Mindset graphics computer
- The Morrow Designs' Morrow Pivot
- The MZ-5500 by Sharp
- The Decision Mate V from NCR Corporation; its version of MS-DOS was called NCR-DOS
- The MikroMikko_2 by Nokia
- The The NorthStar Advantage
- The PC-9800 system from NEC
- The Rainbow 100 from DEC
- The RM Nimbus by RM plc
- The Tandy/Radio Shack TRS-80 Model 2000
- The Texas Instruments TI Professional
- The Torch Graduate by Torch Computers
- The Tulip System-1 by Tulip
- The Victor 9000 by Sirius Systems Technology
- The:YES by Philips was late on the market, ran DOS Plus and MS-DOS, but by using a 80186 it was incompatible with IBM's PC
- The Z-100 by Zenith with an MS-DOS OEM version named Z-DOS

Non-x86-based Systems

Not all manufacturers immediately switched to the Intel x86 microprocessor family and MS-DOS. A few companies continued releasing systems based on Non-Intel architectures. Some of these systems used a 32-bit microprocessor, the most popular being the Motorola 68000.

Others continued to use 8-bit microprocessors. Many of these systems were eventually forced out of the market by the onslaught of the IBM PC clones, although their architectures may have had superior capabilities, especially in the area of multimedia. The PC architectures of that era often only had a CGA display, and no other sound system than the internal PC speaker. Three systems of this era, while now extinct, have thriving legacies:

- The Apple Lisa by Apple Inc. was the predecessor of the Apple Macintosh, inspiring the Macintosh's design. The original Macintosh used a Motorola 68000 chip like the Lisa, and had a sufficiently similar design that some Lisa systems were converted for sale as 'Macintosh XL' computers.
- The Acorn Computers Acorn Archimedes, later named the Risc PC, used a custom-designed microprocessor: the ARM. The ARM architecture continues to be popular, appearing in nearly all mobile phones and in many hand-held devices like Apple's iPhone, iPod and iPad, as well as small UNIX-based systems. The Risc PC's descendants include the A9home, the Iyonix PC and the RiscStation R7500.
- The Sun Microsystems Sun-1 and Sun-2 families of UNIX systems introduced the SunOS UNIX operating system, running on Motorola 680x0 chips. Sun's current large-scale UNIX systems use the SPARC processor family developed by Sun, but run a descendant of SunOS called Solaris.

Other Non-x86-based systems included:

- The Apple IIGS, a 16-bit version of the Apple II series, with extended multimedia capabilities.
- The Commodore Amiga
- The Amstrad PCW series
- The Atari ST
- The Cromemco C-10
- Intertec's Compustar II VPU Model 20
- The Corvus Concept

- The Kaypro 10
- The Fujitsu Micro 16s
- The Micro Decision by Morrow Designs
- The MTU-130 by Micro Technology Unlimited
- The PC-9801 system from NEC
- The Xerox 820
- The Epson QX-10
- The RoadRunner from MicroOffice
- The SGI IRIS series of graphics workstations
- The TRS-80 model 16, 16e and 6000 by Tandy Corporation.

FLOATING POINT

In computing, floating point describes a method of representing real numbers in a way that can support a wide range of values. Numbers are, in general, represented approximately to a fixed number of significant digits and scaled using an exponent. The base for the scaling is normally 2, 10 or 16. The typical number that can be represented exactly is of the form:

- Significant digits × $\text{base}^{\text{exponent}}$

The term *floating point* refers to the fact that the radix point (decimal point, or, more commonly in computers, binary point) can 'float'; that is, it can be placed anywhere relative to the significant digits of the number. This position is indicated separately in the internal representation, and floating-point representation can thus be thought of as a computer realisation of scientific notation.

Over the years, a variety of floating-point representations have been used in computers. However, Since, the 1990s, the most commonly encountered representation is that defined by the IEEE 754 Standard. The advantage of floating-point representation over fixed-point and integer representation is that it can support a much wider range of values.

For example, a fixed-point representation that has seven decimal digits with two decimal places can represent the numbers 12345.67, 123.45, 1.23 and so on, whereas a floating-point representation (such as the IEEE 754 decimal32 format) with seven decimal digits could in addition represent 1.234567, 123456.7, 0.00001234567, 1234567000000000, and so on. The floating-point format needs slightly more storage (to encode the position of the radix point), so when stored in the same space, floating-point numbers achieve their greater range at the expense of precision. The speed of floating-point operations, commonly referred to in performance measurements as FLOPS, is an important machine characteristic, especially in software that performs large-scale mathematical calculations. A number representation (called a numeral system in mathematics) specifies some way of storing a number that may be encoded as a string of digits. The arithmetic is defined as a set of actions on the representation that simulate classical arithmetic operations. There are several mechanisms by which strings of digits can represent numbers. In common mathematical notation, the digit string can be of any length, and the location of the radix point is indicated by placing an explicit 'point' character (dot or comma) there.

If the radix point is omitted then it is implicitly assumed to lie at the right (least significant) end of the string (that is, the number is an integer). In fixed-point systems, some specific assumption is made about where the radix point is located in the string. For example, the convention could be that the string consists of 8 decimal digits with the decimal point in the middle, so that '00012345' has a value of 1.2345.

In scientific notation, the given number is scaled by a power of 10 so that it lies within a certain range—typically between 1 and 10, with the radix point appearing immediately after the first digit. The scaling factor, as a power of ten, is then indicated separately at the end of the number. For example, the revolution period of Jupiter's moon Io is 152853.5047 seconds, a value that would be represented in standard-form scientific notation as 1.528535047×10^5 seconds. Floating-point representation is similar in concept to scientific notation. Logically, a floating-point number consists of:

- A signed digit string of a given length in a given base (or radix). This digit string is referred to as the significant, coefficient or, less often, the mantissa. The length of the significant determines the *precision* to which numbers can be represented. The radix point position is assumed to always be somewhere within the significant—often just after or just before the most significant digit, or to the right of the rightmost (least significant) digit. This stage will generally follow the convention that the radix point is just after the most significant (leftmost) digit.
- A signed integer exponent, also referred to as the characteristic or scale, which modifies the magnitude of the number.

To derive the value of the floating point number, one must multiply the *significant* by the *base* raised to the power of the *exponent*, equivalent to shifting the radix point from its implied position by a number of places equal to the value of the exponent—to the right if the exponent is positive or to the left if the exponent is negative.

Using base-10 (the familiar decimal notation) as an example, the number 152853.5047, which has ten decimal digits of precision, is represented as the significant 1528535047 together with an exponent of 5 (if the implied position of the radix point is after the first most significant digit, here 1). To determine the actual value, a decimal point is placed after the first digit of the significant and the result is multiplied by 10^5 to give 1.528535047×10^5, or 152853.5047. In storing such a number, the base need not be stored, Since, it will be the same for the entire range of supported numbers, and can thus be inferred.

Symbolically, this final value is $S \times b^e$

where *s* is the value of the significant (after taking into account the implied radix point), *b* is the base, and *e* is the exponent.

Equivalently:

$$\frac{S}{bp-1} \times b^e$$

where *s* here means the integer value of the entire significant, ignoring any implied decimal point, and *p* is the precision—the number of digits in the significant. Historically, several number bases have been used for representing floating-point numbers, with base 2 (binary) being the most common, followed by base 10 (decimal), and other less common varieties, such as base 16 (hexadecimal notation), as well as some exotic ones like 3. Floating point numbers are rational numbers because they can be represented as one integer divided by another. The base however determines the fractions that can be represented.

For instance, 1/5 cannot be represented exactly as a floating point number using a binary base but can be represented exactly using a decimal base. The way in which the significant, exponent and sign bits are internally stored on a computer is implementation-dependent. The common IEEE formats are described in detail later and elsewhere, but as an example, in the binary single-precision (32-bit) floating-point representation p=24 and so the significant is a string of 24 bits. For instance, the number π's first 33 bits are 11001001 00001111 11011010 10100010 0.

Rounding to 24 bits in binary mode means attributing the 24th bit the value of the 25th which yields 11001001 00001111 11011011. When this is stored using the IEEE 754 encoding, this becomes the significant *s* with e = 1 (where *s* is assumed to have a binary point to the right of the first bit) after a left-adjustment (or *normalisation*) during which leading or trailing zeros are truncated should there be any. Note that they do not matter anyway.

Then Since, the first bit of a Non-zero binary significant is always 1 it need not be stored, giving an extra bit of precision. To calculate π the formula is

$$\left(1+\sum_{n=1}^{p-1} \text{bit}_n \times 2^{-n}\right)\times 2^e$$

$$=\left(1+1\times 2^{-1}+0\times 2^{-2}+1\times 2^{-4}+1\times 2^{-7}+\ldots+1\times 2^{-33}\right)\times 2^1$$

$$=1.5707964\times 2$$

where n is the normalised significant bit from the left. Normalisation, which is reversed when 1 is being, can be thought of as a form of compression; it allows a binary significant to be compressed into a field one bit shorter than the maximum precision, at the expense of extra processing. The word 'mantissa' is often used as a synonym for significant. Use of mantissa in place of significant or coefficient is discouraged, as the mantissa is traditionally defined as the fractional part of a logarithm, while the *characteristic* is the integer part. This terminology comes from the manner in which logarithm tables were used before computers became commonplace. Log tables were actually tables of mantissas.

Some other Computer Representations for Non-integral Numbers

Floating-point representation, in particular the standard IEEE format; is by far the most common way of representing an approximation to real numbers in computers because it is efficiently handled in most large computer processors. However, there are alternatives:

- Fixed-point representation uses integer hardware operations controlled by a software implementation of a specific convention about the location of the binary or decimal point, for example, 6 bits or digits from the right. The hardware to manipulate these representations is less costly than floating-point and is also commonly used to perform integer operations. Binary fixed point is usually used in special-purpose applications on embedded processors that can only do integer arithmetic, but decimal fixed point is common in commercial applications.
- Binary-coded decimal (BCD) is an encoding for decimal numbers in which each digit is represented by its own binary sequence. It is possible to implement a floating point system with BCD encoding.
- Logarithmic number systems represent a real number by the logarithm of its absolute value and a sign bit.

The value distribution is similar to floating-point, but the value-to-representation curve, i. e. the graph of the logarithm function, is smooth (except at 0). Contrary to floating-point arithmetic, in a logarithmic number system multiplication, division and exponentiation are easy to implement but addition and subtraction are difficult. The level index arithmetic of Clenshaw, Olver, and Turner is a scheme based on a generalised logarithm representation.

- Where greater precision is desired, floating-point arithmetic can be implemented (typically in software) with variable-length significants (and sometimes exponents) that are sized depending on actual need and depending on how the calculation proceeds. This is called arbitrary-precision floating point arithmetic.
- Some numbers (*e.g.*, 1/3 and 0.1) cannot be represented exactly in binary floating-point no matter what the precision. Software packages that perform rational arithmetic represent numbers as fractions with integral numerator and denominator, and can therefore represent any rational number exactly. Such packages generally need to use 'bignum' arithmetic for the individual integers.
- Computer algebra systems such as Mathematica and Maxima can often handle irrational numbers like π or $\sqrt{3}$ in a completely 'formal' way, without dealing with a specific encoding of the significant. Such Programmes can evaluate expressions like '$\sin 3\pi$' exactly, because they 'know' the underlying mathematics.

RANGE OF FLOATING-POINT NUMBERS

By allowing the radix point to be adjustable, floating-point notation allows calculations over a wide range of magnitudes, using a fixed number of digits, while maintaining good precision. For example, in a decimal floating-point system with three digits, the multiplication that humans would write as

$0.12 \times 0.12 = 0.0144$

would be expressed as

$(1.20\times10^{-1}) \times (1.20\times10^{-1}) = (1.44\times10^{-2})$.

In a fixed-point system with the decimal point at the left, it would be

$0.120 \times 0.120 = 0.014$.

A digit of the result was lost because of the inability of the digits and decimal point to 'float' relative to each other within the digit string. The range of floating-point numbers depends on the number of bits or digits used for representation of the significant (the significant digits of the number) and for the exponent.

On a typical computer system, a 'double precision' (64-bit) binary floating-point number has a coefficient of 53 bits (one of which is implied), an exponent of 11 bits, and one sign bit. Positive floating-point numbers in this format have an approximate range of 10^{-308} to 10^{308}, because the range of the exponent is [–1022,1023] and 308 is approximately $\log_{10}(2^{1023})$. The complete range of the format is from about -10^{308} through $+10^{308}$.

The number of normalised floating point numbers in a system F (*B*, *P*, *L*, *U*) (where *B* is the base of the system, *P* is the precision of the system to *P* numbers, *L* is the smallest exponent representable in the system, and *U* is the largest exponent used in the system) is: $2\,(B-1)\,(B^{p-1})(U-L+1) + 1$ There is a smallest positive normalised floating-point number, Underflow level = UFL = B^Lwhich has a 1 as the leading digit and 0 for the remaining digits of the significant, and the smallest possible value for the exponent. There is a largest floating point number, Overflow level = OFL = $(1-B^{-p})(B^{u+1})$ which has *B*–1 as the value for each digit of the significant and the largest possible value for the exponent. In addition there are representable values strictly between "UFL and UFL. Namely, zero and negative zero, as well as subnormal numbers.

IEEE 754: FLOATING POINT IN MODERN OMPUTERS

The IEEE has standardised the computer representation for binary floating-point numbers in IEEE 754. This standard is followed by almost all modern machines. Notable exceptions include IBM mainframes, which support IBM's own format (in addition to the IEEE 754 binary and decimal formats), and Cray vector machines, where the T90 series had an IEEE version, but the SV1 still uses Cray floating-point format. The standard provides for many closely related formats, differing in only a few details.

Five of these formats are called basic formats and others are termed extended formats, and three of these are especially widely used in computer hardware and languages:

- Single precision, called 'float' in the C language family, and 'real' or 'real*4' in Fortran. This is a binary format that occupies 32 bits (4 bytes) and its significant has a precision of 24 bits (about 7 decimal digits).
- Double precision, called 'double' in the C language family, and 'double precision' or 'real*8' in Fortran. This is a binary format that occupies 64 bits (8 bytes) and its significant has a precision of 53 bits (about 16 decimal digits).
- Double extended format, 80-bit floating point value. This is implemented on most personal computers but not on other devices. Sometimes 'long double' is used for this in the C language family, though 'long double' may be a synonym for 'double' or may stand for quadruple precision. Extended precision can help minimize accumulation of round-off error in intermediate calculations.

Less common formats include:

- The other basic formats quadruple precision (128-bit) binary, and decimal floating point (64-bit) and 'double' (128-bit) decimal floating point.
- Half, also called float16, a 16-bit floating point value.

Any integer with absolute value less than or equal to 2^{24} can be exactly represented in the single precision format, and any integer with absolute value less than or equal to 2^{53} can be exactly represented in the double precision format. Furthermore, a wide range of powers of 2 times such a number can be represented.

These properties are sometimes used for purely integer data, to get 53-bit integers on platforms that have double precision floats but only 32-bit integers. The standard specifies some special values, and their representation: positive infinity (+∞), negative infinity (–∞), a negative zero (–0) distinct from ordinary ('positive') zero, and 'not a number' values (NaNs). Comparison of floating-point numbers, as defined by the IEEE standard, is a bit different from usual integer comparison. Negative and positive zero compare equal, and every NaN compares unequal to every value, including itself.

All values except NaN are strictly smaller than +∞ and strictly greater than +∞. Finite floating-point numbers are ordered in the same way as their values (in the set of real numbers).

To a rough approximation, the bit representation of an IEEE binary floating-point number is proportional to its base 2 logarithm, with an average error of about 3 per cent. (This is because the exponent field is in the more significant part of the datum.)

This can be exploited in some applications, such as volume ramping in digital sound processing. A project for revising the IEEE 754 standard was started in 2000; it was completed and approved in June 2008. It includes decimal floating-point formats and a 16 bit floating point format ('binary16'). binary16 has the same structure and rules as the older formats, with 1 sign bit, 5 exponent bits and 10 trailing significant bits. It is being used in the NVIDIA Cg graphics language, and in the openEXR standard.

Internal Representation

Floating-point numbers are typically packed into a computer datum as the sign bit, the exponent field, and the significant (mantissa), from left to right.

For the IEEE 754 binary formats (basic and extended) which have extant hardware implementations, they are apportioned as follows:

Type	Sign	Exponent	Significant	Total Bits	Exponent Bias	Bits Precision	Number of Decimal Digits
Half (IEEE 754-2008)	1	5	10	16	15	11	~3.3
Single	1	8	23	32	127	24	~7.2
Double	1	11	52	64	1023	53	~15.9
Double extended (80-bit)	1	15	64	80	16383	64	~19.2
Quad	1	15	112	128	16383	113	~34.0

While the exponent can be positive or negative, in binary formats it is stored as an unsigned number that has a fixed 'bias' added to it. Values of all 0s in this field are reserved for the zeros and subnormal numbers, values of all 1s are reserved for the infinities and NaNs. The exponent range for normalised numbers is ['126, 127] for single precision, ['1022, 1023] for double, or ['16382, 16383] for quad.

Normalised numbers exclude subnormal values, zeros, infinities, and NaNs. In the IEEE binary interchange formats the leading 1 bit of a normalised significant is not actually stored in the computer datum. It is called the 'hidden' or 'implicit' bit. Because of this, single precision format actually has a significant with 24 bits of precision, double precision format has 53, and quad has 113. For example, it was shown that π, rounded to 24 bits of precision, has:

- Sign = 0 ; *e* = 1 ; *s* = 110010010000111111011011 (including the hidden bit)

The sum of the exponent bias (127) and the exponent (1) is 128, so this is represented in single precision format as

- 0 10000000 10010010000111111011011 (excluding the hidden bit) = 40490FDB as a hexadecimal number.

Special Values

Signed Zero

In the IEEE 754 standard, zero is signed, meaning that there exist both a 'positive zero' (+0) and a 'negative zero' (–0). In most run-time environments, positive zero is usually printed as '0', while negative zero may be printed as '-0'. The two values behave as equal in numerical comparisons, but some operations return different results for +0 and –0. For instance, 1/(–0) returns negative infinity (exactly), while 1/+0 returns positive infinity (exactly) (so that the identity 1/(1/±∞) = ±∞ is maintained).

A sign symmetric arccot operation will give different results for +0 and ‘0 without any exception. The difference between +0 and –0 is mostly noticeable for complex operations at so-called branch cuts.

Subnormal Numbers

Subnormal values fill the underflow gap with values where the absolute distance between them are the same as for adjacent values just outside of the underflow gap. This is an improvement over the older practice to just have zero in the underflow gap, and where underflowing results were replaced by zero (flush to zero). Modern floating point hardware usually handles subnormal values (as well as normal values), and does not require software emulation for subnormals.

Infinities

The infinities of the extended real number line can be represented in IEEE floating point datatypes, just like ordinary floating point values like 1, 1.5 etc. They are not error values in any way, though they are often (but not always, as it depends on the rounding) used as replacement values when there is an overflow. Upon a divide by zero exception, a positive or negative infinity is returned as an exact result. An infinity can also be introduced as a numeral (like C's 'INFINITY' macro, or '∞' if the programming language allows that syntax). IEEE 754 requires infinities to be handled in a reasonable way, such as

- (+∞) + (+7) = (+∞)
- (+∞) × (‘2) = (–∞)
- (+∞) × 0 = NaN – there is no meaningful thing to do

NaNs

IEEE 754 specifies a special value called 'Not a Number' (NaN) to be returned as the result of certain 'invalid' operations, such as 0/0, ∞×0, or sqrt(–1). In general, NaNs will be propagated, *i.e.*, most operations involving a NaN will result in a NaN, although functions that would give some defined result for any given floating point value will do so for NaNs as well, e.g, NaN ^ 0 == 1. There are two kinds of NaNs: the default *quiet* NaNs and, optionally, *signaling* NaNs. A signaling NaN in any arithmetic operation (including numerical comparisons) will cause an 'invalid' exception to be signalled.

The representation of NaNs specified by the standard has some unspecified bits that could be used to encode the type or source of error; but there is no standard for that encoding. In theory, signaling NaNs could be used by a runtime system to flag uninitialised variables, or extend the floating-point numbers with other special values without slowing down the computations with ordinary values, although such extensions are not common.

IEEE 754 Design Rationale

It is a common misconception that the more esoteric features of the IEEE 754 standard discussed here, such as extended formats, NaN, infinities, subnormals, etc., are only of interest to numerical analysts, or for advanced numerical applications; in fact the opposite is true: these features are designed to give safe robust defaults for numerically unsophisticated programmers, in addition to supporting sophisticated numerical libraries by experts.

The key designer of IEEE 754, Prof. W. Kahan notes that it is incorrect to '... [deem] features of IEEE Standard 754 for Binary Floating- Point Arithmetic that...[are] not appreciated to be features usable by None but numerical experts. The facts are quite the opposite.

In 1977 those features were designed into the Intel 8087 to serve the widest possible market.... Error-analysis tells us how to design floating-point arithmetic, like IEEE Standard 754, moderately tolerant of well-meaning ignorance among programmers".

- The special values such as infinity and NaN ensure that the floating point arithmetic is algebraically completed, such that every floating point operation produces a well-defined result and will not by default throw a machine interrupt or trap. Moreover, the choices of special values returned in exceptional cases were designed to give the correct answer in many cases, *e.g.*, continued fractions such as R(z):= 7–3/(z–2–1/(z–7 + 10/(z–2–2/(z–3)))) will give the correct answer in all inputs under IEEE-754 arithmetic as the potential divide by zero in, *e.g.*, R(3) =4.6 is correctly handled as + infinity and so can be safely ignored. As noted by Kahan, the unhandled floating point overflow exception that caused the loss of an Ariane 5 rocket would not have happened under IEEE 754 floating point.

- Subnormal numbers ensure that x - y = 0 if and only if x = y, as expected, but which did not hold under earlier floating point representations.
- On the design rationale of the x87 80-bit format, Prof. Kahan notes: 'This Extended format is designed to be used, with negligible loss of speed, for all but the simplest arithmetic with float and double operands. For example, it should be used for scratch variables in loops that implement recurrences like polynomial evaluation, scalar products, partial and continued fractions. It often averts premature Over/Underflow or severe local cancellation that can spoil simple algorithms. Computing intermediate results in an extended format with high precision and extended exponent has precedents in the historical practice of scientific calculation and in the design of scientific calculators, *e.g.*, Hewlett-Packard's financial calculators performed arithmetic and financial functions to three more significant decimals than they stored or displayed. The implementation of extended precision enabled standard elementary function libraries to be readily developed that normally gave double precision results within one unit in the last place (ULP) at high speed.
- Correct rounding of values to the nearest

representable value avoids systematic biases in calculations and slows the growth of errors. Rounding ties to even removes the statistical bias that can occur in adding similar figures.

- Directed rounding was intended as an aid with checking error bounds, for instance in interval arithmetic. It is also used in the implementation of some functions.
- The mathematical basis of the operations enabled high precision multiword arithmetic subroutines to be built relatively easily.
- The single and double precision formats were designed to be easy to sort without using floating point hardware.

REPRESENTABLE NUMBERS, CONVERSION AND ROUNDING

By their nature, all numbers expressed in floating-point format are rational numbers with a terminating expansion in the relevant base (for example, a terminating decimal expansion in base-10, or a terminating binary expansion in base-2). Irrational numbers, such as π or $\sqrt{2}$ or Non-terminating rational numbers, must be approximated.

The number of digits (or bits) of precision also limits the set of rational numbers that can be represented exactly. For example, the number 123456789 cannot be exactly represented if only eight decimal digits of precision are available. When a number is represented in some format (such as a character string) which is not a native floating-point representation supported in a computer implementation, then it will require a conversion before it can be used in that implementation.

If the number can be represented exactly in the floating-point format then the conversion is exact. If there is not an exact representation then the conversion requires a choice of which floating-point number to use to represent the original value. The representation chosen will have a different value to the original, and the value thus adjusted is called the *rounded value*. Whether or not a rational number has a terminating expansion depends on the base. For example, in base-10 the number 1/2 has a terminating expansion (0.5) while the number 1/3 does not (0.333...).

In base-2 only rationals with denominators that are powers of 2 (such as 1/2 or 3/16) are terminating. Any rational with a denominator that has a prime factor other than 2 will have an infinite binary expansion. This means that numbers which appear to be short and exact when written in decimal format may need to be approximated when converted to binary floating-point.

Rounding Modes

Rounding is used when the exact result of a floating-point operation (or a conversion to floating-point format) would need more digits than there are digits in the significant. IEEE 754 requires *correct rounding*: that is, the rounded result is as if infinitely precise arithmetic was used to compute the value and then rounded (although in implementation only three extra bits are needed to ensure this).

There are several different rounding schemes (or *rounding modes*). Historically, truncation was the typical approach. Since, the introduction of IEEE 754, the default method (*round to nearest, ties to even*, sometimes called Banker's Rounding) is more commonly used. This method rounds the ideal (infinitely precise) result of an arithmetic operation to the nearest representable value, and gives that representation as the result. In the case of a tie, the value that would make the significant end in an even digit is chosen.

The IEEE 754 standard requires the same rounding to be applied to all fundamental algebraic operations, including square root and conversions, when there is a numeric (non-NaN) result. It means that the results of IEEE 754 operations are completely determined in all bits of the result, except for the representation of NaNs. ('Library' functions such as cosine and log are not mandated.) Alternative rounding options are also available. IEEE 754 specifies the following rounding modes:

- Round to nearest, where ties round to the nearest

even digit in the required position (the default and by far the most common mode)

- Round to nearest, where ties round away from zero (optional for binary floating-point and commonly used in decimal)
- Round up (Towards +∞; negative results thus round Towards zero)
- Round down (Towards –∞; negative results thus round away from zero)
- Round Towards zero (truncation; it is similar to the common Behaviour of float-to-integer conversions, which convert –3.9 to –3 and 3.9 to 3)

Alternative modes are useful when the amount of error being introduced must be bounded. Applications that require a bounded error are multi-precision floating-point, and interval arithmetic. The alternative rounding modes are also useful in diagnosing numerical instability: if the results of a subroutine vary substantially between rounding to + and - infinity then it is likely numerically unstable and affected by round-off error. A further use of rounding is when a number is explicitly rounded to a certain number of decimal (or binary) places, as when rounding a result to euros and cents (two decimal places).

5

Web-based Library Services

INTRODUCTION

The due to the tremendous growth and continuous development of technology, the role of library becomes more responsive in making the users techno-savvy. Technological developments have affected not only the formats and sources of the information, but also how and where to provide library services. Libraries and their resources have partially moved to the virtual world of the Internet.

As a result, library users can access the resources from outside the physical library. In an effort to reach users accessing the library via their computers, many libraries and library consortia are extending their services to include virtual reference. Technology now allows users to submit their queries to the library at any time from any place in the world.

Web Based Services, Digital Library Services, Internet Library Services and Electronic Library Services are terms with similar meanings. As more libraries move towards providing services in a digital environment, the improved access to remote library collections is making the use of electronic information resources more realistic and more attractive. Traditional online services had transformed themselves into internet-based online services using web-based technologies. From traditional online services to today, four generations of information retrieval tools have passed that assist users in searching the World Wide Web. The first generation of information retrieval tools was designed for use with bibliographic databases. The first generation provided access to references to the end documents rather than to the documents themselves, and indexing and searching were thus applied to document surrogates, such as titles or abstracts. These tools require considerable human efforts to collect, arrange, code, and annotate the various resources. A primary benefit of the first generation of tools is providing users with easy browsing capabilities.

The second generation of tools attempts to collect and index resources as an automated function. Automatic collection and indexing reduces the amount of human effort. The ability to search through massive amounts of information and locate the desired information for the user is the primary benefit of the second generation of tools.

The third generation deals with World Wide Web Meta search engines, such as Harvester and Meta crawler. The fourth generation involves new ideas such as search agent technology currently being developed to search for information on the web. Web-based search engines are as a means of finding relevant pages on the Internet. Different search engines, directory, meta-search engines, gateways, subject portals, electronic journals and on line databases each type could be used in a different way, from simple keyword searching up to peerreviewed web sites.

WEB BASED LIBRARY SERVICE

A digital Library service manages and develops electronic services, the library Web sites and library staff. According to White, it can be defined broadly as 'an information access service in which users ask questions via electronic means, *e.g.*, e-mail or web forms'.

Library service on the internet requires many of the same qualities as traditional references: accuracy, promptness, courtesy, an understanding of the information need. It provides users with the convenience of accessing information in their own time, saving them traveling cost and time and new options for answering reference questions. The provision of these services is not constrained by the traditional opening hours but can be offered on a 24-hour, seven-days-a-week basis known as 24/7. And while there may be a disadvantage in not having a face-to face encounter, there are many advantages to this new medium and the greatest advantage is that many more users can be helped by using electronic library services. Advantages and disadvantages of electronic access over printed form access are showed in table. Web based services are established due to the following reasons.

- Ensuring the needs of users and the accessible information sources are suitable matched at all times.
- Delivering those information sources to the user in a timely and appropriate fashion.
- Ensuring the information provided is high quality, accurate and appropriate.
- Assisting the user in interpreting the materials, if necessary.
- Promoting user awareness of new services and information sources as they develop.
- Providing users with individualised guidance and support as they build their information search and application skills.

Table 5.1. Advantages and Disadvantages of Printed Form over Electronic Access

Sl. No.	Print Form	Electronic Form
Advantages		
1.	Format is tested and standardised	Format is in the early stages of development
2.	Easy for users to use	Requires some training for users to use
3.	No special equipment needed	Special equipment required (hardware, software, printers, etc.,)

(Contd...)

Sl. No.	Print Form	Electronic Form
4.	Easy to locate (if shelved properly)	Access is currently unreliable (URL problems, internet connection problems, etc.,)
5.	Use is limited only to copyright laws	Use is limited by copyright laws and licensing agreements
6.	Archiving is effective and permanent	Archiving is 'up in the air'
Disadvantages		
1.	Operating costs are considerable (ordering, cataloging, claiming, and binding)	Operating costs are minimal (no cataloging, binding, or clalmlng)
2.	Requires shelving	No shelving required
3.	Often mutilated, stolen, or misshelved	Cannot be mutilated, stolen, or misshelved
4.	Requires extensive storage space	Saves considerable storage space
5.	Allows only one user at a time	Allows for multiple users with simultaneous access
6.	Slow delivery via 'snail mail'	Immediate receipt of issue
7.	Issues are easily lost in the mail or missing	No more missing issues
8.	Slow publication	Fast publication

DIFFERENT RESOURCES FOR WEB BASED LIBRARY SERVICES

Today, users may have access a variety of textual information resources. There are different kinds of webbased reference resources and services for accessing information from libraries such as OPAC, Gateways, Portals, Subject Portals, Electronic Journals, Online Databases, Subject Directories and Search Engines. These resources overlap considerably in the type of information they cover, and sometimes it is difficult to distinguish between some of them. A library should have a good collection of these resources like selected Web links, subscription resources, and library materials in well-organised pages for serving better services to their users.

Many libraries and organisations are providing digital reference service through collaborative services. Existing library consortia are adding digital reference to current shared services, and networks of libraries. Some regional library consortia are offering member libraries the opportunity to share reference questions with each other using the Internet and other technologies.

OPAC

OPAC's - On Line Public Access Catalogues, form an important part of many digital library's collections. It allows users to search for the bibliographic records contained within a library's collections. Now days, some OPAC also provide access to electronic resources and databases, in addition to the traditional bibliographic records.

GATEWAYS

A gateway is defined as a facility that allows easier access to network based resources in a given subject area. Gateways provide a simple search facility and a much-enhanced service through a resource database and indexes, which can be searched through a web based interface. Information provided by gateways is catalogued by hand. Gateways cover a wide range of subjects, through some areas, such as music and religious studies, currently lack subject gateways. Some well-known gateways are as follows:

- Internet Public Library (IPL),
- Bulletin Board for Libraries (BUBL),
- National Information Services and Systems (NISS),

PORTALS

In the library community, portals may be defined as an amalgamation of services to the users where the amalgamation is achieved through seamless integration of existing services by using binding agents such as customisation and authentication services, search protocols such as Z39.50, loan protocols such as ISO10161, and e-commerce.

The result is a personalised service which allows the individual to access the rich content of both print-based and electronic systems. Portals are either commercial or free web facilities that offer information services to a specific audience. The facilities include web search to communication to e-mail to news, etc.There are three kinds of portals; Consumer (or horizontal), Vertical and Enterprise.

- Consumer portals are aimed at consumer audiences and offer free e-mail, games, chat, etc., Examples are Yahoo!, MSN and AOL.
- Vertical portals, target a specified audience, such as a particular industry, and offer many of the consumer portal features. Example includes VerticalNet.
- Enterprise portals on the other hand are similar to consumer portals, but they are offered only to corporations or similar organisations. Examples include Epicentric and Corporate Yahoo! These portals can be best understood as electronic pathfinders for users, pulling together in one place in a web site selected links to subjects or interest-oriented resources located on the WWW.

SUBJECT PORTALS

Web Search Engines had been developed initially by computer scientists, by borrowing techniques from information retrieval search such as best match searching and relevance ranking. Information professional are increasing bringing their skills to help organise the growing wealth of Internet resources.

A good example of their influence is the development of subject-specific web search engines known as subject portals, where evaluation of material covered is a major concern. Two prime UK subject portals are SOSIG (Social Science

Information Gateway), covering social science resources and OMNI (Organising medical networked information) covering medical resources. Subject portal sites can be very helpful, but they should be used with care. Users should bear the following points in their mind:

- The aim of the subject portal is to list and review the most important sites on the web relevant to that subject. The sites are usually constantly peer-reviewed to ensure that the site is relevant and up to date.
- New sites are appearing all the time. Relying on a subject portal site to find everything users require may mean that they miss an important site that has recently appeared and has not yet been reviewed by the producers of the particular subject portal.
- A subject portal is a one stop shop for information on the topic it covers. Users don't have to carry out extensive Internet searches in order to find the information require. They can simply go to the required subject portal site.
- Subject portals save users having to have long lists of bookmarks (saved addresses of web pages), which are often, cumbersome and time consuming to arrange and keep up to date. However, if users do prefer to use bookmarks they can arrange them in an order to suit the way they work and not have an order forced on them by the subject portal.
- A subject portal site is only as good as the reviewers who peer-review the site listed. The reviewers need to have a policy of keeping the portal sites up to date and of constantly reviewing the sites they list, to make sure that they are still relevant and still contain good, timely information.
- A subject portal may be available to everyone who needs to use it to only certain groups of users. A good portal should be publicly available to anyone who needs it.

ELECTRONIC JOURNALS

Electronic journals form a large part of the collection of a library for providing web based services. Today many journals are available electronically - some are full text and some contain only bibliographic information with abstract. Major advantage of electronic journals is that they are constantly updated and easy to access but disadvantage is that breaching of copyright law is very easy.

They are available as bitmaps, PostScript, PDF, ASCII, SGML and HTML. Library services may be delivering to users on CDRom, through e-mail or through web. Some international societies and associations have developed their own digital libraries through which users can get access to all their publications. Services are available to the members of society or associations through subscription.

ONLINE DATABASES

These are large collections of machine-readable data that are maintained by commercial agencies and are accessed through communication lines. Many libraries subscribe to them for easy access and use of current information. The disadvantage is that only bibliographic data is presented and not full text. The information cannot be accessed when the system is down for any reason. Examples Ei Compendex, SciFinder Scholar, Web of Science, Current Contents, etc.

SEARCH ENGINES

Search Engines are huge databases of web page files that have been assembled automatically by machines where as the subject directories are human-compiled and maintained. Search engine indexes every page of a Web site and subject directories linked only homepages.

Search Engine is the popular term for an information retrieval (IR) system. A search engine is computer software that searches a collection of electronic materials to retrieve citations, documents, or information that matches or answers a user's query. The retrieved materials may be text documents, facts that have been extracted from text, images, or sounds. A query is a question phrased so that it can be interpreted properly by search engine. Depending on the type of software, it may be a collection of commands, a statement in either full or partial sentences, one or more keywords, or in the case of Non-text searching, an image or sequence of sounds to be matched.

SUBJECT DIRECTORIES

Subject directories differ from search engines in that search engines are populated by robots that finds and index sites whereas humans making editorial decisions that populate subject directories. Subject directories are basically index home pages of sites and can be classified as general, academic, commercial or portal. Among the well known subject directories are the Argus Clearinghouse and Yahoo. Strengths include relevance, effectiveness and relative high quality of content. Weaknesses are that they lack depth in their coverage of the subjects.

NEW WEB BASED LIBRARY SERVICES

VIRTUAL LIBRARY TOURS

Web sites of libraries provides virtual library guide to the physical facilities including collections, services and infrastructure available in the library. The combination of library maps and floor plans, library departments and photographic views are used for the tour. Virtual library tours are also using new technologies such as QuickTime movies etc and are beginning to replace image maps on main campus Web sites.

ASK-A-LIBRARIAN

Ask-A-Librarian services are Internet-based question and answer service that connects users with individuals who possess specialised subject knowledge and skill in conducting precision searches. Most 'Ask-a-Librarians' services have a web-based question submission form or an e-mail address or both. Users are invited to submit their queries by using web forms or through e-mail. Once a query is read by a service, it is assigned to an individual expert for answering. An expert responds to the query with factual information and or a list of information resources.

The response is either sent to the user's e-mail account or is posted on the web so that the user can access it after a certain period of time. Many services have informative web sites that include archives of questions and answers and a set of FAQs. Users are usually encouraged to browse archives and FAQs before submitting a question in case sufficient information already exists.

REAL TIME SERVICES

A new and exciting method of digital reference service that libraries are attempting to provide more and more now is live reference. These are real-time, interactive reference services in which the users can talk to a real, live reference librarian at any time, from anywhere in the world.

User and librarian can interact using chat technologies, and unlike with e-mail reference the librarian can perform a reference interview of sorts by asking the users to elaborate or clarify if needed before proceeding to answer the question. The librarian can perform Internet searches and push Web sites onto the user's browser, and can receive immediate feedback from the users as to whether their question have been answered to satisfaction.

BULLETIN BOARDS

A bulletin board is an electronic communications forum that hosts posted messages and articles connected to a common subject or theme or interest. It allows users to call in and either leaves or retrieves messages. The messages may be directed to all users of the bulletin board or only to particular users. But all messages can be read by all users. Several libraries are using bulletin boards for their web-based library services. The bulletin board system is also used as an interactive interface to invite suggestions on activities and services of a library. It can also be used as an interface to distribute library services.

WEB-BASED USER EDUCATION

Web guides and teaching tools are found everywhere on the Web because they are easily updated, accessed, and printed on demand. The web-based user education provides a high degree of interactivity and flexibility to the users.

The library web sites can use web-based user education for imparting training to users in teaching the basic library skills along with glossary of library terms, using Library OPAC, locating books, magazines, biographical data and other library materials, understanding how to navigate the libraries Web site and how to select the most relevant database, instructions for searching CD ROM and guidance in locating web-based databases and other electronic resources and instructions on subject searching training, using Boolean operators and searching internet resources through search engines.

WEB FORMS

Library web sites have some web forms for suggestions and comments on the Library Services. Different types of Web Forms are available on web that may be an Indent form for acquiring some publications, interlibrary loan request form for document delivery, Ask-a-Librarian forms, on line reservation form or user survey form, etc.

INDIAN SCENARIO

The Indian libraries also have realised to give web based services to users and they have recognised that working together can accomplish for more than they can do individually. Many Indian libraries in India are not geared up for accessing e-journals due to various reasons including user ignorance, infrastructure and initial funds. The library and information networks in India were initiated in early eighties.

The growth during this period can be linked to some of the policies that Government of India pursued. Some institutions like CSIR, ISRO, DRDO, DAE, ICAR, SIRNET, NICNET, NISSAT, INFLIBNET, MHRD and IIM libraries are actively working continuously to improve the present situation. They spend annually a huge amount of money towards library acquisition, especially towards journals, e-journals and e-databases.

Some initiative include, Indian Institute of Management for accessing bibliographic databases, CSIR laboratories for Science Direct, FORSA for accessing Astronomy and Astrophysics journals, Hyderabad Knowledge park members of J-gate, INFLIBNET (UGC–INFONET) initiative for full text and databases like BIOSIS and CAS and INDEST for a host of full text sources and few bibliographic databases for the benefit of IITs, IISc, NITs and Engineering colleges. In India, library consortia are emerging as one of the important service to users. The Indian consortiums will help the library to provide better services to the users by investing Meagre amount. To expand the access for more number of e-journals, e-books and other eresources, we have to develop the digital library infrastructure as a platform for e-learning.

FUTURE OF WEB BASED SERVICES

Library Web services will continue to spread out, offering more full-text electronic journals and indexes that do not now include full text will begin to do so, or link to external resources. Bibliographic access to full-text periodicals either through cataloging, databases, or vendors will be in improved form. There will be more Web forms for user feedback, and perhaps a virtual librarian who interacts in real time chat or video conferencing. More Document delivery services to distance education or users and Savings on Interlibrary Loan and user convenience are incentives. Information resources through creative consortia purchasing will be popular. A well-developed user education modules or tutorials, especially to support independent exploration of library and Web resources.

Somebody will have to figure out how to keep Word users from saving print documents as XML, without thinking in terms of Web, not print, space. XML will be embraced as a way to control page appearance and Behaviour, but it will take a while for people to figure out how to use it well and there will be trends we haven't thought of yet.

CONCLUSION

The standards for organising web-based resources are still in the early stages of development, and librarians are forced to utilise standards for print resources that were not designed for electronic resources. Additionally web-based information resources are volatile in the sense that may be moved from one site to another or may be removed altogether from web. Web-based library services will become more widespread and sophisticated as the web becomes common place throughout the world, and to be successful players in the E-world. Libraries must continue to address the web design and implementation issues. As we actively transfer library services, our central purpose remain the same, to serve and teach users to find, evaluate, and use information effectively. The librarians should be expert to hold the hands of the users who are moving towards new communication paradigm a shift from face to face human contact to human machine interaction, from paper to electronic delivery, from text centered mode to multimedia and from physical presence to virtual presence. Despite these changes in communication technology, the reference interview will remain at the heart of the reference transaction. To meet these challenges the librarians may play a leadership role in providing better Web Based library Services facilities to their current techno savvy users.

6

Information Economy and Geospatial Information

INTRODUCTION

The recent socioeconomic trends, convergence of telecommunication technologies and the emergence of information as an integral component of the contemporary economy, have had significant effects on individuals and on wider social groups in the population. The current information node infrastructure of the telecommunications industry, which has facilitated that convergence of the telecommunications technology, is comprised of a variety of links.

These links include data clearinghouses, data providers, and data warehouses, which themselves combine to form complex information networks as well as individual links, or single participants. All of these links affect how information flows across the network.

Libraries, as participants in the information network infrastructure, are well suited to affect the nature of data processes in the current information economy. Although the framework of the information economy may have been built by technological innovations and capital investments, there are cultural and political factors about the social milieu in which information is processed that affect how individuals participate in the economy. The composition of the information networks creates a variety of challenges to the successful searching, discovery, and mining of data for users in a variety of situations. Libraries can facilitate the interactions of individuals with different types of information that are integral to successful participation in the information economy. A key informational component of the information economy is how libraries can facilitate participation of their users with geospatial information.

This chapter will explore different socioeconomic aspects of the information economy and the role of libraries. The development of geographic information systems, the importance of 'value added' services and an examination of how information is being increasingly commoditised is also included. Public aspects of geospatial information, such as government-produced GIS, will be discussed. How libraries can play a role in facilitating some of the social aspects of the distribution of the information economy, such as the digital divide, will also be examined.

ROLE OF INFORMATION IN CONTEMPORARY ECONOMY

In the information economy, many private sector firms and government agencies have become consolidated around a framework of telecommunication networks and related information technologies. However, integrating communications and information technologies into their organisations have affected organisational processes, including production, distribution, and administration of products and services.

Researchers have noted that organisational processes in both the public and private sectors have become characterised by applications, such as electronic data exchange, distributed databases, computer-based communication, and client server computing. Other researchers have indicated that geographic concepts, such as space and location, are significant factors in the distribution of data as it flows between individuals and organisations across communication networks, therefore, the use of geographic information systems in the facilitating and analysis of data has also increased greatly. The development and integration of geospatial information in a variety of administrative, production, and service functions within organisations in both the public and private sectors can have an effect on the role that libraries play in the information economy. The geospatial information that is used by individuals and organisations in the information economy is often produced by a mix of private developers and government agencies.

The data used by geographers and geographic information systems analysts in their operations is diverse and distributed across a wide network of server locations, over a complex series of information nodes. Libraries can provide a unique entry point to this multitude of sources. Economic activities during the past few decades have increasingly been characterised by different functional uses of information. The establishment and growth of diverse information industries, such as statistical bureaus, marketing associations, trade journals, and consulting agencies, have integrated information in their operations.

The development builds on early studies of how information not only impacted, but helped define, different economic processes. During the decades following World War II, individuals in the banking and accounting sectors began defining information as having value and affecting production. Statements, such as the 'Statement of Basic Accounting Theory,' asserted that accounting systems could be conceptualised as an 'application of general theories of information to the problem of efficient economic operations'. The National Science Foundation began to fund research about the economics of information.

Other organisations, such as the Organisation for Economic Co-operation and Development (OECD) and the United Nations Economic, Scientific, and Cultural Organisation (UNESCO), were also debating policy issues about the economics of information. However, to develop an information policy, one must first understand that policy is '... the generic name of any formulation, simple or complex, vague or exact, general or special, discretionary or detailed, of guidance for action in the face of circumstances which, lying necessarily in the future, can be approached only by conjecture and imagination'. The first bibliography of information economics was published in 1971.

By the mid 1970s, developments in the literature illustrated how the general theories of information were being investigated by economists and other researchers in the sciences and social sciences. Clearly, "... the existence of learning processes and likely variation in policy criteria in a business organisation imply that the decision-making unit is undergoing continual change".

Further, "those responsible for shaping information policy must determine the appropriate mix of information inputs to achieve social objectives, while at the same time they must have regard for equity considerations". By 1976, the American Economic Association officially recognised information as an economic topic and incorporated it into core ideas. By the 1980s, research into this area was generating much debate among researchers about what comprised information economics. Among the ideas being debated was the emergent issue of how to incorporate information into modes of production and thereby study its effects in different sectors of the economy.

Early economists described three factors of production that included land, Labour, and capital. The competing theories on defining just how these three factors relate, especially capital, in a system is contentious and open to debate. Economists differ on how to define capital. It can be described concretely as something of value as in money or more abstractly as an association with Labour and consumption.

In examining the value of transformative functions of an economic activity, the definition of capital can be more broadly interpreted, in some cases to include information. For example, the definition of human capital is the "sum total of skills embodied within an individual: education, intelligence, charisma, creativity, work experience, entrepreneurial Vigour,

... it is what you would be left with if someone stripped away all of your assets-your job, your money, your possessions". A number of articles and other publications that were produced in the 1990s discussed different forms of intangible capital including information, cultural capital, linguistic capital, and social capital.

Social capital would involve "networks of communication and communication-based institutions and their rules, norms of social practice, and relationships of trust". Networks themselves would be considered as facilitating a sum of knowledge that would have value as a factor in production. Another perspective on integrating information into economic theory was in examining how change in the economy is affected by information.

Braman suggests that "the production of knowledge and its transformation into technologies and other applied mechanisms such as competition can alter the order of different sectors of the economy and thus its equilibrium". More fundamentally, it changes the role, the function, and the perception of economic measurement data. Because information is its key resource and output, the intangible economy is highly data-sensitive and intrinsically self reflective".

However, as researcher suggests, the effects of the applications of information and technology are only apparent over a period of time when it is possible to perform analysis with systematic data. Recent studies have focused on defining the role of technology in causing economic growth. Some researchers consider economic change as being influenced by aspects of the innovation process, aspects that are characterised as being 'information intense' or more developed technologically than what had currently existed. There has been much speculation on the correlation between technological development and economic growth and the social consequences of economic activities. In Marshallian neo-classical economics, externalities refer to by-products of activities that affect the well-being of people, where those impacts are not reflected in market prices; the costs (or benefits) associated with externalities do not enter standard cost accounting schemes.

The backbone of the information economy is in the linkages that combine to form a network. If the network is a combination of technology and human activities that processes information as they traverse the network, then the uneven flow of information across the network can cause externalities to manifest themselves. These externalities can be caused by incomplete information that can result in the fluctuating prices of a commodity.

The effect of content of information on the economy is up to debate. Are the contextual aspects of information processed in the economy irrelevant or do the contextual aspects of information in the economy have distinct sociopolitical value? For those who argue the latter, the contextual aspects of information do shape the perception and understanding of economic processes themselves. The cultural variability of information creates difficulties in determining the locational aspects of data.

Data may be associated with a physical carrier, but it is not bound by the location of that carrier. This aspect of information has created challenges to economists who have attempted to illustrate Braman's concept that would "distinguish between the costs of information at different stages of an information production chain". Further, the value of the information chain hinges upon relevance that "is a subjective question of mapping an utterance on the conceptual map of a given user seeking information for a particular purpose defined by that individual" and the "utility of a piece of information will depend on a combined valuation of its credibility and relevance". Most of the economic models that attempt to illustrate an information production chain have the elements of information creating, processing, flows, and use incorporated into their structure.

A number of organisations have created models that have the elements of information acquisition, production, assembly, storage, monitoring, interpretation, and exchange. United States federal documents describe an information cycle that includes information creation, collection, processing, and distribution as do international organisations. Creators, or individuals who are involved in the innovation of new concepts and new industries, are highly valued.

However, the idea of an information sector is not new. In 1962, over 50 industries were identified that comprised an information sector. Other economists preferred to identify information sector industries by using existing industry classifications, as identified by Standard Industrial Classification (SIC) codes. However, critics of the approach questioned the validity of defining information on so specific a criteria, fearing that existing industrial classifications "ignore a major part of the processes of investment in information in the economy" and that "most significant information activities do not produce goods in tangible form and thus not included in the SIC system". The debate over how to classify industries in the information sector illustrates the variability of trying to define information for econometric purposes.

The debate is further magnified when trying to define the economic aspects of information in an international sense. Cultural context is a factor in defining what comprises the information sector, with definitions varying between countries and methods that describe material and information related production. Even though legal negotiations about the nature of information and production between countries, such as with the General Agreements on Tariffs and Trade (GATT), have attempted to arrive at some definitional parameters for information, the process of trying to understand how information works in an international trade environment is problematic due to the great variability production across different countries. For example, the North American Industry Classification System (NAICS) was adopted in 1997, replacing the old Standard Industrial Classification (SIC) system. Developed jointly by the U.S., Canada, and Mexico to provide new comparability in statistics about business activity across

North America, the NAICS also better distinguishes between manufacturing and information sectors. Although imperfect, the NAICS is an essential tool to determine service and product providers in the information sector, to remain current on industry analyses, statistics, and leading companies. The international economic environment is indeed a complex one, and in defining how information operates within economic systems, one can examine the redefining of economic components such as the agent, the firm, and the market.

As discussed in classical economic theory, agents tend to act in ways that put themselves in a better position than previously held. Braman questions the decision-making processes of economic agents as they improve their position according to economic theory. Processes including 'rationality, perfect information, and individualistic independence' are subject to myriad influences and the amount of information available. Further, there are limits to the amount of information that an individual agent can have access to or even process in order to maximise his position.

Research in the fields of psychology, that is, cognitive miserliness has indicated that there are cognitive and neurological limitations that affect how information is perceived and understood. Technology limitations can also affect the capture, recording, and transmission of information, thereby, affecting its cognition by an agent or organisation. The cultural context of information, as well, can have an affect on how information is understood. The social organisation of society can have an significant impact on the flow of information creating barriers that can slow or impede the finding of information by individual agents. The concept of social organisation and community is also important in understanding how information is processed in regards to economic function. In classical economic theory, economic agents act purposively.

Since, they have an end in mind and find means to attain those ends, the actions of individual agents bear a causal relationship to overall market outcomes. Further, an economic agent uses information in order to "obtain satisfaction or benefits gained from consuming a particular good or service according to a hierarchical ranking of preferences". The social context of how information can be pursued and utilised also affects the actions of an individual economic agent.

An individual may use information and acquire goods and services beyond what is necessary for the maximising of their position and thus, may not make the best use of information in a classical economic sense. Cultural processes can affect preferences for a particular commodity adding or detracting from its value. The decision-making process is interconnected among various individuals in society, which can affect the utility factor in economic activities.

Societies and communities can be conceptualised as components of a larger structure or market in which economic activities are performed. The larger structure can operate as an "informational mechanism" with different types of information arrayed spatially across it. How economic agents operate within markets is subject to much debate as economists advocate different operational models about the functioning of markets.

One model centers on the prices of commodities and services that are distributed across a market. Economic agents enter the market with a certain knowledge level and assumptions about prices that influence their interaction with the market. The search for further price information for an eventual outcome process frames their activities in the market. Social aspects and cultural ties that are part of the market structure affect how information interacts with markets. The distribution of information across markets has an impact on the economic decision process of the firm as well as the individual. If a market is a social arrangement that allows buyers and sellers to discover information and carry out a voluntary exchange of goods or services, the firm is an alternative system of allocation to the market that exists to organise production in a Non-price environment. Although there is a distinction between a market and a firm, most economists admit that the two shade into each other.

A business model describes the elements and relationships that express the business logic of a firm. Just as NAICS classes businesses into sectors, firms are often classed into 'internally consistent sets of firms," referred to as strategic groups or configurations, allowing typologies and taxonomies to explore the determinants of performance. Early studies of information flow within existing business entities usually focused on individual managers. In a market environment in which reliable information was at a premium, business managers made decisions based on an individualised perspective that made use of personal social networks as well as market information.

The growth of larger business enterprises with extensive production and distribution linkages increased the need for accurate market information, which led to the eventual progression Towards extensive record keeping overseen by professional managers. The availability of accurate market information and information on other firms in related enterprises began to affect business decisions.

An increased efficiency in record management usually decreases what some economists have labeled transaction costs, or the searching for information needed for a particular type of economic activity. Early studies in the nature of transaction costs within business processes determined that firms usually invested in those transaction costs that were more expensive, while leaving the more inexpensive transaction costs to the marketplace. The application of advanced telecommunication technology by firms has encouraged commercial enterprises to distribute their transaction costs on an even wider basis for more efficiency. Contemporary studies in the nature of firms and different economic sectors have expanded the focus of study beyond the single firm to a hierarchy of firms or even larger social constructs, such as networks.

Research into the role of information and economic theory bridges the mathematical boundaries of idealised econometric models to account for information sector variability and the irrationality of human Behaviour. Research in the social dynamics of industries that comprise the information sector should take a wider, holistic approach. Studies on the information sector should integrate concepts and analytical methods from other disciplines.

One such discipline is political science, which has often focused on the effect of uneven flows of information and of the impact of imperfect information on decisions. In expanding their descriptive scope of the components of the information sector, economists expanded their idea of the firm and the market by including variables with wider spatial structures. Such structures include telecommunication networks and social communication networks.

It is with the physical network of the telecommunications sector that some researchers, especially in the field of geography, have sought to combine spatial concepts of space, place, and landscape to provide a rigorous and quantifiable platform in which to measure the complex socioeconomic phenomena that comprises the information sector.

GEOGRAPHIES OF THE INTERNET

The study of contemporary geographic spaces and technology inevitably focuses on the ubiquitous telecommunica-tions networks that comprise the Internet. The complex interlocking nodes of the Internet create a variety of physical spaces bounded by technology such as computer hardware, Fibre optics, and communication software. Upon the network of the Internet, geographers have identified a great many physical and virtual places as well. Geographers view the concept of space as more of an abstract expression, but the concept of place is bounded in the social milieu of a given location and can evolve as the local society that identified the space changes, and as new technologies alter the unique expression of the location.

Places can be a unique experience of an individual person, but more often, they are the social constructs of many people with shared experiences. What is unique about places on the

Internet is they can alter the bounded physical locations of places as identified by society and encourage the defining of new concepts of place that use elements of technology combined with historical notions of place, or "cyberspaces coexist with geographic spaces, providing a new layer of virtual sites superimposed over geographic spaces". Using such logic, geographers identify places on the Internet with a variety of parameters, including socioeconomic, political, and cultural factors.

In defining their research about the geographic nature of telecommunications and of the Internet, geographers tend to focus on two broad aspects of research. On one hand, geographers are interested in the technological aspect of telecommunications and the Internet and how society and interacts with the technology. Research by geographers on the Internet "developed lines of research focused on the technology and infrastructure of the Internet and how the use of this technology has blended with existing cultural, political, and economic structures manifest in physical places.

Geographers intent on researching the technical aspects of the Internet tend to focus on analysing locationally referenced Internet infrastructure data, essentially, the locations of nodes, communications networks. Factors in locating the infrastructure across the landscape include: "amounts of bandwidth coming from a populated area, Internet Fibre backbone, and points of presence (POPs) or broadband development". Many of the studies in the locational aspects of the Internet infrastructure depict an uneven distribution of its composition. The most densely developed Internet hubs are located in larger urbanised areas, while less densely developed rural areas lack high bandwidth rates.

The distribution of the Internet has a significant effect on how information flows across the Internet and how the information is used by people. The physical distribution of the Internet is especially relevant to the delivery of library information and resources. In the dynamic environment of the information sector, the library can be an important cornerstone in facilitating information flow between individuals and organisations.

The stable presence of the publicly funded institutions can offer access to information as well as guidance in interpreting information for users. Libraries can also offer other services such as archival functions in an environment wherein information durability can be problematic.

CONVERGENCE OF COMMUNICATION TECHNOLOGIES

Telecommunication convergence in the information economy has had a significant effect on the delivery of library information resources and services. Convergence promises a 'clean slate' approach, where things are reengineered to provide better, more flexible service to the user. Convergence, according to Fowler can be defined in four major categories of the telecommunications industry that correspond to layers, or sets of layers, in the Open Systems Interconnect (OSI) network model. The categories are transport, switching, and applications.

- *Transport*: The same physical pipes and transport technology carry multiple services, usually of different customers, for example, multipleT1 or T3 links. Convergence at this level is primarily used by carriers to provision their infrastructure; it is largely transparent to users as they continue to see and pay for separate services.
- *Switching*: The same cable plant carries different types of traffic and does appropriate switching. Content and presentation to the user is unchanged, with the possible exception of new features. Historically, this has been the layer about which most discussion has centered. The distinction between services becomes less distinct or disappears entirely under network layer convergence; at the present time, Internet protocol (IP), a switching technology, is envisioned as the common medium for all (or many) types of

telecommunications traffic, especially voice and Internet traffic.

- *Application (Content)*: The same end-user device or type of device and network handles and delivers all content; the user does not have separate network interface devices
- *Telecommunications/IT*: There is also a fourth meaning of convergence, which will be considered here, that refers to *blurring.of.the.distinction.between. telecommunications.and.information.processing*. Examples are use of Applications Service Providers (ASPs) and network computing.

With convergence, separate functions are now available through one source or channel, such as an ISP or through a single vendor. Of particular interest to libraries is the technological convergence at the application level. Multiple resources in varying formats, including text, data, images, graphics, audiovisual media, streaming media, games and simulations, and so forth, are now available over one transmission network, through the same user equipment, and through standard, ubiquitous software applications. Previous channels would have included, and perhaps required, delivery via postal mail service or broadcast media, carrying a variety of formats and media. Enterprise systems, interactive video-on-demand, and telecalls/teleconferencing are becoming the norm. What will limit the rapid expansion of these applications will be intellectual property rights issues. As the United States continues to build infrastructure and to recreate how the infrastructure is policed, broadband will undergo a number of changes.

However, increased broadband access will continue to build convergence. The United States Congress has been urged to recognise and "encourage the convergence of voice, data, image and video information into bit streams" to "[e]nsure the greatest possible regulatory flexibility, to allow for unpredictable future service needs, market developments and technological innovation". Congress has also been urged to reduce barriers to competition, restructure the market in the public interest, and increase spectrum efficiency with both licensed and unlicensed models of spectrum use.

Convergence is seen as an evolutionary, rather than a revolutionary process. Initiatives to ensure broadband to the majority of homes in the United States by 2010, if realised, may speed up these trends. Initiatives include the UTOPIA, the National LambdaRail Network, the NorthEast Education and Research Network (NEREN), the Third Frontier Network (TFN), and the hundreds of other Fibre communities in the United States. Integrated media systems that seamlessly combine video, audio, computer animation, text, and graphics into a common digital display medium were noted as a new area of convergence.

Further, Mihram and Mihram predicted that infrastructure installation, product creation, and commercialisation relating to integrated media systems would become areas of research and development for both the public and private sectors. Today, geographic information systems are seen as the next pivotal technology in this convergence, again due to the advances in interoperability and data standards. Again, we see infrastructure installation, product creation, and commercialisation in GIS becoming areas of research for the public and private sectors. Standards development, in particular, is a crucial area for GIS convergence. Many organisations work collaboratively to promote the advancement of open geospatial standards and specifications, especially as the market expands into domains associated with Internet and telecommunications communications technologies.

These organisations include the Open Geospatial Consortium, W3C, and OASIS, as well as national and international standards associations. Since, much of the data in the contemporary information economy have geospatial or geotemporal components, no applications, systems, or technologies are unaffected. Further, it is through the efficient use of GIS/geospatial technologies that we are able to understand and leverage the value of spatial/location based information and processes in the broader context of ICT and enterprise information systems. Convergence continues through business processes and architectures.

Business architectures are the starting point from which to develop related and integrated functional, information, process, and application architectures. These architectures are aided by the rapid development and deployment of open, standards-based service-oriented architectures. Examples include the development of XML and XML Schema; SOAP; WSDL; and XQuery.

In addition, more Web service tiers are integrated with business logic and workflow. There is increased deployment of mobile devices, communications, and services with even newer new micromobility management schema and technologies.

There are also smarter and richer client tools (especially in the GIS world) with more robust and flexible secure information exchange solutions. Certainly, enterprise systems will "serve as a 'unifying' element through their capacity to manage and utilise geospatial content, capabilities and services in enterprise environments". As the landscape of information technology changes through the convergence in the industry, the public sector, including libraries, is affected as well. As academic disciplines transition to newer forms of working and educational environment, the situation necessitates a commitment that encompasses several objectives: to change basic educational tools, to retrofit installations of school- and campus-wide data networks, and to create affordable networks that would link schools, homes, and communities. The development of new media technologies tends to be spatially uneven, often concentrating in one sector of society while marginalising other sectors.

The process of being marginalised by technology can often be through cultural, socioeconomic, geographic, technological and political means. The uneven distribution of technology, computer networks, and of the information they transmit, has been characterised as contributing to a 'digital divide' between those who do have access to the Internet and those who do not.

SOCIAL STRUCTURE OF THE INFORMATION ECONOMY

The digital divide has been described by researchers in a variety of dichotomies in both contemporary American and international settings. In contemporary American society, researchers apply econometrics to socioeconomic data to portray how particular income groups have sufficient capital to purchase computer hardware and software for Internet access, while others do not.

Researchers also look at factors such as race, ethnicity, and educational attainment to further illustrate differences in technology access. Different technological standards are identified, within contemporary American society, that can contribute to uneven access to information technologies.

In international settings, the literature on the digital divide includes many of the factors described in articles about technology and information access in America, though other factors are emphasised, for example, political ones. Many research and policy papers that examine different aspects of the digital divide identify minority ethnic groups, indigenous peoples, and specific groups of people as being disadvantaged in participating in the information economy. Factors include low incomes, few educational qualifications, low literacy levels, unemployment, age or disabled status, and single parent households.

Diverse minority groups often live in large urban centers that have complex telecommunication networks, unlike persons living in rural and frontier areas. However, both rural and urban areas may have older telecommunication infrastructures, affecting access

In every income bracket, at every level of education, in every age group, for people of every race and among people of Hispanic origin, among both men and women, many more people use computers and the Internet now than did so in the recent past. Some people are still more likely to be Internet users than others are. Individuals living in low-income households or having little education, still trail the national average. However, broad measures of Internet use in the United States suggest that over time Internet use has become more equitable.

However, there still exists a significant gap in the number of computers in low-income schools and communities. Prieger also did not find that language was a statistically significant factor in Internet access, though many research reports indicate that English language ability is an important factor in participation in the information economy.

Households with a record of higher educational attainment would be more inclined to use computers, have Internet access, and place a high value on literacy. An important factor influencing participation in the information economy is the acquisition of information and communication technology (ICT) skills. Individuals who are members of the various groups that have been marginalised from computers and of the Internet often lack the necessary skills to use ICT applications. Cullen argues that the interaction of factors, such as cost, restricting access to equipment, low educational achievement, and cultural, age or gender-based exclusion from literacy and computing skills, counteracts against the spread of such skills in disadvantaged communities.

Efforts to improve access to computers and Programmes to improve ICT technology skills among marginalised groups have been incorporated in a variety of community outreach Programmes by both public and private agencies. Many such Programmes try to establish and create a culture that is more conducive to ICT technologies.

COMMUNITY INTERNET INITIATIVES

The combination of municipal and commercial computer networks in some large metropolitan areas has led to the creation of community information networks. Community information networks are often built around existing social networks involved in Neighbourhood activities like employment and economic opportunity centers, youth and family centers, health, education, and affordable housing initiatives. One such project in Chicago, the Chicago Area Northside Neighbourhood Online Network, is an organisation that offers training and Internet access to community based entities throughout the city.

Building on existing human networks in the communities, the project has successfully trained residents and staff of over 60 community organisations, creating a unique multiracial, mixed-economic, and mixed-gender pool of community users. The NeighbourTech Programme works with Chicago's inner city Neighbourhoods. NeighbourTech uses a variety of methods to draw in Neighbourhood residents, small businesses, and Non-profit organisations located in disadvantaged Neighbourhoods. The Erie Neighbourhood House, a Non-profit, multiservice agency in Erie, New York, operates the Erie Technology Center. The mission of the Technology Center is to provide computer and information literacy to West Town residents with limited English proficiency and low educational attainment. By working with other educational Programmes in the area, the Technology Center integrates traditional teaching/learning methods with current technology applications for students ranging from prekindergarten to senior citisens. Grants from federal agencies, such as the U.S., Department of Commerce, are also used to build community information networks outside of urban areas in rural locations.

The ItascaNet network, established in the town of Grand Rapids in north central Minnesota, is mostly rural, with a shrinking population base. Local community leaders used the grant funds to build an online network to increase the community's access to, and use of, the national information infrastructure, reduce disparities in access levels among community residents, increase information available to community members, and facilitate the sharing of data and information among partner organisations. The ItaskaNet network involved five partner agencies that oversaw the purchasing of a server and cable for connections between the agencies.

A significant member agency of the partnership was the public library. Internet-linked computers were made available to students in the public schools and to citisens in the public library, and free computer training classes were offered to the community. Researchers have identified libraries as an important cultural resource in contemporary American society. They can be an important node in the contemporary computer network and provide computer access and information service to the user community.

ROLE OF LIBRARIES IN THE INFORMATION ECONOMY

The emergence of the new information economy comprised of computer networks that link users to one another or to larger organisations is creating a class of singular information users. To aid users in participating in the information economy, libraries designed a virtual presence to deliver information services, usually in the form of a 'digital library.' Digital libraries can offer a more varied informational experience to the community of online users. Libraries, with their traditional strengths of information collection, description, organisation, and dissemination, can provide a more holistic learning experience for these new user communities.

In commenting on the structure and environment of digital libraries, the DLF (Digital Library Federation) has offered the following definition:

> "Digital libraries are organisations that provide the resources, including specialised staff, to select, structure, offer intellectual access to, distribute, interpret, preserve the integrity of, and ensure the persistence over time of collections of digital works".

In elaborating on the concept, researchers define six major characteristics that should be integral to digital libraries:

- *Collection of data objects*: A library holds together a

collection of data objects, items and resources. The items can be books, journals and documents, multimedia objects. The library objects can be available locally, or indirectly, by using a network to access them.

- *Collection of metadata structures*: A library contains a collection of metadata structures, such as catalogs, guides, dictionaries, thesauri, indices, summaries, annotations, glossaries, and so forth.
- *Collection of services*: A library provides a collection of services, such as various access methods for as well as consultation for. different users; management of the library (purchase, shelf arranging, computerisation, communication); logging/statistics and performance measurement evaluation (PME); selective dissemination of information (SDI) or push mode, as it is called on the Internet.
- *Domain focus*: A library has a domain focus and its collection has a domain focus; purpose. For example, art, science, or literature. Also, it is usually created to serve a community of users and therefore, is finely grained.
- *Quality control*: A library uses quality control in the sense that all its material is verified and consistent with the profile of the library. The material is filtered and its metadata is usually enriched.
- *Preservation*: The purpose of preservation is to ensure protection of information of enduring value for access by present and future generations. Preservation includes the allocation of resources for preservation, preventive measures, and remedial measures to restore the usability of selected materials.

As librarians compile digital collections of materials, the networked environment of which they are a part offers access to many more information resources. In describing libraries and the new online environment in which they operate, libraries are placing lesser emphasis on the materials they collect and house, and more emphasis on the kind of material they are able to obtain in response to user requests.

The trend includes libraries forming partnerships to deliver material from elsewhere in time to answer a user's information needs. The shift to on-demand delivery of material from elsewhere is an effect of recent growth in digital networking in an environment where standards for description were established and refined over the past 35 years.

Librarians are also moving primarily away from being caretakers of physical collections to people who identify resources that exist. The earlier survey of the information economy has illustrated a variety of information sector industries and organisations that utilise information, such as geographic data, in their varied production and distribution functions. The flexibility of spatially referenced information, and its applicability to a variety of research techniques and spatially referenced applications, create a powerful tool in which librarians can raise the profile of their institution's involvement in the information sector.

In defining the parameters of geographic information librarianship, the varied applications of geographic information in government functions, community initiatives, and private sector development can offer strategies in dealing with the social effects of trends like the digital divide and information marginalisation. The following section provides an overview of the development of geographic information systems and related applications.

DEVELOPMENT OF GEOGRAPHIC INFORMATION SYSTEMS (GIS)

During the 1960s and 1970s, geographers and cartographers began adapting computer analytical methods to capturing graphical data portrayed on maps. Previously, the emphasis of cartographic research was based on the 'idea of storing graphical features that were displayed on maps in computer files'. Only with the later use of mathematical models and structures based on theory in topology were researchers able to apply 'logically consistent two dimensional data representations'.

By the 1980s, the ability to create stable and consistent representations of map data was integral to research and development in geographic information systems. Kainz describes the impact of the micro- and personal computer in the development of powerful desktop software packages in word processing, database management, and statistical analysis and the development of desktop mapping software that could integrate visualisations of map data with corresponding data in other databases.

He further describes the rapid progression of research on spatial data structures, indexing methods, and spatial databases. A workspace in a GIS software package could contain graphic representations of a spatial dataset, integrate data from relational databases, and have other corresponding information in text formats or numeric formats. The convergence of computer hardware innovations with research into mathematical spatial modeling, and mapping software during the 1980s clearly contributed to better-defined geographic information systems.

A geographic information system (GIS) can be defined as "a computer-based technology and methodology for collecting, managing, analysing, modeling, and presenting geographic data for a wide range of applications". A GIS essentially combines five components, people, data, hardware, software, and methods, for the purpose of finding solutions to issues that have a spatial context. The fundamental operations of a GIS application are capturing, storing, querying, analysing, displaying, and outputting data.

The nature of geographic data can be best understood by three major concepts: *feature.geometry*, *attributes*, and *topology*.

- *Feature.geometry* represents features, such as houses, roads, or property boundaries, and establishes where these features are located in the real world.

All features are symbolised by points, lines, or polygons.

- *Attributes* provide a description of the features and are stored in an associated table that is linked to the features. An attribute field can contain an address, street name, or land-use code, and so forth.
- *Topology,* the most abstract concept of geographic data, defines either the Behaviour or the spatial relationships that exist between features.

For example, a GIS layer representing a transportation network requires topology rules to accurately depict one-way streets, overpasses, and right of way scenarios. Without topology, data integrity associated with sound editing, display, or analysis is not maintained.

Geographic knowledge is represented in five data formats: *maps* and *globes, geographic. datasets, data.models, processing and workflow models,* and. *metadata.* Interactive *digital.maps.and. globes* can query information and present it to the user. Since, digital maps and globes have limited analytical functionality, they are generally used to resolve location and directional questions. *Geographic.datasets* contain feature geometry, attributes, and topology. *Data.models* are templates with defined topology schemas, and are used in the data creation process to ensure data standardisation and integrity are maintained.

Processing and workflow models are necessary when managing GIS projects to visually depict and duplicate the geoprocessing procedures associated with the spatial analysis. *Metadata* documents the four previous data formats, and is the key to organising, discovering, and evaluating GIS data resources.

With the proliferation of desktop computing and numerous GIS mapping applications, geospatial data has become an important part of various socioeconomic processes, political activities, and academic research that comprise the information economy. The following discussion outlines some applications of spatial data and geographic information systems in the information economy.

APPLICATIONS OF SPATIAL DATA AND GIS

The literature of the information economy is rich with descriptions of how computer technology and the Internet are altering socioeconomic processes within organisations and throughout political and commercial networks in which they are integrated.

Some researchers assert that the use of information communication technologies can facilitate closer contact between members of management and other employees of an organisation, thus rearranging lines of command for long-distance interactions, resulting in a direct savings on transportation costs, and improving the decision-making process in the organisational structure. Other scholars have discussed how the integration of information systems into government organisations' infrastructure have affected resource management, such as the decentralisation of decision making. As part of extensive commercial and political networks, organisations exchange information through complex optical and cable networks that comprise the Internet. In summarising research about the information economy, Grubesic and Murray describe the Internet as 'a complex mesh of interconnected computers, Fibre optic cables, routers and human users'.

They further describe the Internet as "a series of smaller networks linked together by hardware, software, and many peering agreements between Internet Service Providers. The distribution of smaller networks across the United States alone amounts to over 166 million users, 7,000 Internet Service Providers, and a large grouping interlinked cable and telephone companies that offer information services". The reliance of organisations upon a telecommuni-cations network infrastructure to transmit different forms of electronic information adds a spatial component to the data.

Grubesic and Murray note that a "unique element of many datasets is the geographical or spatial entities they represent. The geographic component of the data could correspond to a location of a point of presence, central office, or the path a Fibre optic cable traverses". Geographic information systems can analyse, store, and process the spatial data associated with an organisation's datasets.

Since, a GIS is often used to visually organise geographic data in order to facilitate different types of analysis for the data, geographic information systems are described as a 'computer Programme for acquiring, storing, interpreting, and displaying spatially organised information". Besides recording the locational aspects of a particular data set such as Neighbourhood, street, or country, GIS data may have additional information characteristics, such as temperature, cost, Colour, or even detailed demographic information or public health data.

The uses of GIS in the information economy are many, and often GIS databases are built with data from different types of sources in both the public and private sector, such as from ESRI, Inc., the U.S., Census Bureau, and even the Centers for Disease Control and Prevention. Definitions of geospatial data vary within the research literature in geography. Some researchers define spatial data as being "anything dealing with the concept of space, in the geographic context, primarily dealing with the distribution of things on the surface of the earth " while other researchers define spatial data as 'data that occupies geographic space".

There are many types and characteristics of geospatial data. However, most spatial or geographic data have specific location according to a global geographic referencing system and may be illustrated by other characteristics, such as size and shape of a particular dataset. Davis further elaborates that the size would be calculated by the amount of area, and shape would be defined by the position of the shape points of the dataset, for example, an administrative zone or economic zone. Geospatial data collected by government agencies across different areas can include topographic data, hydrographic data, earth science data, and soil and forest survey inventories. Other types of information that can be geospatially referenced include social and economic data (*e.g.*, population and industrial characteristics).

An important aspect of geospatial data is its potential for multiple applications. GIS technology facilitates the integration and comparison of different data sets, which allows for greater statistical analysis of the data content. It was suggested that the annual federal spending on geospatial data activities in the United States was over $4.4 billion. Since, the 1960s, digital spatial data has been produced in a variety of formats and in a number of carriers.

Digital spatial data can include information digitised and recorded by a single researcher, or be in the form of large-scale geographic coverages processed and packaged by private firms. Much digital spatial data is also generated by government agencies at the city, state, and federal level, and is issued in a variety of formats like on CD-ROMs with computer files with accompanying attribute data in relational databases. The proliferation of spatial data and the rapidly evolving technological environment in which spatial data is being used in all manner of research has led some researchers to speculate on the nature of future applications of GIS. Future development in GIS will be in areas such as geocomputation, social informatics, information ecology, and a spatially integrated social science.

Sui notes that the 'diffusion of spatial analytical tools' and their integration with 'visualisation tools' will lead to the use of geographic metaphors important in describing political-economic activities across contemporary social and cultural regions. One research area involving digital geospatial data has been the electronic space of the Internet, or cyberspace. Recent trends involving spatial data and geographic research have focused on defining epistemologies and methodologies using GIS to better explain socio-geographic phenomena across different environments.

Longan argues that geographers have only begun to explore social, cultural, and political aspects of cyberspace. In his examination of the community networking environment across the United States, he attempts to define a sense of place in the online environments that different Neighbourhoods and towns are setting up in their areas.

Other researchers examine the Internet and the effects of telecommunications between communities and social classes and the distribution of wealth, arguing that Internet community networks may help disadvantaged groups overcome the problems of distance by using cyber communications to access needed resources or find that access to telecommunications has positive effects on a community's sense of identity. Still others have used GIS and spatial data in examining urban cultural and political spaces or to study economic production and social consumption. Still other researchers envision continued development of representation of real world data using computer languages.

MAP LIBRARIES IN TRANSITION

In attempting to put some order to the many types of geospatial data produced by government agencies, private firms, and other organisations, librarians can turn to map librarianship for guidelines and best practices in designing procedures for processing spatial data. Map libraries, especially in the United States, have benefited from lengthy depository Programmes wherein maps produced by the United States Geological Survey, Army Map Service, and Inter-American Geodetic Survey were deposited across many libraries.

The experiences of processing the cartographic collections in libraries are beneficial in learning about the scope of map collections in libraries as well as to understand cataloging and classification schemes for maps and cartographic materials. The rapid migration to digitally produced cartographic materials in a variety of formats presents librarians with new challenges in processing spatial data. The same technological changes that have transformed the production of cartographic materials have affected the functioning of library services and collections as well.

The advent of the Internet has provided an opportunity for the traditional academic library to evolve its services and reposition its collection to take advantage of the communication possibilities that the World Wide Web presents. Applications of GIS technology and geographic information can also provide libraries with tools that can be used to overcome technological and social barriers that have come about due to the digital divide.

The public aspect of GIS, especially in terms of government produced and facilitated data, create more of a sense of urgency in providing access to the information. The discussion that follows examines the convergence of communication technologies in the contemporary information economy and its effect on various segments of the private and public sector including libraries.

7

Computer in Library Management

INTRODUCTION

The project titled Library Management System is Library management software for monitoring and controlling the transactions in a library.The project 'Library Management System' is developed in java, which mainly focuses on basic operations in a library like adding new member, new books, and updating new information, searching books and members and facility to borrow and return books.

'Library Management System' is a windows application written for 32-bit Windows operating systems, designed to help users maintain and organise library. Our software is easy to use for both beginners and advanced users. It features a familiar and well thought-out, an attractive user interface, combined with strong searching Insertion and reporting capabilities.

The report generation facility of library system helps to get a good idea of which are the books borrowed by the members, makes users possible to generate reports' hard copy. The software Library Management System has four main modules.

- *Insertion to Database Module:* User friendly input screen
- *Extracting from Database module* – Attractive Output Screen

- *Report Generation module:* Borrowed book list and Available book list
- *Search Facility system:* Search for books and members

SYSTEM ANALYSIS

EXISTING SYSTEM

System Analysis is a detailed study of the various operations performed by a system and their relationships within and outside of the system. Here the key question is- what all problems exist in the present system? What must be done to solve the problem? Analysis begins when a user or manager begins a study of the Programme using existing system. During analysis, data collected on the various files, decision points and transactions handled by the present system. The commonly used tools in the system are Data Flow Diagram, interviews, etc.

Training, experience and common sense are required for collection of relevant information needed to develop the system. The success of the system depends largely on how clearly the problem is defined, thoroughly investigated and properly carried out through the choice of solution. A good analysis model should provide not only the mechanisms of problem understanding but also the frame work of the solution. Thus it should be studied thoroughly by collecting data about the system. Then the proposed system should be analysed thoroughly in accordance with the needs. System analysis can be categorised into four parts.

- System planning and initial investigation
- Information Gathering
- Applying analysis tools for structured analysis
- Feasibility study
- Cost/ Benefit analysis.

In our existing system all the transaction of books are done manually, So taking more time for a transaction like borrowing a book or returning a book and also for searching of members and books. Another major disadvantage is that to preparing the list of books borrowed and the available books in the library will take more time, currently it is doing as a one day process for verifying all records. So after conducting the feasibility study we decided to make the manual Library management system to be computerised.

PROPOSED SYSTEM

Proposed system is an automated Library Management System. Through our software user can add members, add books, search members, search books, update information, edit information, borrow and return books in quick time. Our proposed system has the following advantages:

- User friendly interface
- Fast access to database
- Less error
- More Storage Capacity
- Search facility
- Look and Feel Environment
- Quick transaction

All the manual difficulties in managing the library have been rectified by implementing computerisation.

FEASIBILITY ANALYSIS

Whatever we think need not be feasible. It is wise to think about the feasibility of any problem we undertake. Feasibility is the study of impact, which happens in the organisation by the development of a system. The impact can be either positive or negative. When the positives nominate the negatives, then the system is considered feasible. Here the feasibility study can be performed in two ways such as technical feasibility and economical feasibility.

TECHNICAL FEASIBILITY

We can strongly says that it is technically feasible. Since, there will not be much difficulty in getting required resources for the development and maintaining the system as well. All the resources needed for the development of the software as well as the maintenance of the same is available in the organisation here we are utilising the resources which are available already.

ECONOMICAL FEASIBILITY

Development of this application is highly economically feasible. The organisation needed not spend much for the development of the system already available. The only thing is to be done is making an environment for the development with an effective supervision. If we are doing so, we can attain the maximum usability of the corresponding resources. Even after the development, the organisation will not be in a condition to invest more in the organisation. There fore, the system is economically feasible.

SYSTEM REQUIREMENTS

This management system can be used in windows 98, Windows2000, Windows XP and Windows NT, supported for other platform such as Applet, Macintosh and UNIX.

The system must be running Windows 95, or Windows NT4.0 operating system and must meet the following hardware requirements:

- For Windows 95 based computers, a 486/ 66 MHz or higher processor with 8MB
- For Windows 98 based computers, a 500/88MHz or higher processor with 32 Mb of RAM
- For Windows NT based computers, a 488/ 66 MHz or higher processor with 16 MB of RAM
- For Windows 200 based computers, a 700/850 MHz or higher processor with 512 MB of Ram

SYSTEM DESIGN

INPUT DESIGN

Input design is the process of converting user-oriented input to a computer based format. Input design is a part of overall system design, which requires very careful attention.

Often the collection of input data is the most expensive part of the system. The main objectives of the input design are:

- Produce cost effective method of input
- Achieve highest possible level of accuracy
- Ensure that the input is acceptable to and understood by the staff.

Input Data

The goal of designing input data is to make enter easy, logical and free from errors as possible. The entering data entry operators need to know the allocated space for each field; field sequence and which must match with that in the source document. The format in which the data fields are entered should be given in the input form.Here data entry is online; it makes use of processor that accepts commands and data from the operator through a key board. The input required is analysed by the processor. It is then accepted or rejected. Input stages include the following processes:

- Data Recording
- Data Transcription
- Data Conversion
- Data Verification
- Data Control
- Data Transmission
- Data Correction.

One of the aims of the system analyst must be to select data capture method and devices, which reduce the number of stages so as to reduce both the changes of errors and the cost.Input types, can be characterised as:

- External
- Internal
- Operational
- Computerised
- Interactive.

Input files can exist in document form before being input to the computer. Input design is rather complex Since, it involves procedures for capturing data as well as inputting it to the computer.

OUTPUT DESIGN

Outputs from computer systems are required primarily to communicate the results of processing to users. They are also used to provide a permanent copy of these result for latter consultation.Computer output is the most important and direct source of information to the users.

Designing computer output should proceed in an organised well through out the manner. The right output must be available for the people who find the system easy o use. The outputs have been defined during the logical design stage. If not, they should defined at the beginning of the output designing terms of types of output connect, format, response etc,Various types of outputs are:

- External outputs
- Internal outputs
- Operational outputs
- Interactive outputs
- Turn around outputs.

All screens are informative and interactive in such a way that the user can full fill his requirements through asking queries.

DATABASE DESIGN

The general theme behind a database is to handle information as an integrated whole. A database is a collection of interrelated data stored with minimum redundancy to serve many users quickly and effectively. After designing input and output, the analyst must concentrate on database design or how data should be organised around user requirements. The general objective is to make information access, easy quick, inexpensive and flexible for other users. During database design the following objectives are concerned:-

- Controlled Redundancy
- Data independence
- Accurate and integrating
- More information at low cost
- Recovery from failure

- Privacy and security
- Performance
- Ease of learning and use.

SYSTEM IMPLEMENTATION

Implementation is the stage in the project where the theoretical design is turned into a working system. The implementation phase constructs, installs and operates the new system.

The most crucial stage in achieving a new successful system is that it will work efficiently and effectively. There are several activities involved while implementing a new project they are:

- End user training
- End user Education
- Training on the application software
- System Design
- Parallel Run And To New System
- Post implementation Review.

END USER TRAINING

The successful implementation of the new system will purely upon the involvement of the officers working in that department. The officers will be imparted the necessary training on the new technology.

END USER EDUCATION

The education of the end user start after the implementation and testing is over. When the system is found to be more difficult to under stand and complex, more effort is put to educate the end used to make them aware of the system, giving them lectures about the new system and providing them necessary documents and materials about how the system can do this.

TRAINING OF APPLICATION SOFTWARE

After providing the necessary basic training on the

computer awareness, the users will have to be trained upon the new system such as the screen flows and screen design type of help on the screen, type of errors while entering the data, the corresponding validation check at each entry and the way to correct the data entered. It should then cover information needed by the specific user or group to use the system.

POST IMPLEMENTATION VIEW

The department is planning a method to know the states of t he past implementation process. For that regular meeting will be arranged by the concerned officers about the implementation problem and success.

SOFTWARE TESTING

Is the menu bar displayed in the appropriate contested some system related features included either in menus or tools? Do pull –Down menu operation and Tool-bars work properly? Are all menu function and pull down sub function properly listed ?; Is it possible to invoke each menu function using a logical assumptions that if all parts of the system are correct, the goal will be successfully achieved? In adequate testing or Non-testing will leads to errors that may appear few months later. This create two problem:

- Time delay between the cause and appearance of the problem.
- The effect of the system errors on files and records within the system.

The purpose of the system testing is to consider all the likely variations to which it will be suggested and push the systems to limits. The testing process focuses on the logical intervals of the software ensuring that all statements have been tested and on functional interval is conducting tests to uncover errors and ensure that defined input will produce actual results that agree with the required results. Programme level testing, modules level testing integrated and carried out. There are two major type of testing they are:

1. White Box Testing.
2. Black Box Testing.

WHITE BOX TESTING

White box some times called 'Glass box testing' is a test case design uses the control structure of the procedural design to drive test case.Using white box testing methods, the following tests where made on the system:

- All independent paths within a module have been exercised once. In our system, ensuring that case was selected and executed checked all case structures. The bugs that were prevailing in some part of the code where fixed
- All logical decisions were checked for the truth and falsity of the values.

BLACK BOX TESTING

Black box testing focuses on the functional requirements of the software. This is black box testing enables the software engineering to derive a set of input conditions that will fully exercise all functional requirements for a Programme.

Black box testing is not an alternative to white box testing rather it is complementary approach that is likely to uncover a different class of errors that white box methods like.

- Interface errors
- Performance in data structure
- Performance errors
- Initialising and termination errors.

IMPACT OF INTERNET ON LIBRARY AND INFORMATION SERVICES

Perhaps no other recent innovation has impacted the library profession to such a great extent as Internet. Not only is our world becoming an interconnected global community, but this early use of the Internet has changed the fundamental roles, paradigms, and organisational culture of libraries and librarians as well, which created profound impact on LandIS by offering new modes of information delivery and a vast information source.

There is a continuing evolution of the roles and functions of libraries and librarians, which appears to parallel the growth of acceptance and use of the Internet by library professionals. The innovative use of Internet technologies enable us to reach both local and distant users much more easily and effectively than hither to possible.

Technologies such as e-mail and Web provides tremendous opportunities for library and Inf. Scientists to deliver the information to the desktops of our users. Web offers significant advantage by integrating different library and information services with a common user interface offered by Web browsers. Realising the potentials, many libraries are rushing to getting the connectivity. The following listing will give an idea of which various functions of libraries may take advantage from Internet and Web technologies.

Acquisition:

- Correspondance with Book seller and Publisher.
- Reminders, Price verification
- Biblographic details and downloading of bib. records etc
- Ordering, billing
- Bookshops are on-line, *e.g.*, amazon.com

Classification:

- Network resources
  - Available on the net
  - Subscribed or free or trial basis
- Dewey Online
- Maths. Classification System
- Engineering Electronics Lib. Classification
- Search engines – such as yahoo use DDC.

Collection Development:

- Ownership vs Access
- Subscribe in print or e-form
- Subscribe in print as well as in e-form
- Pay-per-use

- Consortial approach

Cataloguing:

- Cataloguing of network resources
- Online Catalogues
- WorldCat (OCLC)
- WebOPAC – web sites
- MARC adds 856 field
- OCLC Scorpian project- MARC and AACR2
- Metadata standards - Dublin core

Circulation:

- Remote login
- Status check
- OPAC access
- Reminder to users
- User requests
- Direct borrowing
- ILL

Resource Sharing:

- Union Catalogue
  - Access, adding, downloading
- Access to databases over networks
  - Ohionet, ILLINET, WLN, OCLC, BID (UK)
  - Full text journals access, etc.

Services:

- ILL
- Document Delivery Service, *e.g.*, Ariel
- Reference/ Inf. Services
- CAS
  - Recent additions,
  - Contents pages
- SDI
  - From library collection
  - Databases
  - Internet Sources
- OPAC
- Database access
  - Bibliographical

— Full text
— Many vendors and organisations are moving to Internet (web) access

Subject Lists/ Gateways:

- Internet Public Library
- *EEVL* – Engineering
- *SOSIG* – Social Science
- *OMNI*- Medical
- *ADAM* – Arts, Design, etc.

User Education:

- Through E-mail
- Through Web
- Setting Intranet.

Preservation and Storage:

- The Internet is also a medium for the preservation and storage of information. In past, libraries were seen as the main storage facility of information. As society becomes increasingly more digital and more information resides on the Internet, the focus on storage and preservation is shifting. For example, some academic libraries are now faced with the problem of whether or not to purchase serials that can be just as easily accessed on-line. Preservation of these same media also becomes an issue of economics, not the 'just in case' preservation ideology of the past paradigm. Co joined to the function preservation is the destruction of information. Because the Internet can be seen as a medium for preserving information, the process of destruction of information also is affected. As more and more information is created and stored on the Internet, the capacity to store this information is also decreasing.

RETRIEVAL OF INFORMATION

Directories, Search Engines, Meta Search Engines and Information Gateways/Virtual Libraries etc are widely used to retrieve relevant information from Internet.

Search Engines:

- They are also called Meta crawlers or multi search engines
- Do not crawl the web compiling their own searchable databases
- Search the databases of multiple sets of individual search engines simultaneously from a single site and using the same interface.
- They function as intermediary
- Present the results of their searches in two ways
  - Single lists
  - Multiple Lists.
- There are three types of meta search engines,
  - Listing
  - Options
  - Automatic
- While you query, options less
- Cover all major search engines
- Do not return all results retrieved, they take only top ones from the list.
- They are very fast.
- Use them when you are in a hurry
- Helpful when you want to have quick overview on a subject and/or unique term.
- Use them when you are,
  - Conducting a relatively simple search
  - Not having any luck pulling up documents in your search.

RESOURCES AVAILABLE ON THE INTERNET

The advent of IT and other communication technologies changed all means of information services and sources. The Internet has given the world numerous easy-to-use and inexpensive research tools. Internet is changing the way we view information sources. Information bundled in World Wide Web in the form of structured and Non-structured sources create huge problem for professionals who are dealing with information. The shift in publication process takes place as individuals, institutions, publishers, professional associations, business houses and many others are publishing information on Internet.

Electronic publishing is considered as the speedy, accurate and effective way of communication among academia and research community, and becoming a favorite idea among information professionals to experiment with. The library and information professionals have a vital role to play in organising the information and bridging the *information gap*. Internet has become a part of library environment today. Internet for reference work in the library is gaining popularity. It can be successfully utilised for providing short-range and long-range reference service because various primary and secondary sources of information are available online from many sites. As information professionals, we can arrange the sources on net as we come across, in a structured manner.

These can be;

- E-journals
- E-books
- Standards
- E-TDs
- Preprints
- Library catalogue
- Bibliographical Tools
- Share wares
- Old books
- News papers
- Dictionaries
- Magazines
- Encyclopaedias
- Databases
- Directories
- Films
- Maps
- Technical reports

- Audio/Video
- Proceedings
- Patents
- Web sites of Companies, Institutions, Organisations, Associations, etc.

Evaluation of Information Sources

When we access or retrieve something on the Web, we need to decide whether the information is useful, reliable, and appropriate for our purposes. The resources identified can also occasionally contain inaccurate and misleading information. The nature of the Internet and WWW makes it easy for almost anyone to create and disperse information.

People also have considerable freedom and variety in the formats with which they publish information on the Web. We have to double -check the facts before giving it to users. Here we need to use some general guidelines or criteria when evaluating information sources. We should ask the following questions about whatever information we found:

- Who is the author or Institution?
- How current is the information?
- Who is the audience?
- Is the content accurate and objective?
- What is the purpose of the information?
- How easy to use it?

More than that, we can consider coverage, presentation and arrangement of information in the sources to find out its value. The tremendous increase in online information sources made the searching difficult, where organising skill is required for library and information professionals. Libraries role is also enhanced where they will have to adapt to changing environment. The scope is only limited to the imagination of information professionals, where they have to acquire thorough understanding of changes in their profession. Willingness to take up the challenges in information resource management is the need of the hour for us.

WEB SITE FOR A LIBRARY

The roles of libraries and the Internet in providing information in the 21st century are firmly intertwined. It behooves any librarian working today to understand not only how to find things on the World Wide Web, but to have a basic understanding of how it works. Librarians will be called on to become information architects, to be able to create Web sites with clearly stated goals, that are aesthetically pleasing and filled with relevent content and functionality.

As more and more libraries set up comprehensive Web sites, there becomes an increasing demand for librarians who have an understanding of HTML, as well as other types of Internet programming skills such as javascript, SQL, CGI, ASP, and Cold Fusion. Librarians should know the principles of setting up an efficient information resource. As the Internet becomes more interactive, there is a push Towards making databases accessible online; the best example of this is the library card catalog. Other interactive options include e-mail and bulletin board service, and moving from CD-ROMs to online subscriptions.

A library Web site is not merely establishing a presence on the Internet. It can be a virtual addition to the existing library structure, reaching out to patrons around the clock and providing valuable information resources. Additionally, a library's Web site is an important source of information about the library. The library's Internet policies, special programming, and new materials can all be made viewable at any time from the Web site. Libraries, too, should be designing their own Web sites that serve as portals to interesting sites that have been reviewed and annotated by professional librarians. Librarians will continue to play an important role as information professionals in the Information Age, well into the 21st century.

MARKETING OF LIBRARY SERVICES

In recent years, libraries of all types from all countries have found it necessary to compete for both money and clients as major changes have occurred. The Internet brings a whole new dimension of competition that public, academic, and special libraries are facing daily. Whereas budget problems have been around for some time, the recent competition from the Internet can translate into fewer users, despite the fact that the Internet is also a crucial tool used by librarians for research and marketing.

Because of all of these existing challenges and intensifying changes at least a handful of libraries have turned to 'tried and true' business models for improved planning and development, and that they are employing marketing plans as one method for moving forward. As time goes on, libraries must think about marketing of their services and resources to achieve goals. It is important to clarify what marketing means in a library environment.

Marketing is not so much about 'selling' information products to researchers, as it is more about spreading the word about potentially useful new tools. It is also about keeping users informed about library activities and involving them in collection development. It is more about integrating new research tools into existing, effective research processes, and in some way enhancing researchers' work, rather than selling the tool to users as an end in itself.

As librarians market new tools, they should know how the tools may offer clarity, and not simply contribute to noise for the users. Effective marketing can only occur when librarians understand, at least in a broad sense, what the scientists, professors, and graduate students are already doing to keep informed, and what their research projects are about.

BASICS OF NETWORKING AND SECURITY

COMPUTER NETWORKS

A computer network is an interconnection of various computer systems located at different places. In computer network two or more computers are linked together with a medium and data communication devices for the purpose of communicating data and sharing resources. The computer that provides resources to other computers on a network is known as server. In the network the individual computers, which access shared network resources, are known as workstations or nodes. Computer Networks may be classified on the basis of geographical area in three broad categories:

- Local Area Network
- Metropolitan Area Network and
- Wide Area Network.

Local Area Network (LAN)

Networks used to interconnect computers in a single room, rooms within a building or buildings on one site are called Local Area Network. LAN transmits data with a speed of several megabits per second. The transmission medium is normally coaxial cables.

LAN links computers, i.e., software and hardware, in the same area for the purpose of sharing information. Usually LAN links computers within a limited geographical area because they must be connected by a cable, which is quite expensive. People working in LAN get more capabilities in data processing, work processing and other information exchange compared to stand-alone computers. Because of this information exchange most of the business and government organisations are using LAN.

Major Characteristics of LAN:

- Every computer has the potential to communicate with any other computers of the network
- High degree of interconnection between computers
- Easy physical connection of computers in a network
- Inexpensive medium of data transmission
- High data transmission rate

Advantages:

- The reliability of network is high because the failure of one computer in the network does not effect the functioning for other computers.
- Addition of new computer to network is easy.
- High rate of data transmission is possible.

- Peripheral devices like magnetic disk and printer can be shared by other computers.

Disadvantages:

If the communication line fails, the entire network system breaks down.

Use of LAN:

- Followings are the major areas where LAN is normally used:
  - — File transfers and Access
  - — Word and text processing
  - — Electronic message handling
  - — Remote database access
  - — Personal computing
  - — Digital voice transmission and storage

Metropolitan Area Network (MAN)

Networks used to interconnect computers in a city or a town are called Metropolitan Area Networks. Generally telephone lines are used to connect these computers. Alternatively, wireless mode also is used for this purpose. Computers are connected to the telephone lines through devices called MODEMS.

Modems

The word modem is a contraction of the words modulator-demodulator. A modem is typically used to send digital data over a phone line. The sending modem modulates the data into a signal that is compatible with the phone line, and the receiving modem demodulates the signal back into digital data. Wireless modems are also frequently seen converting data into radio signals and back.

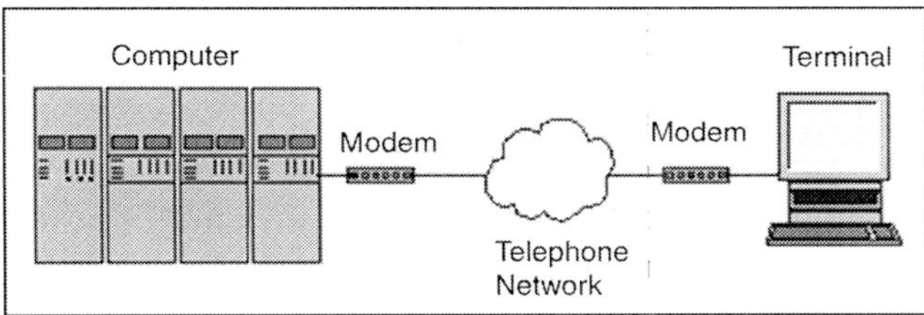

The Modem

Wide Area Network (WAN)

The term Wide Area Network is used to describe a computer network spanning a regional, national or global area. For example, for a large company the head quarters might be at Delhi and regional branches at Bombay, Madras, Bangalore and Calcutta. Here regional centers are connected to head quarters through WAN. The distance between computers connected to WAN is larger. Therefore the transmission medium used are normally telephone lines, microwaves and satellite links.

Characteristics of WAN

Followings are the major characteristics of WAN:

- *Communication Facility*: For a big company spanning over different parts of the country the employees can save long distance phone calls and it overcomes the time lag in overseas communications. Computer conferencing is another use of WAN where users communicate with each other through their computer system.
- *Remote Data Entry*: Remote data entry is possible in WAN. It means sitting at any location you can enter data, update data and query other information of any computer attached to the WAN but located in other cities. For example, suppose you are sitting at Madras and want to see some data of a computer located at Delhi, you can do it through WAN.
- *Centralised Information*: In modern computerised environment you will find that big organisations go for centralised data storage. This means if the organisation is spread over many cities, they keep their important business data in a single place. As the data are generated at different sites, WAN permits collection of this data from different sites and save at a single site.

Difference between LAN and WAN

- LAN is restricted to limited geographical area of few

kilometers. But WAN covers great distance and operate nationwide or even worldwide.

- In LAN, the computer terminals and peripheral devices are connected with wires and coaxial cables. In WAN there is no physical connection. Communication is done through telephone lines and satellite links.
- Cost of data transmission in LAN is less because the transmission medium is owned by a single organisation. In case of WAN the cost of data transmission is very high because the transmission medium used are hired, either telephone lines or sate llite links.
- The speed of data transmission is much higher in LAN than in WAN. The transmission speed in LAN varies from 0.1 to 100 megabits per second. In case of WAN the speed ranges from 1800 to 9600 bits per second.
- Few data transmission errors occur in LAN compared to WAN. It is because in LAN the distance covered is negligible.

NETWORK TOPOLOGY

The term topology in the context of communication network refers to the way the computers or workstations in the network are linked together. According to the physical arrangements of workstations and nature of work, there are three major types of network topology. They are star topology, bus topology and ring topology.

Star topology

In star topology a number of workstations are directly linked to a central node. Any communication between stations on a star LAN must pass through the central node. There is bi-directional communication between various nodes. The central node controls all the activities of the nodes. The advantages of the star topology are:

- It offers flexibility of adding or deleting of workstations from the network.

- Breakdown of one station does not affect any other device on the network.

The major disadvantage of star topology is that failure of the central node disables communication throughout the whole network.

Bus Topology

In bus topology all workstations are connected to a single communication line called bus. In this type of network topology there is no central node as in star topology. Transmission from any station travels the length of the bus in both directions and can be received by all workstations. The advantage of the bus topology is that:

- It is quite easy to set up.
- If one station of the topology fails it does not affect the entire system.

The disadvantage of bus topology is that any break in the bus is difficult to identify.

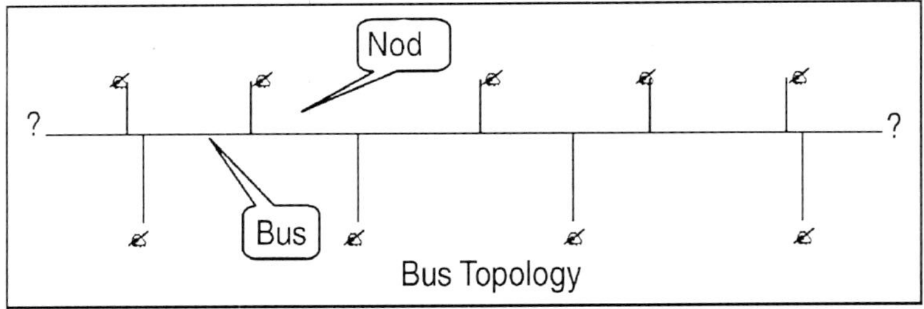

Bus Topology

Ring Topology

In ring topology each station is attached nearby stations on a point to point basis so that the entire system is in the form of a ring. In this topology data is transmitted in one direction only. Thus the data packets circulate along the ring in either clockwise or anti-clockwise direction. The advantage of this topology is that any signal transmitted on the network passes through all the LAN stations. The disadvantage of ring network is that the breakdown of any one station on the ring can disable the entire system.

Communication Devices

Major Communication Devices Used Today

- *Wire Pairs*: Wire pairs are commonly used in local telephone communication and for short distance digital data communication. They are usually made up of copper and the pair of wires is twisted together. Data transmission speed is normally 9600 bits per second in a distance of 100 meter.
- *Coaxial Cables*: Coaxial cable is groups of specially wrapped and insulted wires that are able to transfer data at higher rate. They consist of a central copper wire surrounded by an insulation over which copper mesh is placed. They are used for long distance telephone lines and local area network for their noise immunity and faster data transfer.
- *Microwave*: Microwave system uses very high frequency radio signals to transmit data through space. The transmitter and receiver of a microwave system should be in line-of-sight because the radio signal cannot bend. With microwave very long distance transmission is not possible. In order to overcome the problem of line of sight and power amplification of weak signal, repeaters are used at intervals of 25 to 30 kilometers between the transmitting and receiving end.
- *Communication Satellite*: The problem of line-sight and repeaters are overcome by using satellites, which are the most widely used data transmission media in modern days. A communication satellite is a microwave relay station placed in outer space. INSAT-1B is such a satellite that can be accessible from anywhere in India. In satellite communication, microwave signal is transmitted from a transmitter on earth to the satellite at space. The satellite amplifies the weak signal and transmits it back to the receiver. The main advantage of satellite

communication is that it is a single microwave relay station visible from any point of a very large area. In microwave the data transmission rate is 16 Giga bits per second. They are mostly used to link big metropolitan cities.

Information Security

Information security is characterised as the preservation of:

- *Confidentiality* – ensuring that information is accessible only to those authorised to have access.
- *Integrity* – safeguarding the accuracy and completeness of information and processing methods
- *Availability* – ensuring that authorised users have access to information and relating assets when required.

Information security is achieved by implementing a suitable set of controls, which could be policies, practices, procedures, organisational practices and software functions

Information systems are prone to potential expensive security risk and threats leading to high client concerns for IPR (Intellectual property rights) protection.

According to the '2000 Information Security Industry Survey' published by ICSA (International Computer Security Association), the top 3 IT security concerns are:

- Malicious Code (includes viruses, Trojans, worms, and hostile ActiveX and Java)
- Loss of Privacy/Confidentiality (includes abuse/ misuse of data) and
- Electronic Exploits/Tools (includes cracking, eavesdropping, spoofing and toolkits).

If information assets are not suitable protected, it can be:

- Given away or stolen without depriving you of it.
- Modified without your knowledge to make it worthless.
- List without trace or hope of recovery
- Violation of IPR leading to lawsuits/ loss of customer confidence.

- Corruption/ loss of integrity of importance date, *e.g.*, software codes
- Loss of business due to leakage/ theft of company intellectual property
- Mobile workforce not able to access internal IT systems
- Unanticipated disruption in off-site work due to break down of communication links.
- Leak and unauthorised use of confidential information, business strategy.
- Physical damages/ theft of critical IT infrastructure component.

Information Security through Network Access Control

What is Network access control:

- Imposition of certain controls to restrict access to a shared network based on the access control policy.
- The controls can be implemented by putting firewall at the network perimeter.
- The firewall filters traffic by means of predefined tables or set of rules.

Firewall

Firewall is an intermediate system plugged between two networks, which can act as a security wall. The main purpose of a firewall is to control access to or from a protected/trusted network.

It implements a network access policy by forcing connections to pass through the firewall, where they can be examined and evaluated. Without firewall a site is more exposed to inherently insecure host operating systems, TCP/ IP vulnerabilities and attacks from the Internet. It is also very difficult to maintain same level of security for all the hosts in a network.

Benefits of firewall:

- Protection from vulnerable services, e.g. NIS, NFS, source routed packets
- Controlled access

  - Help to control access to and from a network.
- Concentrated security
  - Additional security measures, *e.g.*, one time password system, etc., can be implemented in single place at the firewall instead of in individual host.
- Enhanced privacy
  - Blocking of services like finger, DNS helps to hide information, which could otherwise be useful to the attackers.
- Logging and statistic s of network use and misuse
  - Help to monitor usage of network services and detection of potential intrusion.
- Policy enforcement
  - Helps to implement organisation network access control policy.

Firewall Components

There are three basic components of firewall

- Firewall Policy
- Packet filters
- Application gateways

Firewall Policy

The policy directly influences the design, installation and use of firewall system. The higher-level policy addresses the services that will be allowed or explicitly denied from/ to the restricted network (including exception). The lower level policy describes how the firewall will actually go about restricting the access and filtering the services that are defined in the higher-level policy.

Packet Filter or Packet Filtering Gateways

Packet filters uses routers with packet filtering rules to grant or deny access based on source IP address, destination IP address, source port and Destination port information of an IP packet. Adding TCP or UDP port filtering to IP address filtering results in great deal of flexibility.

In general the packet filters operates on the each packet in individual and Hence, stateless but Stateful packet filters use some of the state information derived from the past communication.

It can be applied on outbound interface as well as on inbound interface. When IP packets arrive at a network interface of a packet filter and are examined against the rule of filtering. Selection criteria uses information found in packet header and related to the network interfaces, the packets appear.

Application Gateway

Gateways interconnect one network to another for a specific application. Its major function is application specific and used as proxy. If an application Gateway contains proxies for FTP and TELNET, then only that traffic will be allowed and other services are completely blocked.

Packet filter and application gateways are usually combined in a firewall configuration to implement the firewall policy.

Dual – homed Firewall

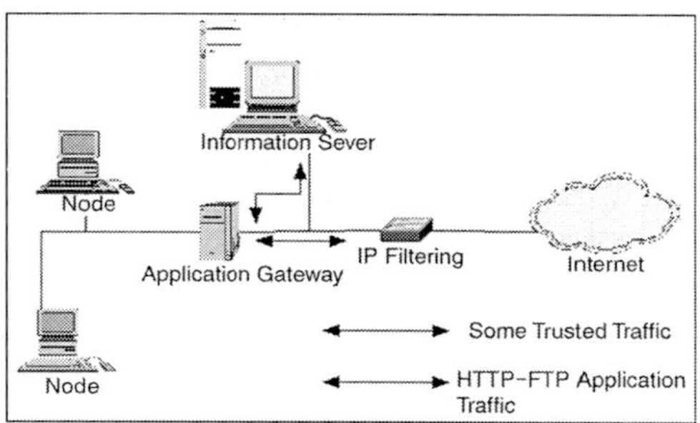

Dual-homed Firewall Configuration

It is a host with two network cards, one connected to the external or untrusted network and other is to the internal or trusted network.

The key security principle is not to allow traffic coming in from an untrusted network to be directed routed to the trusted network. IP source routing and IP forwarding services are disabled in this host.

LIBRARIAN'S COMPUTER AWARENESS AND USE OF IT APPLICATION IN COLLEGE LIBRARIES

Dramatic changes in information technology and society are having a considerable impact on educational institutions and their libraries. Information is a vital and indispensable product of the modern society. Availability of right information accurately, precisely and timely is of critical importance.

IT is the synthesis of computers and communication. Rapid advances in computer and communication technology enable storing, processing and transmission of huge amount of information easily, quickly and inexpensively. Developments in science and technology have brought about reduction in size and cost of IT and tremendous increase in its capabilities. The use of IT enables provision of specialised, user oriented library and information products and services effectively and efficiently.

INFORMATION TECHNOLOGY

Information Technology (IT) can be defined as those processes and technologies which are used in acquisition and dissemination of information based on some electronic technology. Somerville has stated 'Information technology has resulted from a convergence of computing technology and communications technology'.

This means it is essentially the result of advances in the three important areas of computing, telecommunication and microelectronics. Information Technology is the application of a wide variety of electronic technologies to the information-handling activities.

In the domain of library information service, information technologies such as computer, telecommunications, word processing, micro-graphics, reprographics, video recordings and other electronic devices for the storage, retrieval, reproduction and dissemination of information are used.

APPLICATION OF IT IN COLLEGE LIBRARIES

The main functions of a library are acquisition, technical processing, storage, retrieval and dissemination. The traditional methods of doing these result in slow, laborious and repetitive manual routines. With the advent of modern technologies and their applications, manual routines have transformed into machine oriented ones.

The application of modern technology has allowed access to and storage of information quickly. The availability of computers has gradually changed the library scene. The convegence of computers with new developments in telecommunication techniques and equipment is considered as new information technology. The new information technology has a wide range of services which libraries can avail themselves of and offer to supplement the existing ones to users. Some of the areas to which the modern technology could be applied in day to day activities of the libraries are acquisition, cataloguing, circulation, indexing and abstracting of articles, etc.

NEED FOR IT

Twentieth century has been the century of explosions. It has witnessed the population explosion, socio-cultural explosion, and nuclear explosion. The information explosion is due to the fact that information generation is a continuous process.

The interdisciplinary research and multidisciplinary research has led to the creation of new ideas, new knowledge and unprecedented growth in information particularly in science and technology. In this era of information explosion, in which large amount of information needs to be processed, application and use of new technology, i.e., information technology is essential.

COMPUTER AWARENESS

Nowhere has the impact of the computer been felt greater than in the field of library and information services. Already most of the libraries are flooded with documents and records that they simply can not handle efficiently without computers. Computers are changing the way in which libraries collect, store, retrieve and disseminate information. The libraries that can not adjust to these trends will not survive. So computers will come and stay forever in all the library and information centres that wish to function efficiently here after.

ROLE OF COLLEGE LIBRARIAN IN IT ERA

The problem we face today is not of dearth of information, but of excessive information. The developing countries are making an earnest effort to concentrate more on developing and using new electronic gadgets to provide better access to information. With the use of new information technology, the libraries can provide nascent information quickly in great volume.

Today, the librarian plays a significant role in information handling and information transfer. He is rightly known as the information officer and is supposed to provide an active service for maximum use of information with minimum cost and time. Information technology demands trained personnel to handle information storage and retrieval in libraries. A modern librarian has to play a very important role in the process of communication in the contemporary time, for which he must be well educated, highly qualified and professionally competent.

8

Communication Technology in Academic Libraries

INTRODUCTION

Past three decade has witnessed unprecedented developments in computer and communication technology. Computers are being used increasingly to automate various activities in libraries with a suitable off-the-shelf general or specific-purpose software package that are now available in a wide range. Tremendous storage and processing potential of computers are being fully realised through existing communication and networking technologies. The two technologies are interdependent, inseparable and share a symbiotic relationship.

The computer's ability to store and process vast amount of information and communication technology with its ability to transmit this information from one location to another converged to form 'information technology' or 'informatics' or 'Information and Communication Technology'. The information technology refers to mosaic of technologies, products and techniques combined to provide new electronic dimensions to information and retrieval activities.

The term information technology represents convergence of three strands of technologies, namely computer, microelectronics and communications. Information technology is used to describe products and services that came-up with rapid changes in computer and communication technologies and their fusion. Thus, technologies which improve the efficiency and effectiveness of an information system or service fall under the purview of information technology.

Some of these technologies are available to the libraries for many years, while a few are now emerging as important tools for overcoming the barriers in the access and dissemination of information. The emergence of Internet, particularly the World Wide Web (WWW) as a new media of information delivery, coupled with availability of powerful hardware, software and networking technology has further triggered large-scale commercial and Non-commercial digitisation programmes the world over. Increasing number of publishers are using the Internet as a global way to offer their publications to the international community of scientists and technologists resulting in large-scale appearance of STM electronic journals on the web. The Internet and web technology provides an unparalleled media for delivery of information with greater speed and economy.

Moreover, the web-based electronic information products not only eliminated paper, physical storage and transportation costs, it also offers a hosts of other possibilities for incorporating multimedia and hyper-link features to electronic documents hitherto impossible on paper media.

The web-based electronic information products are exerting ever-increasing pressure on the traditional libraries, which, in turn, are committing larger portions of their budgetary allocation for either procuring or accessing web-based online or full-text search services, CD ROM products, online databases, multi-media products, etc.,The libraries and information centres, as consumers of electronic journals and online databases, are benefiting greatly from this technology-driven revolution. The information products of technological revolution, in turn, triggered major shifts in the traditional practices and policies of buying, storing and accessing journals. Rapid changes in information technologies during past three decades have drastically changed the functions and activities of information professionals in libraries. Most functions in modern libraries are being performed using software packages that are now available off-the-shelf. Several libraries have their catalogues available on the Internet with a webbased search interface along with links to resources either acquired through external agencies or created in-house. Most libraries are connected to the Campus network and subscribe to electronic resources to serve the information requirement of their academic community.

Several libraries have taken-up small-scale digitisation projects for part of their collection. The librarians and information professionals are required to develop skills that are required to use, develop and maintain IT-based services and products used by today's libraries. The stage deals with new information technologies, their products, services and applications in libraries. It describes web-based library services.

NEED AND PURPOSE OF INFORMATION TECHNOLOGY IN LIBRARIES

The application of information technology in libraries results in increased operational efficiency. The IT increases productivity of library staff. It relieves professional staff from mundane jobs that involves a lot of duplication so that they can be fruitfully used for user-oriented library services.

It improves quality of services rendered by the library. Use of information technology ensures ease of functioning, accuracy and economy in human labour with greater speed. The exponential growth of information has made manual system redundant giving way to computerised information storage and retrieval tools.

Effective and efficient handling of huge quantum of information is only possible by using computers, which have the added advantage of being highly accurate and efficient that adds value to information. Moreover, the technology also helps in rendering services that were hitherto not possible using traditional means. The new information technology facilitates improved management of physical and financial resources.

The advances in technology and its availability at lower cost, has also raised expectations of users from librarians and libraries.

The new information technology, on one hand, facilitate wider access to information for the library users, on other hand, it facilitates wider dissemination of information products and services generated by the library. The availability of networks facilitates resource sharing and high-speed communication with other libraries.

DEVELOPMENTS IN COMPUTER AND MICROPROCESSOR TECHNOLOGY

Dramatic reductions in the size and cost of computer components and equally impressive gains in the speed, storage capacity and reliability of hardware components have expanded their use rapidly in all activities and functions of a library and information centre. Notable reductions in the size of microprocessors combined with dramatically enhanced capacity have added new dimensions to the computer new hardware technology.

Initially, small silicon chips contained only few components and circuits, but the average number of components has doubled each year Since, 1965. Early small-scale integration efforts first gave way to large-scale integration (LSI) chips that contained thousands of components, very large-scale integration (VLSI) chips that contained hundreds of thousands of components and circuits, and now ultra large-scale integration (ULSI) chips come with millions of components and circuits.

A microprocessor, also known as Central Processing Unit (CPU) of a computer, is a complete computation engine that is fabricated on a single chip. Microprocessors are manufactured by different companies like Intel, Advanced Micro Divices (AMD), Motorola, etc. However, most widely-used microprocessors are manufactured by Intel. The first microprocessor used in a PC was Intel 8080. Introduced in 1974, it was a complete 8-bit microprocessor on a single chip.

Intel 8088 used in the IBM PC in 1979, was the first microprocessor that made its presence felt in the market.

The PC market moved from the 8088, 80286, 80386, 80486, Pentium, Pentium-II, III, IV and now to Intel Dual Core and Quad Core. The new Intel Dual Core can execute any piece of code that ran on the original 8088, but the Dual Core runs about 3000 times faster. The capacity of a microprocessor is measured in terms of the number of bits it can send or receive and the number of bits it can process internally.

The 8088 was an 8/16 bit processor, indicating that it can send or receive 8 bits of data and internally process 16 bits of data at a time. The 80286 was a 16/16 bit processor and 80386 chip had a 32-bit processor with a 32-bit data path and, as a result, was much faster than either the 8088 or the 80286 chip. The 80486 chip, introduced by Intel in late 1989, had a 32- bit processor.

It has architectural enhancements, Hence, it performed better than the 80386 chip. The Pentium is a 32-bit processor with a 32-bit data path. It is three times faster than the 80486. The Pentium II and III had a 32-bit processor with a 64-bit data path. It was three times faster than the Pentium. The Pentium IV is a 32-bit processor with a 64-bit data path, and was introduced in 2000.

It is four times faster than the Pentium. Currently, PCs and laptops are equipped with Dual Core which is a 64-bit processor with 64-bit data path and processing speed of 3.0 Ghz. Like microprocessor technology, digital storage devices have also witnessed notable reductions in its size and cost with dramatically enhancement in capacity of storage.

There are two types of data storage devices, *i.e.*, removable data storage devices and Non-removable data storage devices. The data storage devices come in many sizes and shapes. The storage devices can also be categorised based on media used for storage, for example magnetic storage media, optical storage media, metal-oxide semiconductors or flash memory devices (popularly known as Pen drives or USB drives). Magnetic storage media are commonly used for large volumes of data (*e.g.*, video, image, or remote sensing data). Large amounts of data are stored through tape drives because the capacity on the drives is huge - three billion (or three gigabits) of data per square inch can fit on a single magnetic disk.

Hard discs, floppies, tapes, cartridges, etc., are example of magnetic media. CD-ROMs and DVD ROMs are example of optical storage media which can again be of two types, i.e., i) write-once, read-many: data once written cannot be erased; and ii) Rewritable: the data that is once written can be erased completely and the same storage device can be used again for storing different data. A typical disc used in a computer-based CD drive stores 650 MB.

Digital Versatile Disk or DVD, initially stood for Digital Video Disc. Like a CD, DVD is an optical storage system for read-only, recordable and rewritable applications. The DVD format provides several configurations of data layers, moving from 2D storage to 3D storage. Each configuration is designed to provide additional storage capacity. The similarity between the DVD and the CD gets smaller with each upgraded configuration, however, DVDs in contrast to CDs has storage capacity of 4.7 GB.

Metal-oxide semiconductors-based storage devices, popularly known as pen drives or USB drives or flash memory devices, is Non-volatile computer memory that can be electrically erased and reprogrammed. It is a technology that is primarily used in memory cards and USB flash drives for general storage and transfer of data between computers and other digital products. Flash memory stores information in an array of memory cells made from floating-gate transistors.

In traditional single-level cell (SLC) devices, each cell stores only one bit of information. Some newer flash memory, known as multi-level cell (MLC) devices, can store more than one bit per cell by choosing between multiple levels of electrical charge to apply to the floating gates of its cells. Flash drives are now available with 8 GB storage capacity. Digital collections that are too large to store entirely on a disk use hierarchical storage mechanisms (HSM). In an HSM, the most frequently used data is kept on fast disks while less frequently used data is kept in nearline such as an automated (robotic) tape library.

An HSM can automatically migrate data from tape to disk and vice-versa as required. Intelligent storage networks and snap-servers are now available in which the physical storage devices are intelligently controlled and made available to a number of servers.

A number of RAID (Redundant Array of Inexpensive Disks) models are also available for greater security and performance. The RAID technology distributes the data across a number of disks in a way that even if one or more disks fail, the system would still function while the failed component is replaced.

DEVELOPMENTS IN COMMUNICATION AND NETWORK TECHNOLOGY

Communication technology, with its ability to transmit data and information from one location to another, serve as a tool to exploit potentials and ability of computer to store and process vast amount of information. A computer communication network is an interconnection of a collection of several computers from which the user can select the service required and communicate with any computer as a local user.

A computer communication networks can be viewed as a collection of nodes with computing resources and nodal-switching computers that facilitate communication through a set of transmission links. Developments in communication technology have made it possible to interconnect geographically dispersed computing resources of different kinds and makes.

Users can access the network through PCs and terminals attached to a node and messages traverse these networks through the switching nodes. Since, computer communicates using digitised signals instead of electric signals, it requires different transmission facilities than those used for transmitting analogue electrical signals. It is, however, a common practice to use conventional telecommunication links for data transmission by converting digital signals into analogue signals using a process called 'Modulation' and the device that performs the conversion is called the MODEM (MOdulator - DEModulator).

Currently, terrestrial, satellite-based data networks, Integrated Service Digital Network (ISDN) and wireless networks are available that can handle all kinds of communication requirements (i.e., voice, data, telemetry, facsimile and video) without discrimination.

The computer networks can be grouped into four categories based on geographical locations of its computer terminals, i.e.,

- *Local Area Network (LAN)*: interconnection of many computers within a given local area, more often premises of a single organisation building. A very high speed of data transmission can be attained within a limited geographic area. LANs are typically configured in a star, bus or ring. Low speed LANs use telephone wires or copper cables, optical fibre cables are used to achieve high-speed transmission of data.
- *Wide Area Network (WAN)*: WAN is used to interconnect a number of widely dispersed computers in various cities of a country or different countries. WANs use communication media maintained by telegraph or telephone companies. These networks usually have land telephone lines, underground coaxial cables, microwave communication and satellite communications.
- *Metropolitan Area Network (MAN)*: MAN refers to inter- connection within geographical limits of a city or town.
- *Gateways*: Gateways consist of software and hardware that are required to interconnect networks amongst themselves. Gateways contend with any differences in packet sizes, protocols and addressing methods

between the two networks it connect. Gateways are also used to connect LANs to WANs and WANs, in turn, can be linked through gateways to create national and international data communication networks.

The communications networks can be grouped into the following three categories based on the technology and communication media used by them:

- *Public Switched Telephone Network*: PSTN are managed by common carriers usually telephone companies/ departments the world over. The PSTN generally provide two basic services, the normal dial-up connections to the subscribers and permanent leased connection between two subscriber's points. The permanent leased connections provide single traceable line between two subscriber points. The leased lines are generally less prone to noise than dial-up lines.
- *Public Data Network*: Analogous to the public telephone network, many domestic common carriers provide data communications services via a specialised network called a Public Data Network (PDN). Most Internet Service Providers (ISPs) use combination of PDN and PSTN for providing Internet connectivity.
- *Integrated Services Digital Networks* (ISDN): An ISDN is a network that provides end-to-end digital connectivity to support a wide range of services, including voice and Non-voice services.

Computer networks use physical channels through which information is transmitted between computers in a network. Media may be classified as bounded, i.e., wires (twisted pair telephone wires or UTP CAT 5), cables (co-axial) and optical fibres; or unbounded, i.e., radio waves or microwaves. Data communication is an integral part of the modern information storage and retrieval systems in terms of their online access. Today, network technology works on client server architecture with middleware used for connecting software components or applications on clients and servers.

Technique of packet switching, evolved in 1960s, is used for transferring data between computer systems with an objective to facilitate networked computers to communicate seamlessly across multiple, geographically dispersed locations. The Transmission Control Protocol (TCP) and Internet Protocol (IP), called TCP/ IP suite, is the backbone of Internet and other TCP/IP based networks.

With developments in communication technology, institutions have options to set-up fibre optic-based gigabit LAN or wireless LAN. Depending on the geographical location, institutions have options to buy terrestrial or satellite-based Internet bandwidth its combinations from a number of Internet Service Providers (ISPs).

LIBRARY AUTOMATION

The library automation refers to computerisation or mechanisation of all library activities. It deals with the design and development of process and system that minimize the necessity of human intervention in their operations. The library automation is defined as 'integrated systems' that com-puterise an array of traditional library functions such as acquisition, cataloguing, circulation and serials control, etc., using an integrated library software. A computerised library and information system is a set of functional system encompassing:

- In-house operations of the library; and
- Other applications of the information technologies in libraries including information storage and retrieval.

An automated library is one where a computer system is used to manage one or several of the key functions of a library such as acquisitions, serials control, cataloguing, circulation and the public access catalogue. An integrated library system or an integrated online library system is used for computerisation of in-house activities of a library. Such application packages use a single bibliographic database and a set of interrelated application programmes to support multiple library operations.

Most integrated library software are modular in design consisting of a number of optional and basic modules. Most library packages typically incorporate modules for: Acquisition, Cataloguing, Circulation Control, Serials Control and Online Public Access Catalogue. Online Public Access Catalogue is often a principal motive for the implementation of integrated library software. Several off-the-shelf packages are available in the market that can be used for computerisation of in-house activities of the Library.

These software packages are available for single user in a workstation mode (Windows 95/98/2000) as well in simultaneous multi-user environment on Windows and its variant/ Unix/ Linux/ Sun Solaris Operating Systems. LibSys, SOUL, Alice for Windows, Slim +, Virtua, Librarians Suit, etc., are some of the important software packages available in India. Libraries, besides using integrated library software, also use office automation software like word processing (MS Word), spread-sheet (MS Excel), database management systems (MS Access), presentation packages (MS Powerpoint) and graphic applications (Photoshop or Paint). Librarians and information professionals, therefore, require basic training in use of such general-purpose packages.

AUTOMATIC IDENTIFICATION AND DATA COLLECTION TECHNOLOGY

There are three important identification and data collection technologies that are used in libraries, namely, bar code technology, RFID and Smart card.

BAR CODE TECHNOLOGY

Bar code technology is being used in library and businesses for the past 30 years to minimize data entry errors, speed processes and reduce costs. Most books, journals as well as other consumer products in the market carry black and white thin and thick strips called barcodes. Barcode technology offers a mechanism that can be used for identification, location and tracking of items that are bar coded.

Barcode is not a new technology, it was introduced in 1940 although it was first applied commercially in 1960's as a method for tracking rail road cars. Since, then, it has been used extensively in consumer industry, material handling, industries and libraries. A bar code is a machine readable code consisting of a series of bars and spaces printed in defined ratios.

Bar code symbologies are essentially alphabets in which different widths of bars and spaces are combined to form characters and ultimately, forms a message. Because there are many ways to arrange these bars and spaces, numerous symbologies are possible. Common linear symbologies include UPC/EAN, Interleaved 2 of 5 (I of 5), Codabar, Code 39 and Code 128. While each symbology is in some way unique, the composition of a complete message (bar code) is regardless of the symbology used. Barcode by itself, is not a system but is an identification tool that enables accurate reading of data for sophisticated management systems.

Use of barcode increasing accuracy in data collection, saves time and brings about the efficiency in library activities. Bar code technology is being used in libraries all over the world especially for circulation of books as well as for several other functions including location control or book tracking, stock verification, receipt of issues of journals, cross checking of documents issued from the library, etc.

RADIO FREQUENCY IDENTIFICATION (RFID)

RFID (Radio Frequency Identification) is a term used for a radio-enabled device that communicates with or interrogates a tag or smart label, which is embedded with a single microchip processor and an antenna. The origin of the term lies in the invention of 'tags' that reflects back or re-transmit a radio frequency signal. The two components of RFID are tags and readers. The tags or label is equipped with a single microchip processor, an antenna and an ID code that can be embedded in almost any object. RFID readers are radio-enabled devices that communicate with or interrogate RFID tags or labels wirelessly and obtain the ID code on the tags from a distance of several inches.

The RFID readers can be fixed or made portable just like barcode scanners. RFID can also be referred as a high-tech version of the barcode. In the past few years, the cost of RFID tags have come down drastically. Low cost RFID tags, typically costs less than ₹ 30.00 each for up to 1 metre range making the technology affordable as an alternative to the barcode, magnetic strip or printed label.

RFID has advantages that include tolerance of mis-orientation and obscuration, lower cost over life and ability to 'read'. Most importantly, RFID tags are cheap enough to be disposable and thin enough to go even inside the sheets of paper in some cases. An RFID tag is a means of storing and retrieving data through a radio frequency transmission to the chip inside the tag. An RFID tag is simply an integrated circuit (chip), which includes memory for data storage and a substrate backing material with an antenna pattern.

The chip can typically hold up to 1,024 bits (128 bytes) of information. In a typical library implementation, each book is equipped with smart labels and library patrons are given library cards imbedded with smart labels. Tags or smart labels can be programmed to store i) unique accession number of documents; ii) class number of a document; and iii) a unique security code for EAS. While accession number is used for carrying out functions of circulation, stock verification and other library applications, class number can be deployed for sorting documents according to class numbers and segregating then into bins for different shelving areas.

The RFID tags can also be used as antitheft devices in libraries. Such applications of RFID are called Electronic Article Surveillance (EAS). New forms of RFID perform EAS functions as well, obviating the need for a separate device. An interrogator, or reader, is a radio frequency device used to write data to and read data from the chip. Smart tags used in a library are passive, having no internal power source such as a battery. The interrogator provides enough RF energy to power and activate the tag to reflect or to present information stored on them. RFID tags transmit data, antennas receive or transmit the RF signal through the air and readers decode the RF information received from the RFID tag through the antenna. The data is then transmitted to the host application for necessary processing.

SMART CARDS

A smart card, chip card, or integrated circuit card (ICC), is a pocket-sized card with embedded integrated circuits which can process data. Effectively, a smart card can receive input, process it and deliver the processed data as an output. There are two broad categories of smart cards, memory cards contain only Non-volatile memory storage components and specific security logic.

Microprocessor cards contain volatile memory and microprocessor components. The card is made of plastic, generally PVC. The card may embed a hologram to avoid counterfeiting. Smartcards are generally used as security authentication mechanism for single sign-on within large companies and organisations.

A quickly growing application of smart card is as digital identification cards. In this application, the cards are used for authentication of identity. When combined with biometrics, smart cards can provide two- or three-factor authentication. The libraries generally use smart cards to identify and authenticate its patrons.

INTERNET TECHNOLOGY AND ITS SERVICES

The Internet has revolutionised our society, our economy and our technological systems. Over the past century, important technological developments have created a global environment that is drawing people of the world closer and closer together. About fifteen years ago, most of the world knew little or nothing about the Internet. The Internet was then a private network accessible only to computer scientists and researchers who used it to interact with colleagues in their respective disciplines.

It is estimated that about 60 million host computers on the Internet today serve about 200 million users in over 200 countries and territories. Also, the total numbers of host computers and users have been growing at about 33 per cent every six months Since, 1988 – or roughly 80 per cent per year. The Internet has revolutionised the computer and communications world like nothing before. The invention of the telegraph, telephone, radio, and computer set the stage for this unprecedented integration of capabilities.

The Internet is at once a world-wide broadcasting capability, a mechanism for information dissemination, and a medium for collaboration and interaction between individuals and their computers without barriers of geographic location. The Internet represents one of the most successful examples of the benefits of sustained investment and commitment to research and development of information infrastructure. Beginning with the early research in packet switching, the government, industry and academia have been partners in evolving and deploying this exciting new technology. Today, terms like 'Yahoo' and 'Google' are common part of our vocabulary. Internet-based communication services, content creation and delivery tools applicable in libraries.

INTERNET-BASED COMMUNICATION SERVICES

Libraries use Internet-based communication system while attending their day-to-day routine works. An Internet-based communication system allows communication between computer users hooked into a network.

Internet-based communication system is used for communication between person-to-person, person-to-group and group-to-group. A document or message sent through electronic system may contain text, graphics, image, speech as well as other types of information.

Electronic Mail (E-mail)

Electronic Mail, or e-mail, is a fast, easy and inexpensive way to communicate with other Internet users around the world. It is the most popular and widely used services of the Internet. E-mail is the term given to an electronic message, usually a form of simple text message that a user types at a computer system and is transmitted over some form of computer network to another user, who can read it.

E-mail offers speedy and economical transfer of messages anywhere in the world. Sending e-mail messages are virtually free even to long-distance destinations. Most integrated library system support e-mail-based communication to library users (for circulation and acquisitionrelated activities) and to the vendors/ publishers (for placing orders, reminders, cancellation, etc).

Listserv

Listservs are electronic groups that typically centre around broad topics such as Digital Libraries or Reference Service, etc. Listservers of IFLA with the name IFLA-l, Digilib-l LIBJOBS-l are good example of this. Every e-mail message sent to the listserv is distributed to all members of that listserv, which is potentially hundreds or thousands of people.

It does not cost anything to subscribe to a listserv, but simply requires that the user sends an e-mail message to the appropriate address with the message: subscribe (listserv) Firstname Lastname. Each Listserver has one address where a user sends requests to subscribe, un-subscribe, search the archives, etc., and another address to send actual questions or responses to the readers of the list. Apart from organising discussions, job announcements and conference announcements are popular usage of Listservs.

Chat or Instant Messengers

Chat refers to any live discussions conducted using the Internet, usually between more than two persons using their keyboard to communicate. Chat Programmes allow users on the Internet to communicate with each other by typing in real time. It is a feature offered by many online services or Web sites that allows users to 'chat' by typing messages which are displayed almost instantly on the screens of other users who are using the chat room at a given time.

After entering a chat room, any user can type a message that will appear on the monitors of all the other users. Chatting is one of the most popular uses of the Internet. Generally the users remain anonymous by using nicknames or pseudonyms to identify themselves online. A variation of chat is the phenomenon of the instant messenger. Instant messaging can be used to communicate privately with friends, relatives or co-workers.

To send and receive instant messages, a user needs a connection to the Internet and instant messaging software such as Gmail Messenger, Yahoo Messenger and MSN Messenger. The instant messaging software enables a user to set up a list of contacts who also use the same Programme. Once this list is set up, one can see each contact as they come online. A chat session can be started with them quickly and easily. Most conversations are typed text messages that are sent back and forth, though more advanced users can exchange voice, video, files and more.

Conferencing

One of the most exciting features of Internet is to communicate, talk, and see groups of people in different locations around the world, without the expense of travel. Conferencing can take many forms, such as web chat, audio conferencing, video conferencing, multimedia conferencing, screen-sharing, etc.

The conferencing Programmes, such as the popular CU-SeeMe, allow workgroups to use the Internet to see each others' faces in small windows on the computer screen and to hear their voices through computer speakers. One can use desktop video and audio simultaneously or audio can be used alone, or just use the screen-sharing capability without either audio or video.

Audio Conferencing or Internet Telephony

Internet telephony also called IP telephony is a combination of hardware and software that allows the Internet to be used as a telephone carrier. Internet telephony is the conversion of analogue speech signals used on current telephone systems into digital data, allowing calls to be sent over the Internet, bypassing long distance charges.

While the Internet was first devised as a way of transmitting data, it is now being used to make voice calls. Internet telephony is projected to explode as the costs plummet. After the costs of initial set-up and access to an Internet Service Provider, long-distance voice calls can be made via the Internet free of charge, but current quality of voice transmission over the Internet is not always as good as direct telephone service.

There are also PSTN/ Internet gateways that allow regular telephone callers to make Phoneto- Internet-to-Phone connections. There are PC-to-Phone connections and Phone-to-PC connections.

Video Conferencing

Video conferencing is one of the most exciting areas of development in telecommunications, with applications ranging from business to government to education to home and family. Video conferencing involves sending video signals as well as audio and computer data signals. Conferencing can be done one-to-one, one-to-many (called multicast), and many-to-many (called multipoint). While video conferencing, one can talk as well as see the people sitting miles away as if all are discussing in one room facing each other.

One of the most popular applications is transmission on news from various locations by the TV news channels. It also has enormous potential for enhancing communications for small and mid-sized companies, as well as distance learning. However, video conferencing requires sufficient bandwidth to transfer video files of acceptable quality. Desktop conferencing, therefore, is not yet widely implemented for business and educational use. As bandwidth increases, desktop video conferencing is expected to blossom. The PictureTel and Vtel are two of the largest companies that sell video conferencing equipment.

NetMeeting

Microsoft NetMeeting facilitates a new way of talking, meeting, working and sharing over the Internet. It uses Internet phone voice communications and conferencing standards to provide multi-user applications and data sharing over Intranets or the Internet.

Two or more users can work together and collaborate in reach time using application sharing, whiteboard, and chat functionality. NetMeeting can be used for common collaborative activities such as virtual meetings. It can also be used for customer service applications, telecommuting, distance learning, and technical support. The product is based on ITU (International Telecommunication Union) standards, so it is compatible with other products based on the same standards.

NetMeeting supports text chat, video shared whiteboard, transferring of files, directory of connected users. Files, such as documents or pictures, can be exchanged. One of the problems with net meeting is the break-up in audio that sometimes becomes inaudible when using it on the Internet, though it works fine over a high-speed company network.

News Groups

Another Internet service similar to listservs is a newsgroup. News Groups are like an International bulletin board. Each group is a forum for a different subject, where a subscriber can post his/her questions or answers.

There are thousands of groups covering just about every area of interest. The difference between listserv and news group is that when a user joins a group, the mail is no longer automatically deposited into his mailbox. Instead a user is expected to go to the newsgroup himself to read it. Some listservs can also be accessed as a newsgroup. A good analogy to a newsgroup is a bulletin board, *i.e.,* one can go to it, as opposed to having mail delivered to his/ her desk. The mails from newsgroup does not get cluttered and it can be easily regulate how often messages are read.

A drawback of a newsgroup lies in the fact that a user must remember to go out to the newsgroup to look for the information. There are hundreds of newsgroup communities. They centre around topics such as computing, news, recreation, social, and 'alternative' topics. There are newsgroups dealing with virtually every topic under the sun and new newsgroups appear every day.

INTERNET-BASED CONTENT PUBLISHING AND DELIVERY SERVICES

The World Wide Web- know as WWW, W3 or simply, the Web help people to publish, organise and provide access to information on the Internet. The WWW can be defined as a hypertext, multimedia, distributed information system that provides links to hypertext documents, as well as to many other Internet tools and databases.

The Web serves as a platform for several specialised content publishing and delivery services. Some of the important tools for content publishing and delivery services applicable to libraries and information centres are described here.

Blogs

A blog (an abridged form of term 'web log') is a Web site, usually maintained by an individual, with regular entries of commentary, descriptions of events, or other material such as graphics or video. Entries are commonly displayed in reverse chronological order. Blogs are considered as lightweight publishing tools.

Blogs provide control to an individual or group of individuals for publishing contents or making commentary on it. Technologically, blogs are easier to use, platform-independent, and accessible online over the Internet. Broadly, blogs can be said to be online dairies, however, thousands of blogs are maintained by experts in different subject areas who are willing to share their knowledge, understanding and opinions with other people. Michael Casey, who coined the term 'Library 2.0', for example maintains a blog on Library 2.0 called 'LibraryCrunch'.

The most obvious application of blogs for libraries is to use it as a tool for promotion, publicity and for outreach services. Libraries can disseminate information to their users, make announcements for its new resources and events through its blogs. Blogs can be used to initiate debates and interaction amongst users and staff. Moreover, library staff and user can be encouraged to use Library blogs to get to know each other and interact at personal level.

Wikis

A wiki is a collection of web pages designed to enable anyone who accesses it to contribute or modify content, using a simplified markup language. Wikis are often used to create collaborative Web sites and to power community Web sites. For example, the collaborative encyclopaedia, Wikipedia is one of the best-known wikis, that has broken down one the golden rules of librarianship, i.e., content validation and authenticity of information. Wikis are also used in businesses to provide affordable and effective Intranets and for knowledge management.

Ward Cunningham, developer of the first wiki software, WikiWikiWeb, originally described it as "the simplest online database that could possibly work". Wikis can essentially be equated to open web-pages, where anyone registered with it can publish on to it, add to it, amend it and change it. As in case of blogs, Wikis do not have reliability as traditional resources.

Inspite of this, their value as information resource cannot be undermined. Wikis are not only popular but de-facto source of information for people inspite of the fact that it is not validated or authenticated. The lack of peer review and editorship in case of Wikis is a challenge to librarians. Wikis as items in a collection, and the associated instruction of users in their evaluation, is certainly an important task for libraries. Libraries can use wiki as a communication tool to enable social interaction among librarians and patrons.

Users can share information, ask and answer questions, and librarians can do the same within a wiki. Moreover, a record of these transactions can be archived for perpetuity. Transcripts of such question-answer sessions would serve as a resource for the library to provide as reference. Furthermore, wikis will ultimately evolve into a multi-media environment, where both synchronous and asynchronous audio and video collaborations will take place.

Podcasting

The word 'podcasting' is derived from two words, namely 'broadcasting' and 'iPod' (popular MP3 player from Apple Computer). Podcasting is defined as "process of capturing audio digital-media files that can be distributed over the Internet using RSS feeds for playing-back on portable media players as well as computers.

Users can subscribe to such feeds and automatically download these files directly into an audio management Programme (such as iTunes, Windows Media Player or MusicMatch) on their PCs. When a user synchronises their portable audio device with their personal computer the podcasts are automatically transferred to that device to be listened to at the time and location most convenient for the user. Podcasts can be used with a variety of digital audio formats and play on almost any MP3 player or portable digital audio device - as well as any brand of desktop computer or laptop.

Though podcasters' web sites may also offer direct download or streaming of their content, a podcast is distinguished from other digital media formats by its ability to be syndicated, subscribed to, and downloaded automatically when new content is added, using an aggregator or feed reader capable of reading feed formats such as RSS or Atom. Several libraries use podcasts to support library orientations programmes. Taking advantage of podcasting and other consumer technologies (*e.g.*, PDAs, iPods and other MP3 players) as a deliver media of Library's content and services is a great leap forward for library profession.

Vodcasting

The 'VOD' in Vodcasting stands for 'video-on-demand'. It is identical to podcasting. While podcasting is used for delivering audio files, vodcasting is used for delivering video content. Like podcast content, vodcasts content can be played either on a laptop or on personal media assistant (PMA).

RSS Feeds

RSS stands for Real Simple Syndication or Rich Site Summary. The technology, on one hand allows a web site (or e-publisher) to list the newest published updates (like table of contents of journals, new articles) through a technology called XML, on the other hand, it facilitates a web user to keep track new updates on chosen Web site (s). Like a personal search assistant, RSS feed readers visit pre-defined web sites, look for updated information and fetch it automatically on to the user's desktop.

It provides users a way to syndicate and republish content on the Web. Users republish content from other sites or blogs on their sites or blogs, aggregate content on other sites in a single place, and ostensibly distil the Web for their personal use. Libraries are already creating RSS feeds for users to subscribe to, including updates on new items in a collection, new services, and new content in subscription databases. They can also republishing content from other scholarly web sites on their sites.

DIGITISATION

Digitisation is the process of converting the content of physical media (*e.g.*, periodical articles, books, manuscripts, cards, photographs, vinyl disks, etc.,) into digital format. A digital image, in turn, is composed of a set of pixels (picture elements), arranged according to a pre-defined ratio of columns and rows. An images document file can be managed as a regular computer file and can be retrieved, printed and modified using appropriate software. In most library applications, digitisation normally results in documents that are accessible from the web site of a library and thus, on the Internet. Optical scanners and digital cameras are used to digitise images by translating them into bit maps.

It is also possible to digitise sound, video, graphics, animations, etc. Further, textual images can be OCRed so as to make its contents searchable. Digitisation is not an end in itself. It is the process that creates a digital image from an analogue image. Selection criteria, particularly those which reflect user needs are of paramount importance. Therefore, the principles that are applicable in traditional collections development are applicable when materials are being selected for digitisation.

However, there are several other considerations related to technical, legal, policy, and resources that become important in a digitisation project. Several digital library projects are concerned with providing digital access to materials that already exists with traditional libraries in printed media. Digitisation of printed material is practically the only reasonable solution for institutions such as libraries for converting existing paper collection (legacy documents) without having access to the original data in computer processible formats. Digitisation is the natural choice for large-scale conversions for major digital library initiatives.

Printed text, pictures and figures are transformed into computer-accessible forms using a digital scanner or a digital camera in a process called document imaging or scanning. The digitally scanned images are stored in a file as a bit-mapped page image, irrespective of the fact that a scanned page contains a photograph, a line drawing or text. A bit-mapped page image is a type of computer graphic, literally an electronic picture of the page which can most easily be equated to a facsimile image of the page and as such they can be read by humans, but not by the computers, understably 'text' in a page image is not searchable on a computer using the present-day technology. An image-based implementation require a large space for data storage and transmission. There are several large projects using page images as their primary storage format, including project JSTOR at Princeton University funded by the Melon Foundation.

The project Jstor has a complete set of more than 1000+ journals scanned and hosted on web servers that resides at the University of Michigan and is mirrored at Princeton University. Using technology developed at Michigan, high resolution (600 dpi) bit-mapped images of each page are linked to a text file generated with optical character recognition (OCR) software. Linking a searchable text file to the page images of the entire published record of a journal along with newly constructed table of contents, indexes, permits high level of access, search and retrieval of the journal material previously unimaginable.

Capturing page image format is comparatively easy and inexpensive, it is a faithful reproduction of its original maintaining page integrity and originality. The scanned textual images, however, are not searchable unless it is OCRed, which in itself, is highly error prone process specially when it involves scientific texts.

ELECTRONIC RESOURCES

Electronic resources can be defined as resources in electronic format or computerprocessible format that provide information or an indicator to the information and are generally accessible over the Internet or stored on media like CD ROM/ DVD ROM or other storage devices.

The emergence of Internet and the World Wide Web (WWW) in early 1990s, as a new media of information storage and delivery, came as a real boon for evolution of electronic resources. While searching bibliographic databases became popular, it created demand for actual content in full-text that became difficult for libraries to obtain.

Coincided with evolution of World Wide Web (WWW), display technology evolved, cost of storage came down drastically and networks became faster. It became possible for publishers to deliver content, either as a bitmap page images or other structured formats such as HTML, PDF or RTF. Increasingly larger number of publishers started using the Internet as a global way to offer their publications to the international community of scientists and technologists given the fact that technology is in a position to deliver more content to more users at a significantly lower cost per user.

Electronic resources on the Internet manifest themselves in numerous flavours and categories, although most of them emulate the traditional publishing while others are revolutionary in their design and approach. While the present trend to imitate and emulate the traditional models of scholarly communication may continue for some time, eventually the capabilities added by the new media would be used in more innovative ways. Some of the important types of e-resources are described here.

ELECTRONIC DATABASES

An electronic database consists of electronic resources integrated in highly organised fashion so as to provide controlled access to it by their commercial providers. The first databases were bibliographic in nature and were online version of existing indexing and abstracting services such as Biological Abstracts, Index Medicus, Chemical Abstracts, etc.

By the year 1988, only half of all databases were bibliographic in nature. With introduction of a number of online databases containing textual information, news, statistics, commodity prices, etc., a third type of databases holding text of full-length documents started appearing. Several full-text of encyclopaedia, directories and articles from journals are now available online.

Most of the publishers now provide access to their full-text journals through their web site or through other electronic publishing platforms.

While there are a number of public-domain databases, most online databases require annual subscription for accessing them. Thousands of databases are now available on compact discs (CD-ROM) as well as on the Web.

ELECTRONIC JOURNALS

Electronic journals, or 'e-journals', are used for those journals and newsletters that are prepared and distributed electronically. Electronic journals may be defined very broadly as any journal, magazine, e-zine, webzine, newsletter or type of electronic serial publication which is available over the Internet and can be accessed using different technologies such as WWW, Gopher, ftp, telnet, e-mail or listserv. Several traditional journals are now being published both on the Web and in print.

Content lists for most of the journals are available on the Web or distributed to subscribers as an e-mail text messages or through technologies like RSS and Atom. Internet-based electronic journals started to appear in the beginning of 1990. These journals were mostly delivered as an attachment to e-mail while their back issues were mounted on anonymous ftp sites and users were required to download them from these ftp sites. The libraries and information centres made them accessible through their gopher site.

1995 witnessed peak of Gopher technology which then dropped suddenly and dramatically by 1997. With advent of WWW technology in 1993, electronic publishing became more than a novelty, the web as a means of delivery of electronic information has grown steadily Since, then. As publishers experiment with different publication modes and models, the very definition of a journal is undergoing change in the electronic environment.

New journals have evolved based on the graphic capabilities of the Internet that are available only in electronic form. Like print journals, current and archival issues of electronic journals can be browsed through their content pages. Moreover, e-journals can also be searched not only on their metadata but also in full-text through sophisticated search interface. Currently, there are more than 50,000 peer-reviewed, scholarly electronic journals that are available on the Internet.

ELECTRONIC BOOKS

An electronic book is digital reading material that a user can view on a desktop or Personal Digital Assistant (PDA), laptop or on a dedicated, portable device with a large storage capacity and the ability to download new titles via a network connection.

More and more traditional book publishers, as well as those catering to the professional and business communities, are launching their e-book collections. The electronic books market consists of two distinct components, i.e., i) electronic books consisting of digital material or contents; and ii) electronic book hardware including ebook reading appliance, PCs, laptop or PDA.

The digital material or content that make an electronic book are simply textual and graphical files consisting of bits that can be transported any digital storage media or delivered over a network connection. It is designed to be viewed on some combination of hardware and software ranging from dumb terminals to web browsers, on personal computers to the new reading appliances. More and more books are now being released on the web through enhanced interfaces that offer features such as increased search capacity within a book or entire collection of books, ability to highlight and flag a page, ability to make notes on text without damaging the book, ability to e-mail quotes from the books to other colleagues, etc.

Most publishers like Springer, Wiley InterScience, Taylor and Francis, Cambridge University Press, Oxford University Press, etc., offer their e-book collections on subscription/ one-time purchase basis. Besides, there are a number of e-books aggregators that make thousands of books available online for libraries and individuals at relatively lower cost. Three major ebooks aggregators are Questia, Ebrary and NetLibrary. However, just like other e-resources, e-books come with restrictions such as limit on downloads, in terms of number of pages, *i.e.*, one page at a time or one chapter at a time or no download at all.

ELECTRONIC THESES AND DISSERTATIONS

Theses submitted to the universities as requirement for the award of Ph.D. degree constitute a useful source of information for the new and ongoing research. Doctoral dissertations submitted to universities and academic institutions are originally created in digital format using one of the word processing software packages like MSWord, LaTex, Word Perfect, Word Pro, etc.,

or one of the desktop publishing packages like Page Maker, Ventura, etc. These documents are undisputedly highly valuable collection especially in digital format that qualify to be an important component of a digital library. The documents composed on word processing packages/ desktop publishing packages can be easily converted into PDF, Post Script or XML using appropriate software tools so as to host them on the web.

Several universities and institutions have already implemented electronic submission of doctoral dissertations under the overall umbrella of an international digital library initiative called 'Networked Digital Library of Theses and Dissertations' (NDLTD).

AUDIO, VIDEO AND STREAMING MEDIA

Streaming multimedia is sequential delivery of multimedia content, including video, audio or some other learning objects, over a computer network that is displayed (or played back) to the end-user as it is being delivered by the provider.

The advent of the MP3 players and the iPod resulted in a greater effort to deliver downloadable media. Moreover, web documents are now coming with greater integration of text with media. Encyclopaedia now have articles with audio files, video clips and animation to illustrate a given topic. Media can broadly be categorised into three category, namely.

- Commercial movies that have greater copyright restrictions,
- Educational media typically are lesser controlled and many a time are made available free-of-cost; and

- Media targeted for individual users, such as movies and songs, that comes with restrictions in terms of copying and distributions.

SUBJECT GATEWAYS OR LIBRARY PORTALS

The web, being a hypermedia-based system, allows linking amongst electronic resources stored on servers dispersed geographically on distant locations.

The portal sites or gateways redirect a user to the holders of the original digital material. The librarians, being the earliest users of the web, started to gather and organise link to important web-based resources on various subjects. A subject gateway can be defined as facilities that allow easier access to web-based resources in a defined subject area.

The simplest types of subject gateways are sets of web pages containing list of links to resources. Some gateways index their lists of links and provide a simple search facility. More advanced gateways offer a muchenhanced service via a system consisting of a resource database and various indexes, which can be searched and/ or browse throughout a web-based interface.

Subject gateways are also known as Subject-based Information Gateways (SBIGs), subject-based gateways, subject index gateways, virtual libraries, clearing houses, subject trees, pathfinders, etc. Subject gateway is an important component of a library web site designed for the library users so as to help them discover high-quality information on the Internet in a quick and effective way. In the traditional information environment human intermediaries, such as publishers and librarians, filter and process information so that users can search catalogues and indexes of organised knowledge as opposed to raw data and information. Subject gateways work on the same principle, i.e., they employ subject experts and information professionals to select, classify and catalogue Internet resources to aid search and retrieval for the users. Users are offered access to a database of Internet resources descriptions which they can search by keywords or browse by subject area. A description of each resource is provided to help users assess very quickly its origin, content and nature, enabling them to decide if it is worth investigating further.

In the process users get benefited from the expertise of librarians and subject experts with subject gateways rather than having to locate, evaluate, filter and organise the resources themselves. Specialised software are available as freeware or as priced software to create and maintain professionally developed subject gateways.

INFORMATION TECHNOLOGY-BASED LIBRARY SERVICES

New information technology can potentially support a range of traditional and Non-traditional library services. Most of the library services generated using information technology resemble closely to those generated manually with improvements and modifications to suit the requirements of automated services.

OPAC AND WEBPAC

Remote access to the Library catalogues (OPAC) was possible only through a telnet connection before the Web was launched. The web-based interfaces are now available for most of the integrated library software packages including Libsys. Web sites are increasingly providing links to their webPAC instead of telnet links to their Library OPAC.

Exploiting the provisions of hyperlinking that the web provides, various searchable elements of a bibliographic record in a webPAC are hyperlinks to other records in the database. For example, an author is a hyperlink to all records in the database for that author, a series is an hyperlink to all serial title under that series; a keyword for a record is a link to all records in database having that keyword, etc. In effect, a web PAC adds softwarebased functionality to a conventional OPAC. A user has additional incentives to visit the library web page hosting webPAC.

With web-based resources and services in place, many libraries are phasing out their dumb terminals. The library web sites are increasingly becoming a more logical gateway to the catalogue and other web-based library resources. The acceptability of web-based interfaces to the Library OPAC is much greater because web interfaces are familiar to the users with its graphical and navigational interfaces. The users can click complex subjects instead of typing them or remembering complex commands.

INFORMATION ALERTING SERVICES

As the name implies, information alerting services or Current Awareness Services (CAS) are produced by the libraries for their users to alert them about new developments in a given field of study. Information alerting services are issues periodically by the libraries either for internal distribution amongst staff and employees or externally to other users.

The alerting service may be issued as a newsletter reporting new developments, programmes, forthcoming seminars and conferences, events, training programmes, etc. It may also consist of recent additions of books and other documents in the library for a specified time period. Most library integrated system facilitate generation of such a service organised according to subject category for a given time period.

Alerting service may also consist of an indexing service issued by a library or a commercial publisher or a society that regularly indexes the contents of periodicals and some other publications systematically in a specified subject field. Such indexing services are issued at a regular interval. Abstracting services are essentially indexing services wherein an abstract of articles are included in addition to its bibliographic details. Index India and Reader's Guide to Periodical Literature are examples of indexing services. Biological Abstracts, Chemical Abstracts and Index Medicus are example of abstracting services. Most indexing and abstracting services are now available as web-based databases with sophisticated search interface.

Selective dissemination of information (SDI) is a personal form of Current Awareness Service (CAS). It refers to the mechanism of selectively directing new items of information from primary or secondary sources to individuals based on their current interests in a particular subject. SDI is delivered based on a user interest profile which is matched with updates on databases for finding the items of interest for a given user. Push technology or personalisation are more recent terms that are used in place of SDI.

DIGITAL REFERENCE SERVICE

Reference service and imparting instructional training to the library users are key areas of activities for any library. The technology now allows reference librarians to reach out to the users using the network instead of waiting at the reference desk for users to come by. Besides, imparting instructions on mechanisms of using a library, a reference librarian is also involved in delivering reference service that require deep intellectual understanding of subject.

Although automated libraries are not yet sufficiently advanced to offer interactive reference services, electronically-mediated reference services are increasingly available through libraries and information centres. Digital reference service, also called 'Ask-An-Expert' or 'Ask-A-Librarian' services are Internet-based question and answer service that connect users with individuals who possess specialised subject knowledge and skill in conducting precision searches.

As opposed to static web pages, digital reference services use the Internet to place people in contact with people who can answer specific question and instruct users on developing certain skills. The people who serve as digital reference experts (also called volunteers or mentors) are most of the time information specialists, affiliated to various libraries.

LIBRARY CHAT ROOMS

Several libraries have started experimenting with offering

real time digital reference service, using chat software, live interactive communication activities, call counter management software, web contact software, bulletin board services, interactive customer assistance system or related technologies. Many libraries are experimenting with Internet chat technology as an innovative method to extend and enhance traditional and remote reference service.

While digital reference service is asynchronous method of information delivery, the Internet chat providing the benefit of synchronous communication between a user and a reference librarian (or mentor). Interactive reference services facilitate a user to talk to a real, live reference librarian at any time of day or night from anywhere in the world. Unlike with e-mail reference, the librarian can perform a reference interview of a sort by seeking clarifications from the user.

The librarian can conduct Internet searches and push Web sites onto the patron's browser, and can receive immediate feedback from the patron as to whether his or her question has been answered to his satisfaction. Most libraries currently involved in real-time reference service are part of a collaborative network so that they can share staffing and work around the clock to truly provide reference service any time. Library of Congress Collaborative Digital Reference Service is one of such services.

Several institutions including Cornell University, Internet Public Library, Michigan State University and North Carolina University are offering Internet chat-based services using software like LivePerson, AOL Instant Messenger, Conference Room and Netscape Chat. The librarians have observed that their relatively new chat-based service logged significantly more questions in a relatively short time than their well-established e-mail digital reference service. LiveRef(sm) maintains an online registry of real-time digital reference services.

ELECTRONIC DOCUMENT DELIVERY SERVICES

The term 'electronic document delivery systems' implies

delivery of electronic version of a document that might involve reproduction of an electronic copy of a document if it is not available in electronic format. The libraries had been using fax machines for immediate delivery of photocopies of articles via telephone lines.

The first use of electronic document delivery was based on scanning technology. With maturity of scanning equipment and technology, document supply services started scanning the documents as bitmap page images. Applications are built in such a way so as to automatically produce a hard copy together with a header page containing the address of the applicant which can again be send by snail mail or facsimile. A software package known as 'Ariel' is used in several libraries in developed countries for delivery of scanned articles via Internet.

The Ariel software is loaded on an Internet-enabled computer, can receive and send electronic information to other libraries which have installed Ariel. Availability of most of the peer reviewed research journals in electronic format, inexpensive technology to scan articles and improved electronic delivery mechanisms are some of the enabling factors that have contributed to well-established electronic document delivery system now available commercially. More recently most of the secondary services that were available on CD ROM or through online search services are now available on the Internet where the bibliographic references are linked to their full-text on the publisher's site.

The technology has now been perfected and there are several electronic document delivery services that allow a user to download an article in full-text from their site or deliver them electronically as attachment to e-mails. Most electronic publishers and aggregators like OCLC, OVID etc., are offering full-text of articles through their web sites. Different vendors have various payment options; some charge each time the journal is used, whereas others provide open access for a set annual fee. A user who wishes to have the item delivered can enter a credit card number and specify a delivery method (postal, UPS, fax, e-mail, etc.,) and indicate whether it is a rush item (with a rush order fee attached.) The ADONIS (Article Delivery Over Network information Systems) can be considered as a landmark development in electronic document delivery system. The project was launched by a consortium of five major publishers - Academic Press, Blackwell's Scientific Publications (merged with Wiley InterScience), Elsevier Science Publications, and Springer Verlag.

The project uses combination of laser scanning, printing and digital optical storage technology for storage and retrieval of complete pages of over 650 scientific, technical and medical journal articles. The issues of journals are available on CD ROM with weekly updates for distribution to each centre in various countries licensed to use the system for document delivery.

LIBRARY WEB SITES

Libraries are using web technology to create home pages as starting points or as gateways for searching information about the library. A home page reflects characteristics of an academic institution.

It provides an opportunity to the library to propagate its services and facilities to the academic community worldwide. The home pages of libraries are increasingly used as an integrated interface designed to deliver detailed information about a library as well as to provide access to all computer-based services offered by a library.

Several library web sites facilitate virtual guide to the physical facilities including collections, services and infrastructure available in the library through their web sites. Most library web sites provide library layouts and floor plans to guide users to physical location of facilities and services along with link to relevant information. Besides offering information, the library web sites of academic institutions invariably hosts subject gateways or subject portals that contains links to web resources for subjects of interest to the institution. Most of the IT-based library services mentioned in this article are offered through the web sites of libraries.

The library web sites can have features like have Frequently Asked Questions (FAQ) along with their answers, library calendar listing events or show information for forthcoming events, Web forms for inviting feedback. Moreover, libraries may also use bulletin boards, threaded discussion forum and listservs to help promote and evolve web-based library services.

WEB-BASED USER EDUCATION

The www provides a dynamic environment for distributing information over a large network and web-based instructions is a suitable tool to do so. Web-based guides and teaching tools can be easily updated, accessed, and printed on demand. They may include colour graphics and screenshots. The web-based user education provides a high degree of interactivity and flexibility to the users offering them the benefit of self-pace, graduated to teach from basic to highly advanced levels and designed in a wide range of formats that accommodate diverse learning styles.

The proliferation of digital resources will generate greater demands on reference and instructional services. With availability of digital resources that can be used anywhere at any time, requirement for instructional and reference services would also grow. Failure to develop both the technological aspects and required service components would lead to under utilisation of digital resources. The library web sites can use web-based user education for imparting training to users in the following areas:

- Basic library skills along with glossary of library terms;
- Using Library OPAC/ webPAC, locating books, magazines and other library materials;
- Instructions for searching CD ROM and web-based databases and other electronic resources; and
- Instructions on subject searching training, using Boolean operators and searching Internet resources through search engines.

The web technology provides for incorporating both

synchronous and asynchronous interactivity in the web-based user education.

DIGITAL LIBRARIES

The increasing popularity of Internet and developments in web technologies act as catalyst to the concept of digital library. While the Internet serves as the carrier and provides the contents delivery mechanism, the web provides the tools and techniques for content publishing, hosting and accessing. Today's digital libraries are built around Internet and web technologies with electronic journals as their building blocks. The libraries will not become digital libraries, but will rather acquire access to ever growing digital collections on behalf of their users.

Majority of these collections are being made available by external sources like commercial publishers, collections mounted by scholarly societies, resources at other libraries, electronic journal sites, etc. The electronic journals have become the largest and fastest growing segment of digital collections for most libraries.

The Internet has long been a favorite media for experimenting with electronic publishing and delivery. The technology allows creation of fully digitised multimedia products and make them accessible through the Internet. Technological changes, especially the Internet and web technology, continue to attract more and more traditional players to adopt it as a global way to offer their publications to the international community of scientists and technologists. Most of the important publishers now have their web-based interfaces to offer full-text of their journals. The current electronic publishing market consists of traditional players offering electronic versions of their print journals as well as several new enterprises offering new products and services that are 'borne digital'.

The market also has several subscription agents in their new role as electronic aggregators. Besides electronic journals, there are several online databases that are now available through the web including Medline (several versions), AGRICOLA and ERIC. Most online search services like STN and DIALOG also have their web-based interfaces. Reference works like Encyclopaedia, dictionaries, handbooks, atlases, etc., are also making their electronic appearance on the web. However, amongst electronic resources created exclusively for the web, imbibing all features and facilities offered by the new technology, include web-based educational tutorials called 'online courseware'.

The online courseware is proliferating the web as a strong contender for distant education. Telecampus, Canada lists more than 12,000 online courseware available on the web. Moreover, highly specialised web sites are now coming-up in various disciplines which offer information in totality including all kinds of resources in electronic format, EI Engineering Village, ISI Electronic Library, IEEE/ IEE Electronic Library, Engineering Sciences Data Unit are some of the important examples.

CONCLUSION

Rapid growth of information technology, particularly, the Internet and associated technologies, has opened up an entirely new medium for providing improved information services and resources for the users.

As information professionals, we have the opportunity not only to play a leading role in the organisation and navigation using new tools and technologies, but also in the development and maintenance of IT-based services and resources for our users and organisations. With availability of web-based resources and services, the local collection of a library is not the only source of information for a user. The users are interacting virtually with the library collections and resources as well as with host of resources that the librarian did not select or may not even know about them. The librarians can no longer stay behind the desk to wait for the users to come, assuming that the users would approach at the right time and for the right things. The role of library as a primary aggregator of content for its user is less and less unique.

In an environment of self-service databases, electronic forms, web information and the growth of distance education, a user is likely to approach the librarian after he has already begun his search, but was not satisfied with the results. The future will require the librarians to reorient themselves, think creatively and adopt new technology to generate services and resources where their skills of structuring and organising resources are put to its best use. With myriad of disorganised and unverified information, the web is in need of librarians who are trained in the structuring and organising information, have the ability to locate and evaluate information resources, and have in-depth subject expertise.

If the librarians are committed to sustain their roles as providers and facilitator of information in the emerging and competitive space of higher education, they would need to adopt new technology, interact with users to learn about their requirements and expectations. The librarians have to join the academic community as facilitators and collaborators, guide the students through the complex maze of print and digital resources, teaching them how to search effectively and helping them judge the quality and usefulness of the information that they encounter. The opportunities are limitless especially in the chaotic scenario of Internet.

9

Budgeting for Library Technical Services in an Electronic Age

INTRODUCTION

Library technical services include selection, acquisition, cataloguing, classification, typing, binding, conservation, and related services. They can be classed as the 'behind the scenes' services that are done before users can make use of library services. This paper focuses on technical services in an electronic or computer-based library system and the need for budgeting in libraries, including requirements or considerations when budgeting, technical services in a consortium, and best practices in budgeting. Budgeting standards for automated technical services are recommended.

NEED FOR BUDGETING IN LIBRARIES

A budget is a guide or directive for fiscal management. Libraries need funds for services, and these services must be budgeted for. Fletcher gives two definitions of a budget, calling it "the overall picture of ... allocations and ... income," as well as 'the financial allocation for specific purpose or purposes during a given period.'

Although libraries are service-oriented and have little or no revenue-generating motives or objectives, they still obviously require a budget. Technical services are not a significant source of income in the library system. Very small amounts of income are made from reprography and binding, but the amount is infinitesimal compared to the funds expended on technical services. The need for budgets in libraries is increasingly important.

In public institutions, government funding continues to dwindle. The literature that must be managed continues to grow. There is an increasing demand for online resources and services. Libraries must effectively divide funds between staff and materials, which include acquisitions, services, and equipment. Library fiscal management is becoming more decentralised. Current trends give a measure of financial control to divisional, sectional, and unit librarians. It is within this framework that budgeting for library technical services is approached.

TECHNICAL SERVICES BUDGET CONSIDERATIONS

A number of studies have been carried out on budgets and financing of library services; however, budgeting for technical services has received little attention. Most discussions of budgeting for technical services use a line-item budget as a focus. A line budget itemises elements of the budget, which add up to the totality of what the library hopes to spend in any fiscal year.

Perhaps the most important item to budget for in technical services is personnel.Personnel, for these services can be broken into three: Professional staff, technical staff, and auxiliaries. Tools, equipment, and supplies are also important, and services and functions are also included in the technical services budget, as is equipment maintenance.

Those include cataloguing and catalogue maintenance, labeling, binding, serials control, and reprography, as well as others, depending on the type of library and its goals. Especially when libraries are automated, there should be guaranteed sources of funding. Automation is more expensive than manual systems. When libraries are planning for automation, not enough may be allocated and some costs are either underestimated or overlooked.

Smallen and McCredie prescribe solutions that go beyond 'budget dust,' i.e., using funds that come as windfalls, that come occasionally, and that cannot be relied on to be available on an ongoing basis.

TECHNICAL SERVICES WITHIN CONSORTIA

Consortia are a form of cooperation or resource sharing among groups of libraries and information centers. In technical services, cooperative acquisition, joint cataloguing and classification, and shared union catalogues are aspects that are shared. Library consortia encourage participating libraries to digitise collections, create online catalogues, and improve information technology.

For this to happen, technical services must be up to date in skills, equipment, and technology. Ekpenyong calls for renewed consortial efforts among university libraries while identifying constraints that can militate against such projects, including funds, infrastructure for networking, uninterrupted power supply, and training for technical services personnel. Budgeting is most necessary in an emerging ICT environment. The cost of ICT hardware and software is also very high.

There are automated tools and databases for ordering and cataloging, including OCLC's WorldCat, the public catalogs of the Library of Congress, and vendor databases such as Blackwell's Online. The use of these tools has led to the creation of union catalogues. At the University of Botswana Library (UBL) for example, the selection, ordering, receipt, cataloging and routing of materials are done online.

UBL is a member of SABINET, a library consortium in South Africa, and any materials not available in UBL are obtained from other members of SABINET or other document delivery services through the Inter-Library Loan Service. Generally, consortia eliminate replicating processing of the same materials over and over again, thereby cutting costs, time and energy among consortia members.

METHODOLOGY

A questionnaire was used to elicit responses from technical services librarians in the libraries. An Internet search was also conducted, to examine the Web sites of the university and research libraries.

This was to compare them with libraries abroad that were used as models in this research. The research was carried out over a period of three months by research assistants who traveled to the libraries in different parts of Nigeria. One hundred questionnaires were prepared and some were posted to the respondents with self-addressed envelopes for the responses to be mailed back.

The mailing method was not quite successful as many did not respond. Thirty-two University libraries, ten Research libraries, and ten public libraries were eventually surveyed, totaling fifty-two in all, giving a 52 per cent response.

The questionnaires were administered to the technical services librarians or the chief librarian as applicable. The questions concerned the date of establishment, size of the collection, and budget for the current year. It also asked if they budgeted for technical services, and, if so, how much. Those who did not have budgets were asked if they planned to create one. Their general opinion on budgeting for technical services was also sought.

FINDINGS

The response rate shows that budgeting is not given much priority in Nigerian libraries. In many libraries, expenditures are controlled by the chief librarian. Of those questioned, 45 (86.5 per cent) technical services librarians had little or nothing to do with the budget; they simply took what was given them. For 39 (75 per cent), their interpersonal relationship with the chief librarian determined whether they got what they needed for their departments.

Almost all, 51 (98 per cent) said their libraries had no budget for technical services. In the one library (2 per cent) that claimed to have a separate budget had it contained within the general library budget and it was not clearly demarcated. Twenty one (40.38 per cent) of the technical services librarians surveyed have plans to draw up budgets, 18 (34.6 per cent) have no intention of doing so as it is not part of their responsibilities, and 13 (25 per cent) are undecided.

The Internet search was carried out from May 20th to June 20th 2007. It took this long due to electrical power problems. Searches had to be abandoned and resumed when there were power outages Since, there is no alternative power supply for the facility used. Twenty-one Web sites were searched using google. Results showed that some Nigerian University libraries (70 per cent of the 21 studied) do not have links on their Web sites to the library. None of the Web sites examined included information on the funding of their libraries.

This may be due to the fact that libraries in this part of the world are not run like those in the West, where libraries are given priority and publicity. The public library system in Nigeria also is quite different in terms of administration and financing.

BEST PRACTICES

Libraries are storehouses of knowledge. It is unfortunate, however, that 'libraries rarely feature in the top ten priorities of institutional administrators'. This is one of the reasons why even library administrators sometimes treat budgets for libraries lightly.

Whether out of frustration or a lack of grounding in fiscal management, budgets are often ignored in libraries. This is not a good trend, as pointed out by Oyelude, in discussing the state of the art in academic libraries. This Non-chalant attitude may also be due to the 'invisibility' of libraries in the community.

A library must be highly visible to get adequate funding and recognition. User support is very important in this regard. If the users feel the library's impact, they will make demands on the library's behalf. Ubogu asserts that university librarians should be signatories to their library's account(s). He also recommends that the libraries should budget adequately for personnel, so that trained staff do not migrate to greener pastures; budget for maintenance with a fixed percentage. He further advises that software vendors should have a concrete budget and agreement with the library they are serving and funds for staff development should be part of the technical services budget.

It is also good practice for librarians in technical services to become 'lobbyists' to get their budgets approved and implemented. In a situation where so many things are competing for limited resources, one cannot afford to be politically lethargic. Library administrators should lobby for funds maintaining high standards, compiling statistics, and using the statistics to advantage. By implication, the technical services librarian should lobby the chief librarian who should in turn lobby the head of the institution.

Library friends and the community are good tools in advocacy. Understanding the workplace climate and politics involved are also important. It is also best to set priorities in asking for what is reasonable. It is essential to establish a good relationship with the chief librarian, the library accountant, members of the library committee, and others who may be involved with the technical services budget. The best method is to get other people to argue your case with little or no prompting from you. For example, certain services that should be included in the budget should be asked for directly by library users. Technical services should be showcased at every opportunity, including when the library creates exhibits. Technical services should see itself as part of an integrated system and should speak up for other areas of the library when necessary. This will bring about reciprocity when issues concerning technical services are discussed. Most importantly, funds should be judiciously used and wisely disbursed.

MODELS OF LIBRARY BUDGETS

There are a number of useful models for library budgeting. The Sno-Isle Libraries are a large public library system that provides library service to residents of Island and Snohomish counties in Washington State. Each annual budget includes an increase over the previous year, basing the figures on percentages.

For example, technical services had 25.2 per cent of the total budget in 2005, which was increased to 25.6 per cent in 2006. The technical services budget has an appropriate prominence, receiving a quarter of the total library budget. The University of Alberta Library budgets by committing itself to digital collection research, content creation, and access services. They identify staffing for the digital environment as critical for the next few years. They have also planned extensively for technology replacement through 'lifecycle budgeting.' These budgets can serve as models for Nigerian libraries who are trailing behind in the electronic age.

RECOMMENDATIONS AND CONCLUSIONS

In an electronic age, budgeting for libraries and for technical services are of utmost importance. The technical services budget is the framework for running core library activities. No matter how small the resources, a plan must be made and or implemented. Libraries should cultivate the culture of budgeting.

Libraries are complex entities with enormous resources that require planning. It is foolhardy to depend absolutely on the chief/head librarian for all library financial transactions and administration. Some form of financial management system should be used. Librarians should embrace the principle of decentralised budgeting.

Divisional, sectional and unit heads, and subject librarians would then be involved in preparing and managing library budgets. This will enhance managerial skills and democratise fiscal management resulting in more transparency and accountability in the library's financial dealings. Finally, budgeting in library technical services should necessarily include personnel, tools, equipment, and supplies, among other things. In an electronic age where most things have ceased to be done manually, provision for adequate technical services infrastructure is a priority. Summary of Principles:

- Budgeting is essential.
- Use funds judiciously for their original purpose
- Chief librarians should be signatories to their library's account(s)
- Software vendors must have concrete budgets and agreements.
- Technical services budgets should include funds for staff development
- TS librarians must 'lobby.'
- Compile statistics and use to advantage.
- Get other people (*e.g.,* users), to argue your case for you.
- Technical services should be showcased at every opportunity.
- Start your budget late rather than not at all.

10

Spatial Databases and Data Infrastructure

INTRODUCTION

The emergence, in recent years, of digital libraries and of Internet-based communication applications have led some researchers to propose that the emerging data infrastructure of the Internet and the capabilities of digital libraries can be used to organise and ease data-mining digital geospatial data across the Internet. Digital geospatial data interoperability, the target of major efforts by standardisation bodies and the research community Since, the 1990s, 'has been seen as a solution for sharing and integrating geospatial data, more specifically to solve the syntactic, schematic, and semantic as well as the spatial and temporal heterogeneities between various real world phenomena". Some researchers point to the problem that many GIS systems are singular in nature, are generally isolated, and lack interoperability, due in part to the computer architecture upon which they are based.

This chapter will discuss the emergence of a national spatial digital infrastructure vis-à-vis the development of a national telecommunications infrastructure. Federal policies, standards, and procedures will be reviewed that assist in the management and production of geospatial data. Several examples of current geospatial libraries will be examined. The chapter will conclude with a short implications section on what are necessary next steps and future trends.

CHARACTERISTICS OF SPATIAL DATA

Geographic data are comprised of variables that represent real-world phenomena. These can be natural such as climate regions, topographic features, vegetation zones, and other natural processes. They can also refer to entities and objects that represent manmade activities such as buildings, roads, bridges, cable networks. In representing real-world phenomena, researchers use various abstract models that can represent some or many characteristics of the phenomena under consideration. Having been recorded by the individual researcher or captured by mechanical means, the data representing different aspects of the phenomena are often arranged in layers.

The layering of information is representative of the cognitive process. Individuals tend to perceive information about the particular space they occupy by mentally processing inputs from a variety of senses, thereby building up a mental image or map of the area. The layering or thematic ordering of a particular place is thus rendered. Other attributes of real-world phenomena are its spatial characteristics and its temporal characteristics. The definition of space is integrated with not only the cognitive processes associated with human perception, but also of cultural values as well. Culture affects the value and rendering of a conceptual map of particular place.

Other factors helping to define space are found in various classical and contemporary concepts in mathematics, such as Euclidian notions of geometry and measurement. Contemporary ideas of quantum mechanics further add to the concepts of space in the environment by blurring the boundaries of Euclidean geometries. The concept of space in models representing real-world phenomena are also conceptualisations of the space of data features.

It has been noted that "spatial information is always related to geographic space, that is, large-scale space. This is the space beyond the human body, space that represents the surrounding geographic world. Within such space, we constantly move around, we navigate in it, and we conceptualise it in different ways". The most common form of model used for representation of real-world phenomena is the map. Maps are two-dimensional depictions of a particular aspect usually rendered on paper or other print media.

Maps can be general, thematic, and even topographic in nature. Statically depicted phenomena are bound within the parameters of scale and accuracy of the data captured or recorded for depiction. Map scale determines the spatial resolution of the information. The larger the scale, the more detail can be depicted on the map. Determining the correct scale for a particular rendering of spatial data or map generalisation is part of the processes associated with cartography.

Cartographic concepts of data representation and of the graphical layering of data form essential parts of digital geographic databases and geographic information systems. Creating digital representations of real-world phenomena in a database form are discussed next.

CONCEPTUALISING SPATIAL DATABASES

Much like maps, spatial databases store representations of phenomena in the real world. Geographic information systems (GIS) use spatial databases, aka GIS databases. Spatial databases comprise a system, or hierarchy, of data models. The representations of the data and its potential applications across a network area drive its definition. The data model closest to the level of the end user is referred to as a conceptual data model.

To design an effective database, the developer must know how the spatial data will be used and what the intended product will be. The definition at this level will identify what possible applications the spatial data will have, such as flood zone analysis, voting district redistribution, or library user analysis. The "commonly used conceptual data model is the entity-relationship (ER) model; it uses primitives like entity type to describe independently existing entities, relationship type to define relationships between entities, and attributes to describe characteristic values of entities and relationships". A conceptual database schema is the definition for the entire hierarchy of data models. A central assumption for the design of a spatial database schema is that spatial phenomena in a real-world setting exist in Euclidean space.

Complex relationships exist between all the phenomena in the real world. These relationships have a variety of characteristics that give them specific spatial and temporal attributes. The real-world phenomena depicted can also be classified thematically. The thematic classification of data in layers can depend on the purposes for the data depicted.

The data can thus relate to items such as economic zones, library service areas, hydrographic areas, or physical features. Kainz suggests that "the representations of spatial phenomena are stored in a scale-less and seamless manner. Scale less means that all coordinates are world coordinates given in units that are normally used to reference features in the real world. From there, calculations can be easily performed and any (useful) scale can be chosen for visualisation".

As in print maps, the accuracy of the data being recorded or captured is significant in the composition of a spatial database. Information derived from direct observation of phenomena should have the geographic coordinates defined. The accuracy of spatial database attributes is also affected if the data was derived from a secondary source of cartographic information such as a map. The scale of the data from the map would shape the feature coordinates in the database.

An advantage of digital spatial databases is that a database does not depict boundaries between spatial phenomena, such as in map sheet boundaries or other partitions of the geographic space, other than imposed by the spatial features themselves. Spatial databases are real-world models in "that they are scale-less, potentially three-dimensional, dynamic, and seamless. It is easy to query a database, and to combine data from different layers. Spatiotemporal databases consider not only the spatial and thematic but also the temporal extent of the features they represent". (The number of spatial, temporal, and spatiotemporal data models that have been developed is too large to address in this volume). However, the basic elements of a spatial database schema provide a structure in which to design a system for spatial querying and retrieval of information.

ELEMENTS OF DATABASE DESIGN

As discussed earlier, spatial data are representations of real-world phenomena. The digital representation of the real world is often referred to as a digital landscape model (DLM). With the flexibility to represent different characteristics of the features of data at different levels of scale, the DLM is a central component in the processing of spatial data and for analysis. Model generalisation, or conceptual generalisation, refers to the process that uses a geometric component in the model. Generalisation means the reduction in the complexity of information.

Unlike in cartography, which means suppressing unnecessary detail, in database development, generalisation means information abstraction, or the suppression of detail in order to widen the meaning of the information. Utilising the digital landscape model, the user can derive graphic representations of different aspects of spatial data in either digital form or traditional cartographic processes. A common model is the ANSI/SPARC layered model of database architecture.

Three schema, a physical schema, a conceptual schema, and user views, comprise this model. For example, using this model in the building of a spatial database provides organisation to a data set. A schema adds order to the variables in a database. An overall framework (or logical structure that defines the database) is identified and defined as the physical schema. Database variables are mapped and their attribute relationships identified. Concepts can be mapped as well and their relationships are also identified. The first step in organising a spatial database is defining a logical schema for a set of variables. This initial step recognises data categories that outline the parameters of groups of data.

Table 10.1. ANSI/SPARC Architecture Data Models and Schemas

Schemas	Models
Schema	Models used to derive the schema
Extermal views	Based on diffirent in user perspectives, a spatial model is created by defining and describing a subset of the real world.
Conceptual schema	External views synthesized to create conceptual schema using semantic data modelling techniques, for example, the entify-relationship approach.
Logical schema	Conceptual schema transformed into a logical schema using the ralational model. Emphasis is on redundancy removal.
Physical schema	Logical shema mapped into data stuctures and algorithms. A 'hidden' process not accessible or seen by user.

The framework allows for inserting attribute information, which further describes the attributes of the variables. Populating data categories creates a DLM. Since, the DLM is an object-orientated topographic database, its data structure facilitates spatial analysis and linkage of geographic objects to external data. A DLM uses the vector as its primary geometric form, and often contains explicit or implicit topological information.

The objects, their attributes, and the relations between the objects are referred to in terms of real-world entities. Entities are comprised of type classification, attributes, and relationships.

An entity may have one or more attributes, such as a building's (entity) attributes may be its characterising material, such as block, brick, or frame. Attributes describe quantitative data ranked by three levels of accuracy: ordinal, interval, and ratio.

Ordinal (ranked) may rank an entity from 'worst to bad to good to better to best,' interval (numeric) may address an entity's age or income, and ratio (scale) may address the length or area of an entity. Another aspect of designing a database is in evaluating user perceptions of the data.

Since, a database generally serves multiple users or user groups, users may have very different perceptions of the attribute data collected. Each user (or group) receives his or her external view of the database to create a personalised conceptual database schema. Database designers then merge the external views of the data into a single conceptual schema of the database. In designing a database, a conceptual schema is not determined by the parameters of a measurement tool, technique, or paradigm, but by its flexibility, which allows it to deal with the vagueness and uncertainty of defining different aspects of humancentered phenomena in the real world.

After the phenomena types are defined, the conceptual schema is transformed into a logical schema using one of the logical data models, such as a relational data model. Since, each fact should be stored only once in a database, the logical schema allows the development of a redundancy-free dataset. A physical schema is the result of the implementation of the logical schema with particular database management software.

Table. 10.2. Data Modelling

Physical Reality	Real World Model	Data Model	Database	Language
Phenomena	Entity	Object	Object	Symbols Lines
Properties	Type	Type	Type	Text
Connections	Attributes	Attributes	Attributes	Images
	Relationship	Relationship Geometry Quality	Relationship Geometry Quality	Tables Charts

The structure of spatial databases provides a method for libraries with digital geospatial data collections and services to create a system for the discovery and querying of geographic information across the online environment of the Internet. Many of the sources of digital geospatial data, such as private corporations and government agencies, reside in locations across the United States and the globe.

Besides spatial databases, building a digital geospatial collection in an online environment will use a variety of software applications and hardware tools that will assist in the administration of information as it passes from host to user. Next is a brief discussion of the development of some of the applications and protocols utilised in data transfer in the online environment of the Internet.

EMERGENCE OF A TELECOMMUNICATIONS NETWORK

The contemporary information economy emerged as industries in established economic sectors, such as manufacturing and production services, incorporated computer technologies to their daily operations. The concentration of industrial, technological, and social capital of such industries in urban areas enabled the building of advanced telecommunication services.

Firms were able to take advantage of existing telephone lines and exchanges to build new information networks that were quickly using new communication software applications. In 1961, a researcher at RAND for the U.S., Department of Defence, working on how the U.S., telecommunications infrastructure could survive a "first strike, published a proposed digital data communica-tions system based on a distributed network concept".

He introduced the concept of redundancy and the use of message-block (packet-switching) networks with no single outage point as a method of building communications systems to withstand outages. This became the underlying data communications technology for the Internet. The development of ARPANET, created by the Advanced Projects Agency of the U.S., Department of Defence in 1969, was an early catalyst in the integration of computer and telephone technologies, and enabled the exchange of information related to scientific study occurring in advanced computing centers.

In the beginning, ARPANET's architecture consisted of 4 nodes (sites) located at the University of California at Los Angeles, the University of California at Santa Barbara, the University of Utah, and Stanford Research Institute. Early experimentation with the system resulted in the creation of Telnet, an openly accessible public packet data service that allowed a computer operator at a terminal or PC to log onto a remote computer, run a Programme, and initiate FTP, an early file transfer protocol (FTP). The CCITT (International Consultative Committee on Telephony and Telegraphy) approved the first guidelines for X.25, a network protocol using virtual circuits that became the backbone of the TCP/IP (Transmission control protocol/Internet protocol) protocol.

Table. 10.3. TCP/IP Protocol

Layer	Function	Protocols Used
Process (Application) Layer	'Higher level' protocols, such as SMTP, FTP, SSH, HTTP, and so forth operate in this layer.	SMTP, FTP, SSH HTTP, DHCP, IMAP4, IRC, MIME, POP3, SIP, SNMP, TELET, TLS/SSL, RPC, RTP,SDP, SOAP.
Host to Host (Transport) Level	Flow control and connection protocols live here. Opens and maintains connections. Ensures packets are actually received.	TCP, UDP, RSVP DCCP, SCTP.
Internet (Internet) working Layer	Defines IP addresses and routing schemes for navigating packets from one IP address to another Performs network Segmentation/desegmentation desegmentation and error control functions.	IP, UDP, BGP, ICMP, IGMP IGP, RARP.
Data Link Layer	Responsible for node to node (hop to hop) packet delivery	ATM, Bluetooth, DTM, Ethernet, FDDI, Frame relay, GPRS, PPP Modems, Wi-Fi

(Contd...)

Physical Layer	Describes the physical equipment necessary for communication, such as twisted pair cables, the signaling used on level protocols using that signaling. communication	Bluetooth RF, Ethernet physical layer, ISDN, Modem, RS232 SONET/SDH, USB, Wi-Fi, Power line

Why is a communication protocol important? Communication between computers means sending messages from one machine to another. There are three types of communication. Simplex communication is message travel in only one direction. Half-duplex communication is asynchronous message travel in both directions.

Halfduplex communication is not simultaneous, for example, much like using ham radio, the first person must say 'over' at the end of his communication so the person at the other end knows that it is his turn to talk. Full-duplex communication is simultaneously sending and receiving messages in both directions simultaneously, with no lags or gaps in the transmission or receipt.

Obviously, addressing mechanisms that allow unique identification of senders and receivers are very important. Other critical mechanisms are rules on how data travels, error-detection and error-correction, disassembling and reassembling long messages, avoiding data overflow due to fast transmitters and slow receivers, and routing of messages.

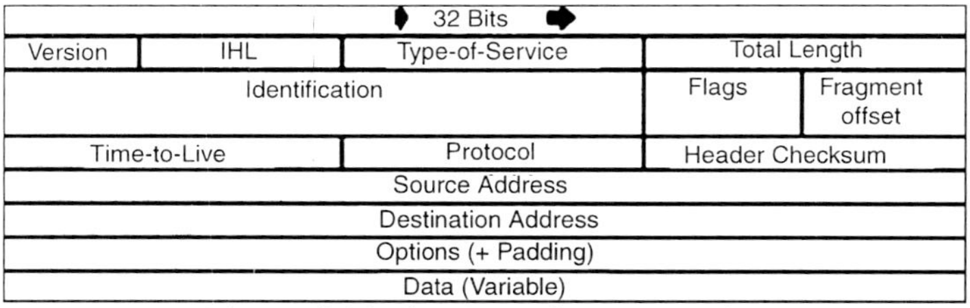

32 Bits				
Version	IHL	Type-of-Service	Total Length	
Identification			Flags	Fragment offset
Time-to-Live		Protocol	Header Checksum	
Source Address				
Destination Address				
Options (+ Padding)				
Data (Variable)				

The 14 Fields that Comprise an IP Packet

TCP/IP is the basic communication language, or protocol, of the Internet and for private networks (*e.g.*, intranets or extranets). TCP/IP communication is primarily a point-to-point protocol (PPP), meaning each communication is from one point (or host computer) in the network to another point (or host computer). There are five layers to the TCP/IP protocol. The higher layer, the transmission control protocol, disassembles a message or file into smaller packets that are transmitted over the Internet and received by a TCP layer that reassembles the packets into the original message.

The third layer, the Internet protocol, handles the address part of each packet so that it gets to the right destination. TCP/IP and the higher-level applications that use it are collectively said to be 'stateless' Since, every client request is considered a new request and unrelated to any previous request. Being stateless frees network paths so that everyone can use them continuously, unlike 'dedicated' lines, such as plain old telephone service (POTS) or fax lines.

By the late 1980s and early 1990s, the Web was accelerating away from a dedicated mainframe environment to a distributed client-server system. This distributed system challenged the development of new protocols. Considering the variety of personal computers, simple terminals, servers as well as platforms, and operating systems, requirements for new protocols had to be simple, cross-platform, and Non-computer specific.

Based upon the idea of HyperCard, Berners-Lee of the Conseil Européen pour la Recherche Nucléaire (CERN; European Council for Nuclear Research) developed hypertext transfer protocol (HTTP) and its accompanying text format, hypertext mark-up language (HTML).

HTML was based on SGML (standard generalised mark-up language), an internationally agreed upon method for marking up text into structural units, such as paragraphs, headings, and so forth, that was Non-machine, Non-platform specific. Two significant components of HTTP and HTML are the use of hypertext links to 'anchor' items to each other inside and outside the 'page' and the 'www' naming protocol (URL) used for addressing Websites.

A uniform resource locator (URL) consists of three parts: the name of the protocol (http), the host name where the page resides, and the name of the hypertext document (home.htm). HTTP, TCP/IP, FTP, Telnet, and SMTP form a 'suite' of protocols that Internet users use as a matter of course. Building on a basic design of a document-sharing protocol, the Web eventually developed into a medium for the creation of a variety of Web sites that met myriad individual and organisational demands and needs. Although many of the top-level domains of the net were still educational, much of the early development of the Internet occurred in the private sector, with Internet service providers (ISPs), such as America Online (AOL).

From its beginning as a specialised dial-up service for Apple Macintosh users in 1989, within 6 years AOL had a million subscribers. This was a substantial inroad in an environment where there were about 20 to 30 million users. The success of these early Internet service providers triggered tremendous growth in the number of Websites during the second half of the 1990s. The availability of inexpensive access through local land telephone lines and relatively cheap cost of transmitting data. The number of commercial (.com or dot com) domains increased from around 1 million in 1994 to nearly 25 million at the beginning of 2000, while other categories of users (.net,.mil,.org, and.gov) added another 19 million domains, of which 15 million were cable-based net service providers.

The development of HTTP and HTML spawned thousands of new sites and inspired new information services, such as 'browsers', 'search engines', and 'portals' to enable net users to find information of interest. More specialised and powerful search engines continue to emerge, including the current leader, Google.

Additional Web-based services, and continued growth depended on the established telecoms or cable TV systems and their telephone wire infrastructure. Rapid development of the Internet in the 1990s was accompanied by a simultaneous investment in construction of new telephone access lines in the United States.

Investment in new lines by major carriers in the United States increased 32 per cent between 1990 and 2000 from 119.8 million to 157.6 million lines. The number of the new lines that incorporated ISDN (integrated services digital network) technology was 129.6 million, an increase of over 850 per cent from the previous number of 13.6 million.

Transmitting data at speeds ranging from 128 kilobits per second to over 150 megabits per second, ISDN networks support a wide of range of simple to complex voice and Non-voice services, and allow for the transmission of multiple channels of information, such as voice, data, fax, and video, over a single wire.

The spatial distribution of ISDN-technology-enabled networks across the United States is uneven, with a concentration of high-speed data lines in areas that have the necessary infrastructure for its development. Broadband, defined as 200 megabits per second of data output, is about fourtimes faster than a 56 Kbps dial-up modem and about eight-times faster than most people's actual download speeds, Since, many IPS's modems offer a maximum of 28.8 Kbps. Since, many contemporary computer applications, for example, music clips, video clips, and streaming video, use considerable amounts of bandwidth, broadband access is growing as an essential Internet service expectation. These graphics intensive applications have many business and entertainment functions, and are not possible at lower dial up Internet connections.

Broadband Internet access is usually provided through digital subscriber line (DSL) technology. Data on the Regional Bell Operating Companies indicate that more than 56 per cent of all cities with populations above 100,000 had DSL available, but less than 5 per cent of cities with populations less than 10,000 had DSL service. A number of ISPs have been building data lines in predominately rural areas. These ISPs tend to be small businesses that fill in gaps in data line access where no larger telecommunication firms are present. Since, the costs of establishing Internet service warrant a subscriber base of at least 200 households, some small telephone exchanges are too small to sustain an ISP of that size. The rural ISPs offer dial-up access in low bandwidth transmission formats. Most of the Internet services in rural areas tend to be related to e-mail and e-commerce transactions. If access to more services or larger bandwidth is required, costs are significantly higher for the user as well as the ISP, Hence,, Internet use in rural areas is held down by higher costs.

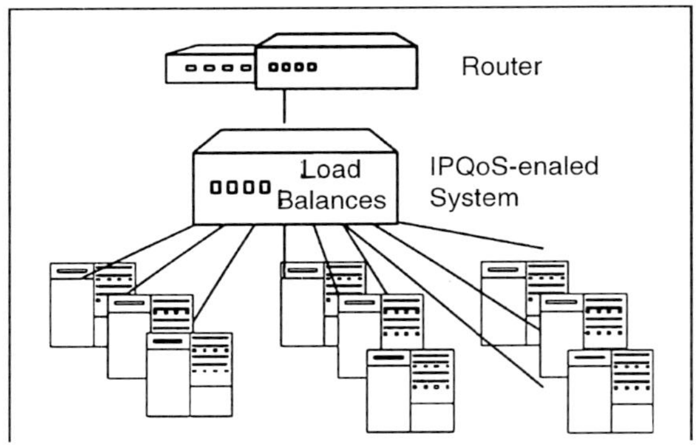

Serer Farms

The economics of Fibre optics can be expensive for urban connections as well. In situations where new trenches must be dug for the cable, installing Fibre in metro areas can run in the hundreds of thousands of dollars per mile.

Although installation cost can often be reduced by intensive use of existing infrastructure, it is difficult to justify the investment when existing phone lines can deliver adequate bandwidth via ADSL (Asymmetric Digital Subscriber Line) technology. ADSL is a modem technology that transforms POTS (plain old telephone service) lines into high-speed digital lines. By splitting an existing telephone line signal into two, one for voice and the other for data, ADSL technology can work at up to 8-Mbps download. Since, the baseband is occupied by POTS, should ADSL fail, POTS service is guaranteed. Similar to telephone switching centers, the Internet requires specialised host computers called servers and routers. Servers are typically clustered in so-called 'server farms' around the world, located in urban areas where most of the traffic originates. Server farm capacity is currently increasing at an annual rate of 50 per cent.

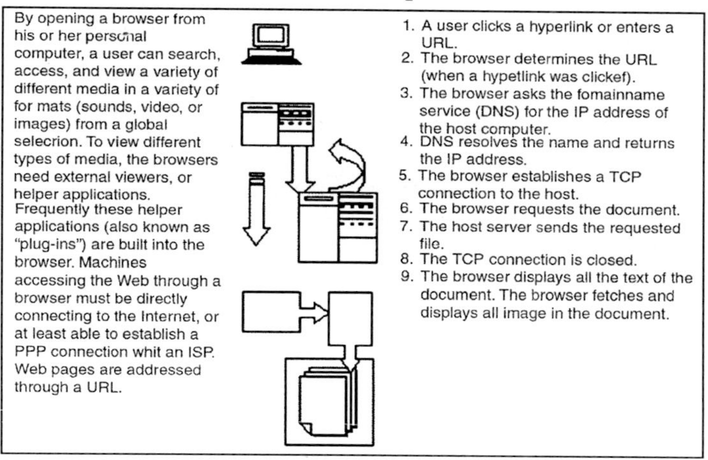

Putting it all together: Retrieving Data from the Web

One of the biggest providers is Exodus Communications, with 9 server farms in Silicon Valley alone and 35 more in big cities around the world. Think of server farms as 'wholesalers' in the Internet and the 'data caches' as retailers, located around the world near consumers of content. Technically, the function of the data caches is to recombine the individual packets of data, dispatched by the routers by different routes (because of changing conditions from moment to moment), into coherent streams designated for final customers. The leader in this field is Akamai, with 11,000 caching servers in 62 countries. Akamai's customers are the content providers (including CNN and Yahoo!).

The net result of all this investment was to create an oversupply of long-distance Fibre-based carrier capacity, without a matching growth in local broadband access capacity for which the established telecoms retained their monopoly (except where cable TV was also available). As of early 2002, long-distance optical Fibre channel capacity is said to be only 2 per cent–5 per cent utilised, whereas local access in many places outside the biggest cities, still dependent on copper wires, is badly congested. The limiting factor is electric power consumption, especially as the farms get larger (one new server farm, being built by iXguardian near London, will have its own gas-fired power plant). By opening a browser from his or her personal computer, a user can search, access, and view a variety of different media in a variety of formats (sound, video, or images) from a global selection.

To view different types of media, the browsers need external viewers, or helper applications. Frequently these helper applications (also known as 'plug-ins') are built into the browser. Machines accessing the Web through a browser must be directly connected to the Internet, or at least able to establish a PPP connection with an ISP. Web pages are addressed through a URL.

- A user clicks a hyperlink or enters a URL.
- The browser determines the URL (when a hyperlink was clicked).
- The browser asks the domain name service (DNS) for the IP address of the host computer.
- DNS resolves the name and returns the IP address.
- The browser establishes a TCP connection to the host.
- The browser requests the document.
- The host server sends the requested file.
- The TCP connection is closed.
- The browser displays all the text of the document. The browser fetches and displays all images in the document.

Building on the data transfer capabilities of the Internet, also known as the World Wide Web, and its accompanying telecommunication infrastructure, the online environment of the Internet is rapidly becoming a standard platform for GIS as government agencies and private companies begin to exploit the data exchange capabilities of the Internet.

CHARACTERISTICS OF DISTRIBUTED SPATIAL DATABASES

Spatial data infrastructures are based on large amounts of spatial data distributed over many agencies. The survey of the information economy indicates that industries in the information sector rely on efficient data transfer between organisations and users for their operations. Even though spatial databases may have useful socioeconomic purposes, a system linking many spatial databases would have far greater applications in the distributed environment of the information sector. What is the structure of a distributed spatial database system? First, two components, a database and a database management system, comprise a database system. The database (DB) is an organised collection of stored data; the database management system (DBMS) is software for building and maintaining a database. The strength of a database system is in its design. It contains a number of features, such as 'persistency, storage management, recovery, concurrency control, ad hoc queries, and data security,' that allow for the efficient processing of data. A persistent storage capability allows data to exist independently of the application of a Programme.

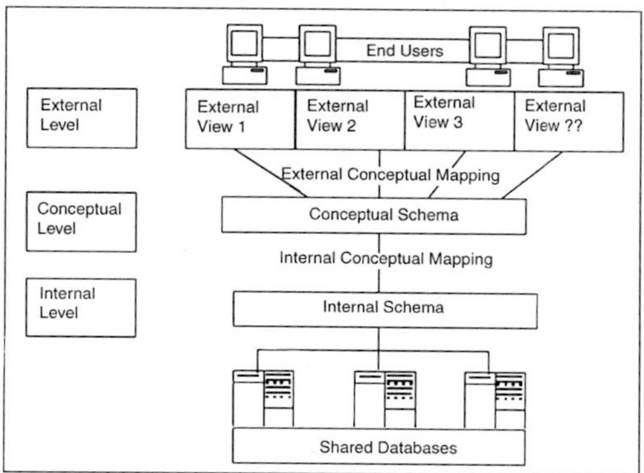

Visual Representation of the ANSI/SPARC Architechure

The ability to recover data is important in the workings of a spatial database system. If in the execution of a Programme is not successful, the database management system can return the database to its former state before the attempted software application or to its former uncorrupted state. A concurrency control mechanism is also part of the normal operations of a distributed spatial database system. Its purpose is to avoid inconsistencies caused by concurrent read and write operations to the database and security access to the server on which the database is located.

The ability of the database system to offer access to multiple users is also based on having data access security delineations. The architecture of most databases is based on the standards of the ANSI/SPARC Study Group on Database Management Systems. These databases have three levels: internal, conceptual, and external level.

The external level is closest to the user, the internal level is closest to the physical storage, and the conceptual 'exists in the middle.' Although individual users may have different external views on the database, there is only one conceptual view and one internal view. A data definition language (DDL) defines the views.

A data manipulation language (DML) describes the processing of the database objects. Databases store models of conceptualised real-world phenomena. In the design process of a database, several data models are used to describe the various feature attributes of the variables in the database. A data model describes the contents and organisation of the data. As discussed earlier, they can be classified into conceptual, logical, and physical data models. Proceeding with the variable feature descriptions as defined by the various data models, the data are then organised as conceptual model.

The next step would be to construct a logical data model. A database management system can then implement the logical data model. An example of a logical data model is the relational data model, which is in widespread use among desktop GIS users using commercial software. A relational data model is characterised by a clear distinction between the graphical and descriptive data of features representing real-world elements.

Graphical elements are stored in layers of the digital map file and attribute data is stored in the form of a relational database table. Spatial features on the digital map are linked through the identifier with the record of the relational database table containing further descriptive data of the feature. A commonly used language for the relational database model is structured query language (SQL). Supported by all major relational DBMS vendors, SQL is both a data definition and data manipulation language.

In a spatial data infrastructure, many databases are distributed over many organisations across a network, and are interconnected through a communication network. Every site runs a unique database management system. Local applications operate on local hardware, while distributed or global applications can involve multiple sites on the data infrastructure. The design process for distributed databases builds on the design process for most database design, that is, it has a conceptual step, logical step, and physical design phase step.

An additional design dimension is the distribution design step. The integration into a network introduces a number of design ideas to the building of distributed databases, such as distribution transparency, fragmentation, and replication. Distribution transparency indicates that most users do not know where the data in a database is actually located. Replication, where duplicate datasets may be stored in different locations, and fragmentation, when different parts of a dataset may be stored on different servers, are frequently performed for security and practical reasons.

In both cases, the user always perceives a centrally located database. Kainz notes that 'there are two possible approaches to the design of distributed databases: top down and bottom up. The top-down design is applied to new databases that are designed from scratch'.

Many GIS data producers and providers participate in the United States Federal Geographic Data Committee (FGDC) data infrastructure initiative. A system of distributed spatial databases that provide users with access to myriad federal, state, and local datasets, the central component of the data infrastructure is the 'clearinghouse'. Originally defined as a 'system of software and institutions to facilitate the discovery, evaluation, and downloading of digital geospatial data,' today the FGDC defines a clearinghouse as "a community of distributed data providers who publish collections of metadata that describe their map and data resources within their areas of responsibility, documenting data quality, characteristics, and accessibility. The FGDC clearinghouse(s) also address the descriptive component of the data through the use of metadata". The clearinghouse computer systems integrate many interoperating metadata servers, using a distributed, client-server architecture.

On the client side, the most common software application is usually browser-based, such as Internet Explorer or Netscape Navigator. A client residing on computer X can interact with server Y, located at another location, using a set of instructions called protocols. Since, most traffic on the Internet uses the TCP/IP (transmission control protocol/ Internet protocol), the TCP/IP software suite is frequently embedded in a computer's operating system (OS) software, such as in Microsoft Windows, MAC OS X, Unix, and Linux free ware.

One protocol selected to provide search interoperability among different servers is the ISO 10163-1995 search and retrieve protocol. The Z39.50, initially developed for the library community, contains client and server software that establishes a connection, relays a query, returns the query result, and presents retrieved documents in various formats.

DATABASES, WEB SERVICES, AND INTERNET GIS

There are a number of advantages to a GIS that is available from the Internet including world wide accessibility, use of a standard interface, and cost-effective maintenance.

The traditional model of GIS is a system that consists of a single software package, and accompanying data on a single machine. With the advent of distributed producers and consumers of digital geospatial data, this model is no longer valid. As Green and Bossomaier note "many GIS projects are often multi-agency, multi-disciplinary, multi-platform, and multi-software. Large numbers of contributors may be involved, and there may be a large pool of potential users". Further, "a central practical issue is how to provide widespread, device-independent access to GIS for large numbers of contributors and users".

The essential differences between a traditional GIS and an online GIS are the 'separation of user interface, data storage, and processing'. In stand-alone GIS, all of the elements are within a single machine; in an online environment, the elements are distributed across many computers. During the 1980s, GIS was conceptualised strictly as a software application: A computer based system that provides the following four sets of capabilities to handle georeferenced data:

- Input;
- Data management;
- Manipulation and analysis; and
- Output.

This definition is accurate when conceptualising GIS as an application; however, it does not address GIS as an interactive system where hardware, software, data, methods, and people come to create geographic knowledge for distribution. In the early 1990s, the concept of a GIS system evolved.

ESRI, a privately held consulting firm, defined GIS as an "organised collection of computer hardware, software, geographic data, and personnel designed to efficiently capture, store, update, manipulate, analyse, and display all forms of geographically referenced information".

The exploitation of geospatial data within diverse policy environments, allied with the increasing attention being afforded to cross-discipline social and environmental issues, has led to the demand for infrastructures to assist in the discovery, dissemination, and exploitation of geospatial data. The authors also note that the structures are often referred to as spatial data infrastructures (SDIs). " Most SDIs will integrate geospatial data and metadata, which can provide the means to access the data and also establishes the needed licensing agreements between users to make use of the data". The diverse information services of SDIs mirror information services of digital libraries, the latter defined as a collection of services and the collection of information objects that support users in dealing with the information objects and the organisation and presentation of those objects through electronic means.

Three significant factors of SDIs are the provision, organisation, and presentation of information and services to a specific group of users. By integrating with the digital library environment, the process of mining through digital geospatial data becomes more varied with additional data added to the original projection datum. In delivering digital geospatial data over the Internet, the identification, retrieval, and delivery of information in a virtual environment is described as a "URL-addressable resource that performs functions and provides answers". Web services are described as an "encapsulation of existing software functionality in a common form that allows the services it performs to be visible and accessible to other software applications".

The single Web services-based application can request services from other Web services, and can expect to receive the results or responses from those requests in an expected form. One advantage of Web services technology is its ability to interoperate in a loosely coupled manner, an 'ask and wait' approach. The user can request a certain type of service across the network, and wait for responses. Web services can also be found and used by other applications, agents, and clients on the Internet.

In a digital geospatial data retrieval system, a Web service can be published inside or outside the host's firewall by providing a document describing its operation and function. Using the Web services definition language (WSDL) mark-up language, the core of the document may illustrate a service when interpreted on a national grid reference responds with relevant coordinates on the host's mapping system. The document then described how the service is prompted and what the executables are.

The document can also be published to a node, a clearinghouse, or other Internet site using the Universal Discovery, Description, and Integration (UDDI) registry. Parson also notes that communication between Web services pass "XML messages wrapped in an interoperable framework to allow the messages to cross different networks, use different application architectures and systems". The widespread use of digital geospatial data by a number of different individuals and agencies in both the public and private sectors will continue to create large amounts of archived data.

To make such data sets searchable across the environment of the Internet, librarians must be willing to take a varied approach in determining the appropriate metadata scheme to enable effective mining across the World Wide Web. A significant factor in the development of Web GIS services and in online services in digital libraries has been the National Spatial Data Infrastructure initiative by the Federal Geographic Data Committee.

ORGANISING A NATIONAL DATA INFRASTRUCTURE

In 1994 the Federal Geographic Data Committee (FGDC) recommended that a National Spatial Data Infrastructure (NSDI) be organised. The NSDI would be an "umbrella of policies, standards, and procedures under which organisations and technologies interact to foster more efficient use, management, and production of geospatial data". The NSDI was conceptualised as fostering more cooperation and interaction between different organisations from the public and private sector.

The recommendation was a response to alterations in the traditional flows of data across the government based on new convergences of information, computer technology, and communication. A significant component of the data being used in government transactions and commercial transactions was digital geospatial data.

The FGDC considered digital geospatial data as being critical to solving many 'environmental, economic, and social problems.' The FGDC had also recognised that 'the use of GIS technologies for the digital analysis of spatial problems had become pervasive'. With the integration of GIS and increased use of geospatial data into problem-solving operations, a major goal of the NSDI was to make 'an environment to respond to the current need of digital geospatial data.'

The FGDC envisioned building the framework around the procedures, technology, and guidelines that enhance integration, sharing, and use of these data, and the institutional relationships and business practices that encourage the maintenance and use of data. The framework would represent the best available data for an area, and be certified, standardised, and described according to a common standard. Today, the FGDC standards provide a foundation on which organisations can build by adding their own detail and compiling other data sets.

MEETING DIGITAL GEOSPATIAL DATA NEEDS

The FGDC reported that many billions of dollars are spent by organisations on an annual basis in both the public and private sector in attempts to manage digital geospatial data. With digital geospatial data becoming a valuable asset within the business practices of many public and private sector organisations, most organisations can only afford to collect or purchase only a small portion of information they require. Often only the most basic digital geospatial data is acquired by organisations, usually a dataset that pertains to a specific geographic area or that has some unique attribute characteristics.

The datasets are often incompatible with other datasets, due to differences in software platforms. Researchers at the FGDC found that data collected by differing organisations may be similar in geographic extent use different geographic bases and standards. Hence, many of the resources organisations spend on geographic information systems (GIS) go towards duplicating other organisations' data collection efforts. The same geographic data themes for an area are collected again and again, at great expense.

A data framework would improve the ability for organisations to share data. The framework would provide a basic geographic data in a common format and an accessible environment that anyone can use and to which anyone can contribute. In this environment, users can perform cross-jurisdictional and cross-organisational analyses and operations, and organisations can funnel their resources into applications, rather than duplicating data production efforts.

Researchers at the FGDC further noted in their findings that "geographic data users from many disciplines have a recurring need for a few themes of basic data: geodetic control, orthoimagery, elevation, transportation, hydrography, governmental units, and cadastral information.

Many organisations produce and use such data every day. The framework provides basic information for these data themes. By attaching their own geographic data, which can cover innumerable subjects and themes, to the common data in the framework, users can build their applications more easily and at less cost. The seven data themes provide basic data that can be used in applications, a base to which users can add or attach geographic details and attributes, a reference source for accurately registering and compiling participants' own data sets, and a reference map for displaying the locations and the results of an analysis of other data. Researchers at the FGDC envision the information framework to be an evolving data resource to which geographic data producers can contribute.

Integral components of the information network incorporate procedures, guidelines, and technology to enable participants to build, integrate, maintain, distribute, and use framework data. These elements ensure that users can depend on accurate, detailed data that can be certified and integrated into the framework to create a trustworthy data source; users can update their data holdings from the framework data; and users can attach additional information to the framework". These procedures would ensure the standardisation of datasets and enable the efficient transfer of digital geospatial data across the Internet.

The FGDC envisions the information framework integrating data from all types of organisations in both the public and private sector. The framework environment is designed to be responsive to the needs of the geographic data community in terms of 'data creation and maintenance, and provides unrestricted access to data'.

A COOPERATIVE INFORMATION NETWORK

The FGDC also envisions organisations building the information framework by coordinating data development activities. Organisations can coordinate framework data along two dimensions. The first dimension emphasises opportunities for organisations with similar needs. An example is a metropolitan area in which local governments, their customers, state and federal agencies with facilities in the area, utilities, and others require high-resolution spatial data for their operations.

In this case the framework provides a starting point for sharing the commonly needed geographic base information and allows each organisation to add the unique information it requires to meet its business needs. The second dimension emphasises opportunities for organisations needing different amounts of detail for an area. For example, a local government, a regional transportation planning organisation, and a state transportation agency may require road data for an area, but at different levels of geography.

For efficient data sharing the organisations would have to share the results of their individual efforts and would benefit from using a common geographic base and generalised data created from this base. The framework provides a starting point for a base and the data generalised from it, providing the organisations with contemporary and consistent data for decision making and helping them avoid confusion caused by differences in the vintages, common attributes, and other characteristics of the base data. The framework is being developed by this entire community, with organisations from all areas playing roles.

For some, the framework will supply the data they need to build applications. Others will contribute data, and some may provide services to maintain and distribute data. Some organisations will play several roles in framework development, operation, and use. An essential community partner in the information network can be libraries. Librarians have the skills and experience needed to help the information network to facilitate digital geospatial data and to aid in its search and mining procedures. Some researchers have advocated the 'geolibrary' as a possible model for a library to facilitate digital geospatial data.

DIGITAL GEO-LIBRARIES AND DIGITAL COLLECTIONS

One approach used by librarians in making digital geospatial data available to their users is to incorporate Web-based mapping functions with their library geospatial information holdings. Such efforts combine the locational aspects of the metadata descriptions of the geospatial data in the catalog with the mapping capabilities of GIS software. In building Web-based functions into their geospatial collections, some libraries have termed their collection a 'digital geolibrary.'

Different perspectives about geolibraries have been discussed in the scholarly geography and information science literature such as from Boxall and Goodchild. Goodchild refers to a geolibrary as being comprised of georeferenced information that can be accessed by a geographic footprint. Likewise, in his discussion of geolibraries, Boxall notes that their scope extends beyond the traditional map library if the construct of a geolibrary is based upon the idea that information has a geographic footprint. His discussion references earlier research that explains georeferenced information as including such things as photographs, videos, music, and literature that can be given a locational variable that defines a footprint. The collection areas of geolibraries extend beyond the traditional scope of map libraries and archives to include almost all information contained within libraries.

He later mentions that it can include information outside of libraries as well. This is the theoretical basis for what we now view as geolibraries. Boxall discusses that a significant focus of geolibraries is on digital information and metadata, as well as the distributed nature of the libraries and 'collections.'

He adds that "... Distributed geolibraries provide a useful framework for discussion of the issues of dissemination associated with the National Spatial Data Infrastructure (NSDI)". The vision is readily extendible to a global context. Boxall feels any discussion of 'Digital Earth' (DE), the 'Global Spatial Data Infrastructure' (GSDI), and 'Distributed Geolibraries' should be framed around the broadest definitions of information and infrastructures; namely to include and focus upon the people, technology and organisations which give rise to and sustain such infrastructures'.

An early significant effort at establishing a digital spatial library was the Alexandria Digital Library at the University of California Santa Barbara. The Alexandria Digital Library was one of six federally funded library projects. The U.S., National Science Foundation founded it in early 1994.

The Library's collection and services focus on georeferenced information: maps, images, data sets, and other information sources with links to geographic locations. Much of the information in the collection was primarily of the University's service area, or Southern California. A key aspect of the collection is the ability to perform data queries and retrieve results by geography location. The basic means of describing and finding information is with a geographic footprint. A footprint depicts the location on the surface of the earth associated with either an object in the collection such as a map, remote sensed image, or aerial photograph, or with a user's query.

The footprint may be represented as a point or polygon, with latitude and longitude coordinates. As a user queries the collection through a user interface, the user creates a footprint or an interactive map to indicate the area of interest. The query area is matched with the object footprints in the metadata to retrieve relevant objects about the query area. This approach to query structure allows the user to choose arbitrary query areas and is not limited to geographic areas with place names. The objects in the collection that fall within a particular query area do not have to have the names associated with them that the user enters for a text based query.

By translating a user's textbased query into a footprint query for a certain geographic area, the user can retrieve all types of information about a location such as remote sensed images, data sets, aerial photographs, and textual information. The catalog for the Alexandria Digital Library is configured for searches that will retrieve objects that are either in an online format or physical location as a map. Using the Alexandria Digital Library as a model, the Idaho Geospatial Data Center was started in 1996 by a team of geographers, geologists, and librarians. The aim of the team was the establishment of digital library of public domain geographic data for the state of Idaho. As a theoretical and practical foundation for their digital spatial collection, which they termed a 'geolibrary,' the team used a set of parameters as defined by Goodchild.

Goodchild defined a geolibrary's components as including a browser or specialised software application running on the user's computer and providing access to the geolibrary through a computer network. A geolibrary also includes a 'basemap' or geographic frame of reference for the browser's queries. A basemap would provide an image of an area corresponding to the geographical extent of geolibrary collection. The basemap would depend on the scale of the search being performed from a large geographic area, such as a state, or a smaller location, as a city block.

A gazetteer or index that would link place names to a map would also be included. A large collection of collection catalogs would be maintained on distributed computer servers. The servers would be accessed over a network with the browser, using basic server-client architecture. A geolibrary would ideally provide open access to many types of information with geographic referenced queries regardless of the storage media. Using a grant from the Idaho Board of Education's Technology Incentive Programme, the team built a geographic digital data repository or the Idaho GeoSpatial Data Center (IGDC).

The library contained a number of digital geospatial datasets that was searchable through a flexible browsing tool. The collection contained a number of public domain information such as Digital Line Graphs and Digital Raster Graphics from the United States Geological Survey and U.S., Bureau of the Census TIGER boundary files for the state of Idaho. The site provided an interactive visual analysis of selected demographic/economic data for Idaho counties.

The site also contained interactive links to other Idaho and national spatial data repositories. A key aspect of the IGDC's collection was the development of the GeoLibrary's browser, which was implemented using MicroSoft Visual Basic 5.0 and ESRI MapObjects technology. The interface of the browser consisted of three panels resembling the Microsoft Outlook user interface.

A first panel, a map panel, would be used to explore the geographic coverage of the geolibrary and to select an area of interest. A second panel in the interface was where the query would be performed. The final panel is where the query results would be displayed for analysis and to download spatial data. In many ways, librarians are well aware of the ideas outlined in the discussion on the concepts and components for digital data infrastructure. Library collections and services in electronic form, such as a digital library, integrate many aspects of the client-server architecture in providing access to materials in an online distributed environment.

Digital libraries have in them collections of digital information objects of various formats in an ordered database defined by descriptive data standards. Organised in a regular manner, the database is searchable using query applications via a user interface, usually through an online catalog. Information is compartmentalised in short descriptions using metadata tags to ease search and retrieval applications. The overall structure is guided by administrative oversight that takes into account the needs of the various users involved in the community.

Researchers, such as researcher, envision an intersection of the concepts of the digital library and that of the spatial data infrastructure in a sort of 'geolibrary'. Goodchild envisions a geolibrary as a library filled with 'georeferenced information that can have a geographic footprint.' Including multimedia, images, and music that could be assigned a location attribute, geolibraries would thus extend beyond the scope of a traditional map library, and provide new services and resources for users to discover.

The survey of the characteristics of spatial data databases and related infrastructure indicate the involvement of many different factors in assembling a data infrastructure. However, in addition to data providers, databases, metadata, data networks, technology, and institutional arrangements, there is also a significant in organisational and human resource factors. Researchers. offer six talking points that are essential to consider in building a spatial data infrastructure. These include technology, policies and standards, human resources, institutional arrangements, spatial data and metadata, and data networks. They suggest that spatial data infrastructure should not recreate the wheel in its technology development. It would be prudent to look at what information technology has accomplished to date, and then integrate that knowledge with GIS expertise, regardless of the difficulties involved. Integration of existing technology also applies to standards and policies. Standards enhance communication and development with a common language and concepts, leading to guidelines that affect architecture, processes, methods, or policies. There should be a common consensus of minimal guidelines that can accommodate those working with geospatial data, retrieval, and discovery.

User-guided development is also critical when examining the human resources side of GIS information and technology. Further, the use of qualified researchers and developers is essential. To create institutional frameworks, agreements have to be certified to establish national, regional, and global spatial data infrastructure. These spatial data infrastructures should be created over the geographic data, stored in the spatial databases, and their description in rich, descriptive metadata. Finally, open systems and ease of access is of strategic importance to ensure quality and accuracy from remote systems.

The need for data description standards for digital geospatial data is especially apparent in the proliferation of WebGis applications in the wake of spatial data distribution enabling initiatives, such as the NSDI. WebGIS describes a type of geographic information system. WebGIS basically consists of client, server, and network model, wherein the client is integrated in a Web browser. While creating many opportunities for librarians in making available unique geospatial datasets, the tremendous growth in WebGIS has created many challenges for libraries in trying to incorporate digital geospatial data in their services and legal considerations in the use of distributed data.

WEB GIS AND LIBRARIES

In recent years the number and scope of WebGIS applications has grown tremendously. In their survey of WebGIS applications, Researchers discuss a wide number of interactive mapping sites available on the Internet. They note that many users of the Internet have already experienced using WebGIS software tools through interactive mapping tools available on the Internet. Such sites include: Yahoo Maps, National Map, and GoogleEarth.

Other WebGIS applications that are available on the Internet give access to a varying amount of specialised geospatial data. Many local government Web sites for city and county governments across the United States offer interactive mapping sites such as the City of Albuquerque and City of Durham for users to access technical data about their municipalities. These mapping sites give access to socio-economic, demographic, and planning data.

Many government sites use ESRI software products such as ArcGIS and ArcWEB services to facilitate data searches for information. Other WebGIS applicatiosn include environ-mental planning, agricultural planning wetlands management, archaeological research, health planning research, transportation planning, citisen political participation, and education planning. Other developments in WebGIS include different data visualisations to offer unique perspectives on information for analytical purposes, such as three-dimensional modeling and combinations of software such as multimedia and WebGIS to offer comprehensive views of geospatial data A net effect of the increasingly popularity of WebGIS.

The popularity of WebGIS applications among the public has led to unequal data distribution across the Internet, Since, bandwidth is constrained. In their study of WebGIS, Yang identify two issues related to improving access to digital geospatial data on the Interent. The first issue concerns the sharing of and interoperability for heterogeneous data among different systems, different communities, and different users. The second issue is a quality of service issue, that of how to improve the system performance so data are delivered to the users within a reasonable time span.

In regards to the first issue, the authors identify international organisational efforts at creating accepted conventions in data descriptive standards in regards to interoperability and data access, such as the OpenGIS Consortium (OGC) and the Technical Committee 211 of the International Organisation of Standards. The strides being made by the aforementioned organisations and agreement between international geospatial data producers and providers is creating an environment wherein libraries have access to geospatial Web Services, such as ESRI's Geography Network and Geosptatial One Stop. Web service Internet sites essentially provide access to GIS data, software, educational and mapping, or related services.

For libraries, the services can give access to current and large amounts of geospatial data are usually available in a timely manner. In his study of how academic libraries can integrate digital geospatial data into their collections and services, Morris provides a good overview of the issues involved in trying to facilitate Web Service data in an academic library. Some drawbacks of attempting to integrate Web services into a library environment can include lingering technical issues like linking data resources, developing sustainable licensing models, and negotiating access rights to digital geospatial data.

Bibliography

Altheide, D.: *Socially Responsible Librarianship Champions Privacy*, London: Cambridge University, 2000.

Atkinson, P.: *Imagining the Digital Library in a Commercialized Internet*, New York: Oxford: Pergamon Press, 2003.

Bernard, H.: *Authentication and Trust in a Networked World*, New York: F.S. Crofts & Company, 2004.

Boyle, J: *Privacy: The Next Challenge*, England: University Press, 2006.

Burnette, D.: *Library Patrons and the Law*, Alexandria: Council on Library Science Education, 2003.

Cohen, M.: *Maintaining the Privacy of Library Records*, London: Waverly Book Company, 2003.

Dean, R. G.: *The Transparent Society: Will Technology Force us to Choose between Privacy and Freedom*, London: Smith College Studies in Library Science, 2002.

Denzin, N.: *Privacy in the Information Age*, Chicago: American Hotel Register Company, 2004.

Dasmann, J.: *Using Qualitative Data Analysis Software: Merits and Hazards*, New York: Computers in Human Services, 2001.

Drisko, J.: *Issues in the Information Age*, New York: Journal of Library Science Education, 2003.

Gilgun, J.: *The New Battle Over Workplace Privacy: Safe Practices to Minimize Conflict*, USA: American school of Chicago, 2001.

Giorgi, A.: *Computerized Monitoring and Online Privacy*, Pittsburgh: Duquesne University Press, 2005.

Glaser, B.: *Confidentiality in the Use of Library Materials*, Mill Valley: Sociology Press, 2001.

Guba, E.: *RSS for Non-Techie Librarians*, San Francisco: Jossey Bass Press, 2003.

Hyde, C.: *Online Resources for Adaptive Information Technologies*, Boston: William J. Nagel Company, 2001.

LeCompte, M.: *Computers in Libraries*, San Diego: Academic Press, 2004.

Mishler, E.: *Accessibility in the Virtual Library*: London: Harvard University Press, 2002.

Padgett, D.: *Information Technology and Libraries*, New York: University Press, 2000.

Strauss, A.: *Assistive Technology in Special Libraries*, San Francisco: Harper Bowling Green State University, 2000.

Van Maanen, J.: *Library Assistive Technology: Predictions and Trends*, Chicago: The Hotel Monthly Press, 2006.

Vygotsky, L.: *Adaptive Technology Equipment for the Library*, New York: Columbia Press, 2001.

Index